*Gender in Crisis: Women and
the Palestinian Resistance Movement*

Gender in Crisis: Women and the Palestinian Resistance Movement

BY

Julie M. Peteet

COLUMBIA UNIVERSITY PRESS
NEW YORK

Columbia University Press
NEW YORK   OXFORD

Copyright © 1991 Columbia University Press
Library of Congress Cataloging-in-Publication Data
Peteet, Julie Marie.
    Gender in crisis : Women and the Palestinian resistance movement /
by Julie M. Peteet.
        p.   cm.
    Includes bibliographical references and index.
    ISBN 0–231–07446–8
    ISBN 0–231–07447–6 (pbk.)
        1. Women, Palestinian Arab--Lebanon--Political activity. 2. Women
Revolutionists--Palestine. 3. National liberation movements-
-Palestine. I. Title.
DS80.55.P34P47 1991
305.4'095692--dc20   90–25824
                                                              CIP

Casebound editions of Columbia University Press books are Smyth-sewn
and printed on permanent and durable acid-free paper

∞

Printed in the United States of America
c 10 9 8 7 6 5 4 3 2 1
p 10 9 8 7 6 5 4 3 2 1

This book is dedicated to *ayyam Beirut.*

Contents

Acknowledgments

■

Many people have contributed to the research and writing of this book. All deserve a warm thanks. Some can be mentioned by name; others are better left unidentified.

This book would have been impossible without the generous hospitality of Ghada Kanafani and Ziad al-Turk, who accepted me into their home and gave unflagging support. Our lengthy discussions were of immense help in focusing my research. Rosemary Sayigh was a good friend and consistent source of encouragement and support who never failed to share her vast knowledge of Palestinian exile society in Lebanon. Um Khalid graciously opened her home to me and tolerated my at times intrusive questions. She was instrumental in helping to acquaint me with daily life in a refugee camp. Sami and Muna Musallem introduced me to several key people in the women's movement. Special thanks go to Fatmi and her husband in ʿAyn al-Hilwah camp for their warm hospitality.

They went out of their way to ensure my comfort and introduced me to many women in the camp. I would also like to extend my appreciation to Jamila and her husband, who always received me warmly and took an active interest in this project. All these people not only helped in the research process but also were great sources of critical commentary on their society. Their experiences are the stuff of which this book is made. A special thanks goes to Imad Elhaj, who was always ready with creative insight and critical comment throughout the research and writing. Most of all, I owe a tremendous debt of gratitude to the Palestinian community in Lebanon for their hospitable reception and openness to intellectual inquiry and critique in an exceedingly difficult situation.

I gratefully acknowledge the advice and support of Barbara Aswad and Carole Browner, who were instrumental in preparing me for this research project. Mary Hegland was a continuous source of invaluable advice while I was writing and was always available for discussion. Muna and Rashid Khalidi provided helpful comments on the manuscript. I also extend my thanks to the reviewers, and whose detailed inquiries and challenging comments were particularly helpful in the final preparation of the manuscript. I want to extend my gratitude to my editor, Kate Wittenberg, and to Susan Pensak, of the Editorial department, for their direction and encouragement. Zeina Azzam Seikaly was essential in trans-literating Arabic terms.

Institutional support was provided by the Center for Contemporary Arab Studies at Georgetown University, where I was a visiting scholar in 1987–88 and 1988–89. Initial financial support was generously provided by the Diana Tamari Sabbagh Foundation.

My family, Imad, Jenna, and Dannah, and my parents, are to be commended for their patience and forebearance.

Introduction

> *Everything that will happen to*
> *my people will happen to me.*

Then who are your people?
The whores? the thieves?

∎

An intricate maze of quiet, narrow alleys—the playground of small
children—lies behind the camp's main streets. Sheltered from the chaotic
city traffic, the alleys are bordered by a profusion of tiny one- and two-
room cement block houses. Most are so narrow that people must walk
single file. Women balance the heavy, round metal trays of freshly baked
bread on their heads and walk gracefully through the alleyways on their
way home from the camp's bakeries. Although open drains running the
length of the alleys are still common, the houses are impeccably tidy.
Overcrowded as they are, one still feels a sense of privacy behind the
large walls enclosing some homes, especially in the rural camps of the
south. The walls are an attempt to recreate the traditional peasant households of Palestine.

The numerous offices of the Resistance movement, where one finds
groups of young men, the *fida'iyyin*, guns in hand, animatedly discussing

1

the latest political developments, line the main streets and are tucked away in quiet corners of the camp.[1] The collagelike pattern of the posters of the martyrs pasted on the bullet-pocked walls, the pervasiveness of Kalasnikovs, the Soviet assault rifle, and the rocket-propelled grenade launchers (RPGs) slung casually over the shoulder of the *fida'i,* and the Palestinian flag, potent symbols in a national movement, express an unshakable determination to define a present and ensure a future.

Shatila camp on the southwestern fringes of Beirut, Lebanon, part of the "poverty belt" encroaching on the city since the 1960s, was the principal site for this ethnography of Palestinian women, exiles in Lebanon since 1948.[2] Wittingly or unwittingly, ethnography is historically specific, and this study is no exception; it examines women's lives and the process of change in gender relations and meaning during a clearly bounded period in Palestinian history. The focus is microprocessual—to describe and analyze events at the level of experience within a larger, regional political-economy and cultural framework.

In the years 1968–69 to 1982 the Palestinian national movement in Lebanon enjoyed unprecedented military, political, and social autonomy as well as a large measure of support from the exile community. The history and experiences of Palestinian women in the other countries of the diaspora such as Jordan, Kuwait, or Syria, and those remaining in historic Palestine are excluded from this study. To include their experiences would be to deny them the seriousness of scholarship that they merit. Their lives are situated in contexts quite different from those extant in Lebanon and thus deserve a focused study of their own. Nor can one extrapolate generalizations from one Palestinian community and apply them to another. Yet this is not to deny the real sentiments, arising from the experience and state of exile, that bind together, in a commonality of sorts, all Palestinians.

As a result of the 1948 Arab-Israel war, Palestinians became exiles in the surrounding Arab countries and abroad, where they remain until this day, usually stateless, temporary residents. Estimates of the number of refugees fleeing or expelled from Palestine in 1947–48 are around 714,000 (Kossaifi 1980:18).[3]

Now into their second and third generation, the women of Shatila are the refugees, and their descendants, of the nearly 100,000 refugees who came to Lebanon in the wake of the establishment of the state of Israel in Palestine. They were predominantly residents of villages and towns in northern Palestine, bordering on South Lebanon. Provisionally settled into refugee camps and the towns and cities of Lebanon, by the early 1980s this number had swelled to between 300,000 and 400,000.[4] Official Palestinian sources give a figure of 492,240 Palestinians in Lebanon in 1983–84. This is the same figure reported for 1981, the last year of an official Palestinian census in Lebanon.[5] Meanwhile, a succession of Israeli governments has refused to allow them to return to their homes or to claim monetary compensation for the loss of property and livelihood.

At the time this research was conducted in the early 1980s, estimates of the worldwide Palestinian population were 4.5 million distributed as follows: still resident in Israel, the occupied West Bank, and the Gaza Strip: 1,835,000 or 40.8 percent, living outside Palestine: 2,665,000 or 59.2 percent. Of the latter, those living in Lebanon (375,000) are only 8.3 percent of the Palestinian population (Said et al. 1983:14). Nevertheless, aside from Jordan, this is the largest single concentration of Palestinians living outside historic Palestine, and at the time of this study their political influence in the area was far out of proportion to their numbers.

The quote at the beginning of the section poignantly underscores women's consciousness of the embeddedness of their lives in the social fabric. This study sketches a portrait of "ordinary" camp women[6] and politically active Palestinian women in Lebanon: the emergence of their political consciousness and its relation to feminist consciousness, how they are mobilized into political organizations and the tasks they perform, and what political activism implies for concepts of gender and gender relations.

The second and third generations of refugees proved to be fertile ground for the political recruitment of young women, though women of all ages have been drawn into the national movement. As we shall see, in camp Palestinian society there were sharp and vivid contrasts among women and between men and women. The mother with her large family and pressing domestic priorities and loyalties can be juxtaposed to the armed militant who fights side by side with men or staffs the Resistance offices and institutions. The above description of Shatila camp subtly underscores the typical wartime sexual division of labor—men carry the gun and fight; women provide sustenance. However, this arrangement of tasks by gender has been subjected to innumerable challenges and cracks have begun to appear in the once seemingly solid structure of the sexual division of labor. At critical junctures these divisions dissolve, revealing a fluidity of boundaries and the fragility of gender definitions. During crisis, housewives, or "ordinary" women, often participate in the defense of the community, giving expression to solidarity in the face of wrenching adversity. A transformation in relations is also occurring between women themselves. Continuities among women, in life-style, types of labor performed, values, and aspirations, are being undermined and replaced by discontinuities, particularly in their sense of self, stemming from their active involvement in the national movement.

An understanding of gender constructs among the exile community in Lebanon derives not just from daily involvement with activist women but equally from the multitude of ordinary women—workers, students, and housewives—who comprise the bulk of women in the camps. Women active in what is often labeled the domain of "formal politics"[7] are not a large category, but if we account for other, less easily defined and categorized types of political affiliation and activism the picture becomes more detailed. Women are affiliated to the Resistance in a variety of ways: as full-time members, or "cadres,"[8] as members, friends, students, and employees.

The women represented in this study ranged from university-educated to illiterate, from single to widowed, and from well-off to poor. Some had two children; some had seven or eight. For some the transition to political activism was a relatively smooth process; others encountered serious familial and social obstacles. Some suffered the trauma of enforced migration and the death of loved ones during military conflict; others escaped with their lives largely intact. This variety of women and life-styles mirrors the diversity of Palestinian women in exile, their variable conditions, and the rich repertoire of responses to them.

The question of theory is problematic in Middle East anthropology. In a review article Fernea and Malarkey starkly observed that "with few exceptions, contributions to anthropological literature based on Middle East research have failed to have an important impact upon theoretical concerns in the field of ethnology" (1975:183). However, this assessment certainly warrants some revision in light of the recent works of Middle East anthropologists, particularly in North Africa, where studies of the ethnographic process and encounter, the relationship between the ethnographer and those observed, have had a substantial impact on the wider discipline (Rabinow 1977; Dywer 1982; Crapanzano 1980). Bourdieu's work on North Africa has, without a doubt, made lasting contributions to the development of theories of culture and the relationship between practice and ideology (see Abu-Lughod 1987).

If we place Middle East anthropology within the larger context of both feminist anthropology and Middle East studies as a whole the picture is rather dismal. As regards feminist studies and feminist anthropology, Abu-Lughod states: ". . . the anthropology of Middle Eastern women is theoretically underdeveloped relative to anthropology as a whole. More disturbing is its theoretical underdevelopment relative to feminist anthropology which itself . . . has not kept pace with feminist theory or scholarship in other disciplines" (1987:40). In terms of Middle East area studies, Said argues that "the whole theoretical dimension is completely absent in Middle East studies. . . . Furthermore, Middle East studies seems to be governed the most by what you might call pragmatic and policy-oriented issues" (1988:33). Where does this assessment of the field leave an anthropology of gender in the Middle East? With this critical assessment in mind, an ethnography of Palestinian women that makes a theoretical contribution seems a daunting task.

On the theoretical level, this study presses for a conception of relations between political economy, practice, and cultural ideologies as one of mutual influence. These elements of social life shape and yet simultaneously constrain the potential for influence of one upon the other. However, one must ask whether there are instances in historical time when pronounced crisis upsets or recasts this relationship. Do external forces bear down so hard as to give rise to realignments in what would otherwise be a rather circular flow of influence? The atmosphere of turmoil and crisis that has gripped Palestinian exile society is one such historical moment, engendering a rapid and culturally creative human response. This approach to social change centrally locates human agency in the process of recasting the flow of influence in social life.

On a substantive level, this study explores the relationship between a national revolutionary movement in a state of embryonic state formation, a society experiencing continuous crisis, and women's political activism and their implications for transforming the meaning of gender. This relationship is illuminated by examining the potential for structural and ideological transformations in gender-based asymmetrical social relations in the context of a national liberation movement and crisis and, correspondingly, the limitations imposed by such a framework. It is hardly surprising that in the process of the Palestinian national movement's emergence profound changes occurred in the realm of gender relations. Research on women in national movements or during war and political crisis illustrates their rich and varied response to conflicts and the nature of changes in social position and the meaning accorded to gender assignations.[9]

The overall orientation of this study does not revolve around the oppositional poles of liberation and subordination, but around the process of transformation and yet the simultaneous reproduction of gender structures and meaning. My concern is less to present the connection between political economy, social practice, and cultural ideology and more to index the nature and direction of the relationship in a historically located, culture-specific instance. A number of general questions are posed as frameworks for organizing an inquiry. I will show how women's political participation informed a realignment and, in part, a reconceptualization of gender relations. Not only relations between men and women were effected. Equally critical, relations between women themselves were sites of transformations. At the same time, central elements of the hierarchal dimension of gender were reproduced.

Class emerges prominently as an analytical mode. Women's individual experiences and their meaning are only comprehensible within a class framework. Gender is not an exclusive or totalizing category indicating essence, experience, and a concept of self. To accord it such exclusivity would be to deny the complexity of women's lives, reducing them to sex —its cultural interpretation alone. As the material presented here will show, how women experience the world around them is mediated by their class affiliation and the power that accrues from it.[10] Power is not just the capacity to have one's will done vis-à-vis others. It is also the availability of options, choices of which influence how one experiences externalities. A recognition of the genderedness of power points to a conception of power as a phenomenon "which is never localised here or there." Foucault offers a view of power where "individuals circulate between its threads; they are always in the position of simultaneously undergoing and exercising this power" (1977:98). Women, as a gendered category, are constituted by power, but at the same time, women as members of different class-power structures are vehicles of power.

War and the national movement were catalysts, undermining the operation of extant asymmetrical gender relations and exposing them to scrutiny. New social realities—women's presence in the public political sector, usually associated with men—have disturbed and unsettled gender relations and ideologies. New ideas took hold and new forms of social relations emerged with a measure of legitimacy. Yet it is necessary to inquire into the process by which a once predominantly peasant society in the process of revolutionary transformation consciously retains traditional social practices and ideologies in order to gain legitimacy and ensure a successful mobilization of the community. The political leadership may co-opt elements of tradition—that is, assign themselves the task of defining their social location and content and the potency of meaning and thus efficacy in shaping behavior. Those structures, practices, relations, and symbols usually designated as "traditional"[11] are suffused with the legitimizing powers of representing cultural authenticity, the latter a process in which women play a paramount real and symbolic role. The potential for sweeping change presented by women's activism was, at some points, counteracted by the meanings with which they endowed their new activities. Many women conceptualized political activism in ways that, in terms of meaning, did not substantially distinguish it from traditional gender ideologies. Just as significantly, altered but dominant-subordinate gender relations were pervasive in the Resistance movement itself.

The construction of gender and gender relations was a conscious process among women who were vividly aware of the historical moment. Women leaders were acutely cognizant that wartime and continuous crises were periods of cultural ambiguity. Patterns of expected behavior were suspended as people mobilized to resist their conditions. While women participated in these crises through domestic tasks, some younger women broke gender boundaries by fighting and staying away from homes for extended periods of time, behavior that, in many cases, was grudgingly tolerated by their families. To exploit the situation to their advantage, at such times women strove to introduce new norms of female potential and meaning to gender relations. The problem was to sustain these changes, forged in the heat of the moment, long enough to inform long-term structural and ideological transformations.

Embryonic state formation and the rise of a national movement were central, though not isolated, factors in this instance of gender transformation. A host of other factors were at work. The historical period in which this study was situated was one dominated by continuous life-pervading and life-shattering events in the form of military threat and assault. The Lebanese civil war and its aftermath have been punctuated by direct assaults (Syrian, Israeli, and Lebanese) on the Palestinian community. Although fragmented in time and space, they were fused by a common denominator—an intent to diminish, at the minimum, the Palestinian military-political presence in Lebanon and its influence in the regional balance of forces and, at the maximum, to compel the Palestinians to flee their camps. The significance of these assaults in shaping Palestinian social life and the decision-making process inside the national movement cannot be underestimated. One of the clearest aspects of this, relevant to our purposes in discussing women, was the determination of priorities for allocating scarce resources and prestige within the national movement, a point developed throughout this book.

The divide between war and private life has little relevance in contemporary studies of Palestinians. Nor do private/public dichotomies carry much analytical weight. This is not to cast aside the notion of a private domain largely associated with women or a public domain largely associated with men (see Rosaldo 1974). Such divisions do exist but are so culturally variable as to preclude generalization or universalization. However, as societies are drawn into the capitalist orbit and as the kin-based organization of labor is seriously undermined by capitalist relations of production these divisions may become more real and pronounced (Reiter 1975). Rather than being useful as explanatory devices, these divisions are better examined as they articulate with one another and for their ideological content (Rapp, Ross, and Bridenthal 1979). In a society in the throes of a war of national liberation and organizing to preserve and perpetuate their identity, these divisions are sites of unsettling disruptions. Long-term conflict makes for flux as gender roles and ideologies are blurred and subjected to conscious reexamination. Households are mobilized for communal defense, and women take on tasks usually associated with men. Yet there also occurs a process of feminization of specific sectors of the national movement. Both processes involve a complex reconceptualization of gender.

The problematic of women underscores the need for the development of theory in the direction of historical specificity, for asymmetrical gender relations acquire their distinctive features in specific historical instances informed by prevailing relations of production and reproduction, state agendas for women and the family, the structural position occupied by religious hierarchies and ideologies within the state and society, prevalent forms of social control of women vested in the family and the legal system, and ideological constructs of gender. Although there are uniformities in women's position that may prevail across class boundaries in Palestinian society, the form and content of their position and the severity of social control to which women are subject is mediated by class.

A brief overview of pre-1948 Palestinian social life and the experience of exile in Lebanon (chapter 1) is followed by a review of the early women's movement, its relations with the Palestinian national movement, and its social bases (chapter 2). Chapter 3 examines various forms of political consciousness (class, national, and feminist) in the context of exile, focusing on transformations in consciousness arising from continuous crises, discrimination in the host country, and a community in the throes of developing a culture of resistance. Chapter 4 explores the process of women becoming politically active and the various avenues of mobilization. Chapter 5 describes what women do in the Resistance, the kinds of organizations they have formed, and their relationship with the larger nationalist movement. Chapter 6 investigates how women have managed the opposition generated by their open challenge to normative traditions of gender and examines how political activism has transformed them and the boundaries of meaning.

Research and Ethnography

One of the problems pertaining to the study of Palestinian society in general is its geographical fragmentation. The community in Lebanon presented a particular aspect of this general problem. This was a society without a clearly bounded and unambiguously identified territorial base, nor was there a clearly identifiable Palestinian economy. Palestinian capital and labor were well integrated into the Lebanese economy, as major investors, property owners, corporations, and a large pool of labor—both an incipient working class and a *lumpenproletariat* (Smith 1984). Yet since the 1970s the Palestinians had been moving, in very nascent form, toward establishing the foundations of an independent economy, directed toward self-sufficiency.[12]

The absence of an independent territorial base, an institutionalized state structure and a set of laws with universal applicability, and a geographically fragmented community in the midst of the host country casts the crucial issue of theoretical approach in a problematic mold. An anthropological approach that views societies in the wake of the colonial encounter as cultures of resistance seems appropriate. In locating a prominent and defining motif of ethnography, that of "salvaging cultural diversity, threatened with global Westernization, especially during the age of colonialism," Marcus and Fischer (1986:24) conclude that such a motif no longer bears much relevance in our contemporary world. "Yet, the function of ethnography is certainly not outmoded just because its enduring narrative motifs have worn thin. The cultures of world peoples need to be constantly rediscovered as these people reinvent them in changing historical circumstances . . ." (ibid.). Caulfield (1974b:69) equates the "conscious affirmation of cultural difference in the face of wholesale denigration" with cultures of resistance in colonial encounters. Palestinians have responded to a unique form of colonialism[13] with cultural reinvention and invigoration. The construction of a network of quasi-statelike institutions and the refashioning of the body politic in the form of a broad-based, popular national movement are the exemplars, or building blocks, of this creative culture of resistance and regeneration, as are the new meanings accorded to traditional symbols and the elevation of some cultural elements to positions of preeminent meaning. However, these are not disparate, autonomous sectors of society or thought; they are drawn into a form of unity, however tenuous, by their consciously formulated common objectives and a set of shared symbols that endow each with vibrancy and meaning.

Ethnography: The Fieldwork Experience

Research for this project was carried out among the Palestinian community in Lebanon from September 1980 to June 1982. I had previously lived in Lebanon and so felt a certain degree of familiarity with the political climate and the Palestine question. Participant observation, the observation of women's behavior and participation in their daily lives, and the collection of life histories and structured in-depth interviews were the main research methods. Arabic was the primary language of research, especially in the camps and with women not educated in a foreign language. In this instance, class and linguistic skills clearly intersect. English was used often with Palestinian women who had been educated in one of the many foreign schools in Beirut, most of whom are from the middle and upper classes.

Since I was interested in studying politically active women, I initially planned to focus on women members of political organizations. As so often happens during anthropological fieldwork, it soon became apparent that social life was not as neat and well ordered as we initially think. The distinction between ordinary and activist women that I had assumed existed was ambiguous and untenable as a device for planning research strategies. The pervasiveness of the crisis had left few women out of the political arena. I revised my research focus to encompass women who were not formal members of the Resistance but who were considered activists nonetheless by themselves and others. Vast numbers of camp women are active in the political arena without being official members of any organization. I tried to focus on women for their representativeness of the main features of the community—class, age, level of education, and camp-urban residence. I purposely chose not to select women according to political affiliation with one group or another. More than men perhaps, women are quite adamant that there are only minor differences between political groups on the question of women.

There was no one single geographical location that was defined as solely Palestinian. The community was spread across Lebanon, and in some camps, sites we tend to think of as largely Palestinian, resided substantial numbers of Lebanese Shites. "Palestinian" was more a shared idea, a national sentiment, a sense of political belonging, and a common identity predicated on similarity of both history and experience. The geographically common areas, those spatial junctures where Palestinians came together in a position of control, security, and cultural unity, were the camps and Resistance-controlled areas of Beirut such as al-Fakhani, a Beirut neighborhood adjacent to the camps and site of numerous PLO offices. The population of the area was indeed largely Palestinian.

Most of this field study was conducted in Beirut, in Shatila camp and the surrounding urban area where were located the Resistance headquarters, offices, and social institutions. Some of the camps outside Beirut were visited for extended periods of time to arrive at an idea of the differing economic and social bases of women's lives, ranging from the extremes of Damur, a small coastal town halfway between Beirut and

Saida to the south, where there were a substantial number of women without men, to the more stable townlike camp of ʿAyn al-Hilweh near Saida, to the more rural-like camp of Rashidiyyah in southern Lebanon. These camps differed not only in their economic potential for women's work but also in the degree of crisis each experienced. Shatila was relatively stable, undergoing only occasional shelling during the civil war, whereas Rashidiyyah, near the border with Israel, had been subjected to fairly continuous but intermittent bombardment over the past ten years. ʿAyn al-Hilweh was somewhat in between these two extremes; it had experienced air raids and shelling over the years but had never undergone anything comparable to Rashidiyyah, which had several times been emptied of its inhabitants.

I made extensive visits to PLO institutions employing substantial numbers of women, such as Samed, the Red Crescent, and those that served what were defined as "women's needs" such as nurseries, day-care centers, and literacy courses. Interviews were conducted with employees, managers, and clients.

Working in a politically charged setting such as pre-1982 Beirut, the issue of protection of subjects becomes of critical importance. I informed the women interviewed that all information was confidential and would not be used for any purpose except that stated, and it was made clear that each would be given a pseudonym to avoid revealing her identity. This imperative takes on added importance in light of the 1982 Israeli invasion of Lebanon and the massive arrests and severe interrogation to which prisoners have been subjected. Some of the women whose lives are featured in this book are from the south of Lebanon and have been arrested and imprisoned without charges or trial. Those who had been in prominent positions would be easily identified if one knew where they worked and what their husbands did. For this reason many of the specific, potentially identifying details of their lives have been omitted or camouflaged.

Fieldwork in a Community in Crisis

It has become an established anthropological tradition to convey to readers the ethnographic encounter, to situate oneself vis-à-vis those studied, to describe the process of acquiring knowledge about others (Abu-Lughod 1986; Marcus and Fischer 1986; Said 1979). The first few months were spent doing lengthy interviews with activists. By this time, participant observation in the camps had made it unavoidably clear that to understand transformations in gender nonactivist women could not be excluded. To gain entrance to Shatila camp, normally closed to outsiders and tightly guarded, I contacted the Resistance offices in Beirut, explained my project, and asked for permission to use the camp as a research site. Since I already knew many Palestinians, obtaining permission was a relatively smooth process. I was sent to Faten, second-in-command in a Resistance office in Shatila, who was to arrange introductions for me. After several months of interviewing activists and participating in their daily round of activities, I decided to find a family where the mother or female head of house was semiactive, i.e., not a full-time militant but one that I would later dub one of the ubiquitous "politicized housewives." Faten arranged that another young woman militant from her office would take me around to visit with families in the camp and I would be free to choose whomever I thought I could best work with and who, naturally, would agree to work with me on a daily basis. I chose to seek formal, institutional assistance in finding a family in the camp rather than using my informal networks so that my daily presence would have legitimacy, both for me and for them, and allow me mobility in the camp and its environs.

After several days of visiting, drinking coffee, and exchanging pleasant formalities, I met Um Khalid, one of my key informants. She served as my introduction to the camp and its "ordinary" women. When I reflect about why I chose to work with her, perhaps it was because she herself was interested in the issue of women and eager to participate in a research project. She received me in an informal way—no hushing of the children and the formal, ritualized exchange of greetings. When I entered her home she and the children were in the midst of the morning cleaning and cooking. As we talked she carried on, rolling out her bread dough and shouting orders to the children to continue with their chores.

Um Khalid was eager to express herself about changes in Palestinian society since the emergence of the national movement. She was vividly aware, for example, of the changes in women's lives as a result of their access to free elementary education and had many hopes for her daughters' futures. Her husband was a full-time militant and a representative on *al-lijneh al-sha'biyyeh,* a popular committee that functions as the camp municipality. Aside from tending to her house and eight children, she taught two hours daily (except Sundays) in the PLO literacy campaign that had recently been initiated in the camps.

It turned out to be a fruitful relationship. Um Khalid straddled the line between the activists, with whom she was friends and occasionally worked, and the ordinary housewives of Shatila, who were a constant source of information, as her house was something of a women's gathering place during the day. Her extensive visiting network around the camp allowed me to meet many families.

Before interviewing proceeded, I first made an effort to become acquainted with each woman. Nearly everyone I interviewed was introduced to me by women previously interviewed. It was a chain reaction; often after an interview a woman would say, "I have a friend or relative who is active [or is interesting]. You should talk to her. Let me take you to her house." I proceeded in this way to build up a network of women to serve as interviewees and guides to their organizations' policies and institutions.

I preferred meeting with activists in their homes rather than their offices, since in the latter women more readily assume a formal air. A peculiarly journalistic ethos would emerge during interviews in offices, especially with women in leadership positions. The setting tended to define the nature of the dialogue; in such a physical setting women felt compelled to present and represent the Resistance to an outsider and therefore presented the official organizational line and less of their own personal ideas and experiences, imposing a distinction between public and private domains that was hard to sustain in reality.

Before actually doing an interview, I made several visits to a woman's home. Having made her acquaintance, I would then ask if she would be interested in participating in an interview; since no one ever declined, I feel confident that this was an appropriate approach. Interviews were conducted informally—women would continue to prepare food, breastfeed their children, and embroider and interrupt themselves to scold the children or direct their studies or chores. Lengthy interviews were always broken by small breaks for tea and coffee or for lunch. Some interviews were carried out under shelling; one that I recall vividly was in ʿAyn al-Hilweh camp with Um Fadi. The camp was being shelled by the Israeli-sponsored South Lebanese Forces, then under the command of Major Saʿd Haddad. As full-time guerrillas, her eldest son and husband were on duty, yet she seemed unconcerned by the whole affair, as if it were simply a minor inconvenience, gesturing animatedly and yelling above the din of bombs and antiaircraft fire, "If I were young enough I'd carry the gun myself and defend the camp!"

I tried to avoid interviews when a woman's husband or father was present. The atmosphere would become overly formal, and she would often be too intimidated to speak frankly. Occasionally when men were present they tried to speak for their wives or daughters, appropriating the right to represent their experiences and present the revolution to outsiders.

The questions I asked were open-ended, and I made a habit of beginning by collecting basic data about household composition, births, marriages, etc., and then I would make the transition to more political and personal issues. Some interviews lasted an hour; others took several days, depending on the loquaciousness of the woman and her willingness to present her life. Some women's life stories were gathered throughout the whole period of fieldwork, more a result of participant observation than actual interviewing; with Layla, for instance, in whose home on the edge of Shatila camp I stayed for about six months, I became a member of the household, doing housework and cooking and going with the family on weekends to her parents' home. Aside from partaking in her daily activities, we spent hours and hours discussing her personal and political life and the Palestinian dilemma.

The general pattern of recording anthropological data may be similar across the discipline, but individual and situational variations must make for a richness in methods.[14] I'm sure nearly all anthropologists have had field experiences where note taking sometimes seems very inappropriate and may disrupt the spontaneity of the situation. Doing research in the midst of a resistance movement punctuated by violent incidents made for some interesting field methods. Aside from interviews, I usually recorded events as soon as possible after the fact. Some examples spring to mind of settings or incidents where note taking or overt observation would have been unwise. During funerals note taking would have been perceived as insensitive and as setting me too apart from the local population. The same could be said of national events such as demonstrations, anniversary celebrations, or cultural events where I wanted to interact with women rather than observe them formally. During an *istinfar* (military alert), when the camps were shelled and we huddled in the shelters or the interiors of the house, it would have been the height of insensitivity to formally and obviously observe people during such an extremely stressful and life-threatening situation. Formal observation in these instances involves distancing oneself at moments where it is precisely such involvement that constitutes the essence of participant observation. Participant observation does not dissolve the distances between ethnographer and subject of research or even allow some kind of transcendental glimpse of understanding and identification. But participation in daily events does elicit empathy.[15] This is not the empathy "that involves a single moment of quasi-mystical identification or fusion with the Other." Rather, it entails the experience of oneness and separation simultaneously. Empathy in this context implies that one can become the Other only in a "limited but meaningful sense, yet clearly remain inside one's own skin" (Kirschner 1987). The context of danger heightens the sense of empathy—such dangers are life-threatening to all subjected to them.

Naturally interviewing required on-the-spot recording. I taped some and took notes during others, depending on how women felt about the tape recorder. Few felt it was an intrusion; most took it lightly and were not at all intimidated. Indeed, camp Palestinians are quite accustomed to the ubiquitous Western journalist with tape recorder in one hand and camera in the other. Although I always carried my notebook, I did not always have it out and ready. Probably the most interesting and revealing events and interactions take place so spontaneously as to preclude note taking. Occasionally during the day I would quietly sit in a corner of Um Khalid's house and jot down a few relevant points to be written up later in the evening. When I would ask Um Khalid detailed question about her life or the camp or Resistance activities, I took notes, since she was understanding of why I was doing so and was not put off by it.

Regular, observable sociocultural patterns eventually emerged from the combination of interviews and participant observation. For example, some commonalities among nearly all women became apparent—the experience of national discrimination. Other patterns had a class dimension, such as how women had been mobilized. What emerges from interviews is a sense of how women weave the presentation of events in their own lives around those of major importance in Palestinian social history such as exile, life in the camps, the emergence of the Resistance, and women's political mobilization. Participant observation gives insight into the kinds of relations into which women enter and their meanings, as well as lending immediacy to data garnered through interviews. One can see how women actually cope with crisis, how it affects them, and how their political activism has informed changes in their lives. It was through participating on the endless round of visits, at the bakery, in the *nadwat* (seminars or political sessions), in the literacy courses, and on visits to recent widows or mothers of martyrs and in national events in Shatila and through intimate friendships that I came to understand the transformations in the structure of gender relations and meaning.

The Dialectic of Oppression and Militancy: Women's Lives as Text

On the whole, women were fairly open to talking about themselves and their society. They regarded research about their society in a positive light, considering that it would likely be a contribution to their struggle.

Perhaps this was an indication of their sense of empowerment to transform their lives. Palestinians in Lebanon were actively engaged in cultural reconstruction via institution building, a revival of their traditional folklore, and new concepts of self. This attempt to reinvigorate portions of the past went hand in hand with the desire and intent of the people and the national movement to develop "modern" social institutions and relations. In this context, Palestinian culture was consciously dynamic, constantly in movement, responding to new challenges and demands. Cultural authenticity was less of a thorny issue than it has been in other colonized or postcolonial societies (Peteet 1986).

Although the national struggle was accorded priority in terms of praxis and allocation of resources, other forms of struggle were deemed an important part of the overall process of nation building and social development. It was widely recognized that women suffered a burden from war and crises different from that suffered by men. Whether or not their struggle had a specificity to it arising from a dynamic of gender subordination was a topic of some debate.

It is in such a context that Palestinian women are so willing and even eager to discuss their lives. But another context loomed large—the political one. Ethnography and ethnographers are situated in both a local and international political context. In Said's *Orientalism,* he brilliantly critiques Western scholarship's interpretation of the East, or the Orient, illustrating the relationship between knowledge and power. Knowledge, its acquisition, content, forms, and deployment, is itself a form of the exercise of power. As compelling and thought-transforming as the book is, the subject of Western discourse—the uniform Oriental—seems voiceless, as passive as Said accuses the Orientalist of rendering and presenting him. Yet in the ethnographic encounter the subject of research is him/herself actively engaged in dialogue—regardless of his/her position vis-à-vis the researcher in the encounter. In other words, subjects bring to the ethnographic encounter their own agenda. This is not to either belittle or deny the asymmetrical power equation in which the research encounter is embedded. It is simply to assert that within this power equation the ones being studied strive to present themselves in a particular fashion, either by stressing some aspects of their culture or holding back others, often for a particular purpose. The precise historical moment and its power dimension color the relationship between researcher and subject. As we shall see, Palestinian women had a specific intent when participating in, researching or talking to outsiders.

The women I worked with viewed me as a foreigner to whom by telling their story they would be conveying it to the West. To them the ethnographic experience was an experience in dialogue in international politics. This is not to place fieldwork in the category of public relations; it is to recognize that the subjects of study often have just as much reason for agreeing to be studied as the ethnographer has for studying them. Palestinian women viewed their own lives as commentaries on suffering, as embodying the whole dialectical experience of national dispossession and resistance. Changes in their position and relations with others, of which they were vividly aware, were usually placed against the backdrop of international and local political events. That they did so reflected a clear understanding of their own position in the global political system.

To surmount the role of outside observer conveying their plight required persistence in probing and encouraging women to go beyond the formal discourse reserved for foreign delegations and journalists. Women used to tell me, "We're all liberated now because of the Resistance." The length of time spent in the field and observations of interactions and situations quickly dispelled these claims, components of a discourse reserved for visitors whom these women think should be presented a positive and endearing portrait of the national movement's ability to transform traditions and confront family-based authority. As I became friends with women—visiting often, going to events with them—the presenting of an ideal situation generally was dropped. I was able to gauge my own acceptance into the community and its openness to me by the progression of titles given me. Um Khalid initially introduced me as a "researcher" studying Palestinian women. Within a few weeks this gave way to a "friend" of the Resistance. Soon her children were calling me *khalti* (my mother's sister) after she herself referred to me as such in relation to them. Finally she alternated between the kinship term at home and *rafiqah* (comrade) in public. The other women in the camp followed suit, calling me *rafiqah* or *ukht* (sister).[16]

Objectifying Culture

Keesing poses a fundamental question when he asks whether anthropological research is possible only in situations of colonialism or postcolonialism where culture has become "a 'thing' to be articulated and objectified to an alien at once situated within the colonial framework of domination and more or less distanced from it" (1985:37). Nader suggests that anthropologists engage in "studying up" the power spectrum —examine the "culture of power rather than the culture of the powerless, the culture of affluence rather than the culture of poverty" (1974:289). Like Keesing, she questions whether the power component of fieldwork is affecting its theoretical results.

In studying a Palestinian community in exile such questions of the power relationship between researcher and subjects took on added dimensions, as did the question of the objectification of culture. What appears as the reality of a culture when during the ethnographic relationship the communication process is a negotiated one? In explaining his or her culture, the informant must objectify it in ways that may not necessarily be used within the society itself. In the case of the Palestinians the negotiation of presentation had decidedly political overtones.

First, Palestinians in Lebanon were an uprooted, dispossessed people, but at the same time they were members of a well-armed militant society, where the Resistance movement enjoyed a substantial degree of control and support. They determined who went in the camps and talked to both ordinary people and Resistance members. I had to have their support to do research and a permit from them to gain entrance to the camps and meet people. Once I was inside, they did not, as far as I know, try to prevent me from seeing or talking to anyone, nor did they ask to see the results of my research. Undoubtedly some people felt that they should cooperate since the Resistance had asked them to, but I certainly did not feel anyone was intimidated into cooperating with me. If anything, the Resistance having supported my project made it easy for those who wanted to talk to do so. If I hadn't had their support it is doubtful people would have responded to my multitude of questions.

Second, it was in such a context that Palestinians had objectified their culture. On the one hand, they were eager to present it to outsiders, and yet on the other, they were fearful that knowledge about them would be used to cause further harm to and control over them. Objectifying Palestinian culture became a way of reclaiming the past and controlling the future. It assumed a stringent importance in the face of Israeli expropriation of Palestinian culture—the land, art and architecture, culinary arts —and denial that it ever existed. Palestinian women were articulating their culture from a position of strength and also from a position of weakness. I was to be a medium to transmit this culture to the public in the Western power center where Palestinians are anxious for recognition and legitimacy, but I was only able to do so on the basis of Palestinian acceptance, tolerance, and hospitality. Like the Kwaio, who had made of custom a potent political symbol (Keesing 1985), the presentation of Palestinian culture has been politicized. The idiom of discourse is a militancy that pervades social relations and is the foundation of a new, dynamic cultural authenticity. The reaffirmation of a Palestinian culture underscores their existence in an international arena that refuses to accord them recognition, and it lends authenticity to the movement that has been organizing for the return.

1

Gender and Culture in Exile

Palestinians refer to 1948 and its immediate aftermath as *al-ghurbah* (exile) and *al-nakbah* (the disaster), terms that evoke sentiments of loss, alienation, tragedy, and betrayal. The year 1948 marks the transition from the tangibility of Palestine to a state of exile. This chapter sets the social context from which a women's movement and transformation in the meaning of gender were to emerge by briefly outlining the contours of pre-1948 Palestinian society and politics, the initial stages of exile in the refugee camps, and the rise of the PLO.

Pre-1948 Palestine

Early twentieth-century Palestinian social structure was composed of a small but wealthy urban merchant, religious, and landowning class, a mass base of peasants, and an emerging petit bourgeoisie of small merchants, traders, and an incipient intelligentsia. Society was fissioned along both horizontal and vertical lines—that is, crosscut by class, clan, regional, and religious cleavages inhibiting, for the most part, collective consciousness, organization, or action. Undoubtedly, the more salient division was rural-urban, a social division that survived the exodus of 1948, as peasants settled into refugee camps and urbanites into towns and cities.

Palestinian peasants were politically organized according to village and family ties to the landowning class by patron-client ties. Political elites were members of wealthy merchant and landowning families, though they themselves, doctors, lawyers, civil servants, and teachers, were often personally less well off (al-Hout 1979). Palestinian political organization during the Mandate has been described as "blocs of notables organized around a powerful individual of social, religious, political or economic prominence. And those who followed a given leader were likely to be drawn to him by personal, clan and regional rather than national or ideological considerations" (Nashif 1977:120).

In Palestine, political power was not allocated on the basis of sect (as in Lebanon). The geographically dispersed Christian minority constituted at most about 15 percent of the population, and the peasants were predominantly, but certainly not exclusively, Sunni Muslims. Palestine's sectarian composition, along with exile and repeated assaults, has structured a society where national identity has assumed a paramount position vis-à-vis sectarian identities.

The majority of Palestinians (75–80 percent) were small landowning peasants or sharecroppers. In the Mandate period, Palestine was increasingly integrated into the capitalist orbit. Land had become a commodity, subject to spiraling prices as it changed hands. As peasants faced a diminished access to land, wage labor increased. The emergent industrial sector was largely under Zionist control. The embryonic Palestinian urban proletariat was soon to be displaced by an exclusivist Jewish-only labor policy and subsequent exile to surrounding Arab states.

Nineteenth- and twentieth-century Palestinian social structure with its vertical cleavages, primordial loyalties, and factional politics was a fragmented society; class formation and class consciousness were underdeveloped. Salim Tamari (1982) argues that patronage and factional politics, which crosscut both rural-urban and peasant-landowner or elite divisions, functioned to deflect class politics. With the country under Mandatory rule, the growth of an indigenous bourgeoisie was stunted. Palestinian elites had access to the channels of power but no actual control over the state apparatus (Miller 1985:47–70).

Very little of a specific nature is known about women in pre-1948 Palestine. Granqvist's (1931) studies of a West Bank village in the 1920s and 1930s provide the most detailed descriptions of the lives of peasant women. For urban women very little exists that would allow anything more than a cursory glimpse of their daily lives. Overall one could speculate that Palestinian women's status was informed by structures and ideologies specific to the social formation. Kandiyoti (1987) argues that continuities in Middle East women's experiences are embedded in the culturally defined systems of control over women's sexuality that crosscut class and sect and are expressed in an honor/shame complex that constrains women's public and sexual behavior and the norms and structures of segregation that govern male-female interaction. Corporate control of female sexuality and reproductive potential was expressed in the practice of early and arranged marriages and a sexual double standard. Discontinuities arose from women's specific class position and the nature of the state. Discontinuities would include women's educational status and position in the labor force, which derive from her class position, and her legal status, which varies by sect.

Women were certainly not marginal to agricultural production. Peasant women like Um Nabil, now in her eighties, were an integral part of the family labor force and expressed an awareness of their valued position and how much it has changed since then:

As peasants we didn't feel above doing any kind of work. We women worked all day long in the fields, leaving the children at home with the in-laws. We breast-fed the babies and went home in the evening to cook. During the tobacco harvest we collected tobacco leaves and strung them to dry. When it was time to harvest wheat we helped the men do that, and we picked the olives in the fall. We used to work a bit less than the men in the fields because we also had to work at home. If the family became very large, the man would have to hire a male helper, since his wife would be too busy with the children and the house.

We used to get up very early in the morning. When the day was hot we arose at 3:00 A.M., before morning prayers. We were raised to do this kind of work. Today I wake up before the call to prayer, by myself. No one else gets up until it is time to leave for work, around 8:00 A.M. Had I still been in my country, by this hour I would have rolled up my sleeves and be fast at work plowing or picking figs or olives. By God, nowadays girls don't even know how to wash their underwear [author's note: a sign of incompetence in housework and personal hygiene and thus an absence of femininity]. Who is going to marry a girl if she can't wash her underwear!?

Urban elite women managed the large households necessary to maintain the status and social standing of their husbands' economic and political position. Um Hussein, member of a prominent Jerusalem-based landowning and religious family, lived in a large family compound with her extended family. When she married her paternal cousin, she assumed household duties, which didn't necessarily revolve around cooking and cleaning for a large number of family members, but organizing the household to do so and assuring that the home was open day and night and able to display the standards of hospitality expected of an elite family to visitors from all over Palestine. She said, "I didn't actually do housework. I had servants for that. My husband gave me money for the household, and I did with it whatever I wanted. I hired and fired the servants and organized their work. The house is the realm of women; men are outside of it."

Nor were women marginal politically. As we shall see in chapter 2, women were defining their own place in the national political sphere in the twentieth century.

Exile in Lebanon: 1948–1969

The bulk of the Palestinians who came to Lebanon were abruptly transformed from landowning or sharecropping peasants to stateless exiles in an often hostile and alien environment. Along with the loss of lands and livelihood, political and social institutions, with the exception of the family, begin to disintegrate. Social relations that revolved around land tenancy arrangements, such as patron-clients ties and trading arrangements with urban merchants, were severed with exile.

Caulfield cautions against a too hasty application of the concept of "deculturated" man (1974a:201–202). Exile and the dissolution of indigenous institutions cannot be equated with deculturization, since humanity is by definition cultural. Exile and dispossession did create a cultural void —old institutions were now hardly functioning, but new ones were to emerge in their stead.

A multiconfessional country with seventeen officially recognized sects, Lebanon was from independence in 1943 until the civil war of 1975–76 a parliamentary republic. The 1943 National Pact is an unwritten agreement between Maronites (Eastern Catholics) and Sunni Muslims that distributed Lebanon's political offices by sect. Lebanese belong to three main sects: Christian, Muslim, and Druze. It is now generally accepted that Muslims form a majority. The official allocation of political power, however, continues to rest on an assumed Christian majority. The civil war and its fifteen-year aftermath can be seen as an attempt to rewrite the sectarian-political map of Lebanon and challenge the economic and political dominance of the largely Maronite Christian community.

As Lebanon unwittingly found itself host to a large refugee population, tension and eventually conflict were perhaps inherent in the situation for both internal and external reasons.[1] The refugees were socially unwelcome to the working class, who viewed with trepidation the competition of the unskilled labor. In addition, the refugees found their right to work, travel, and engage in political activities circumscribed by the Lebanese government. Work permits were necessary to be legally employed and were not easy to obtain, travel was restricted to specific areas, and political organizations and events were forbidden.

The Maronites were quick to sense a threat to their economic and political hegemony from the largely Muslim refugees and feared their presence would upset the precarious sectarian balance and political status quo by serving as a focal point for the growing discontent of Lebanon's Muslims and their eventual mobilization against Maronite domination.

To further compound matters, in the late 1960s and throughout the 1970s Israel sustained a policy of military attacks on Lebanese civilian targets in an effort to compel the government to control armed Palestinian activity and turn the local populace against them (Khalidi 1986: 20–21).

When this study was conducted in 1980–1982, the Palestinian community in Lebanon was still recovering from the effects of the 1975–76 Lebanese civil war, which had caused dislocation on a large scale of both Lebanese and Palestinian communities. In effect, some Palestinians were now refugees twice—once from their original homes in Palestine and now from their camps. In largely Christian East Beirut, sustained military campaigns and wipe-up operations by the Lebanese Forces succeeded in depopulating Dbayyeh, Jisr al-Basha, and Tal al-Zaʿter camps of Palestinians and Lebanese Muslims and the camps were razed. Their residents took refuge in predominantly Muslim West Beirut. Since the early 1970s, southern camps, such as Nabatiyyeh, had been targets of Israeli bombing raids and incursions. The residents of Nabatiyyeh migrated northward in a gradual pattern—first to the southern, urban coastal center of Saida and then to Beirut, although some did leave Nabatiyyeh directly for Tal al-Zaʿter.

The Refugee Camps

With unimaginable rapidity, Palestinian peasants from different villages and regions found themselves inhabiting the same space. In spite of the attempt to recreate the structure of Palestinian villages in the camps, the refugees felt powerless in the wake of the sudden loss of control over their destiny and an intense frustration over the inability of any person, institution, or government to remedy their situation.

The ambiguity of exile can be likened to a collective trauma.

> Apart from the harsh conditions of the first few years, there was the psychological trauma of separation from home and property. The village—with its special arrangement of houses and orchards, its open meeting places, its burial ground, its collective identity—was built into the personality of each individual villager to a degree that made separation like an obliteration of the self (Sayigh 1979:107).

United Nations Relief and Works Agency (UNRWA) statistics indicate that 59 percent of the refugees in Lebanon were from the Galilee (ʿAkka, Bisan, Nazareth, Safad, and Tabariyya), 28 percent came from Haifa, 11 percent from Lydda (Jaffa, Ramle), and 1.5 percent from Jerusalem.[2]

Fifteen refugee camps were formally established throughout Lebanon[3] operated by the UNRWA, a special international agency charged with responsibility for the Palestinian refugees until they are either repatriated or compensated for their losses. The UNRWA provided the poorest refugees with tents, monthly rations of basic food supplies, primary and eventually secondary education, medical services, and refugee residency in Lebanon. Those with their own means, primarily townspeople or better off peasants, settled into Lebanese towns and cities where they attempted to reestablish their livelihoods.

Clustered around the Lebanese urban centers of Beirut, Tripoli, Saida, Sur, and Bʿalbak, the spatial distribution of the camps, from the far north to the southern border area, was intended to prevent the emergence of a geographically contiguous, cohesive Palestinian sociopolitical entity. Although in many instances clans and lineages were broken up and scattered, families and villagers did attempt to reside together. Thus the refugees settled themselves, as much as possible, according to village and family affiliations. The camps came to resemble a microcosm of pre-1948 Palestine, structurally arranged to re-form villages. Internally, the camps are roughly divided into sections defined by former village boundaries. Even today, one can find one's way by locating village areas. If you want to find the home of someone from Safad, you would ask, "Where do the people from Safad live?" Since the early 1970s, Resistance offices and facilities have been augmenting villages as spatial locators. For instance, people will give you directions to someone's house, saying, "That house is next to the Resistance co-op [or the kindergarten or office]." Thus the way Palestinians define and refer to space in the camps is in flux as Resistance institutions augment or in some cases replace village and neighborhood boundary markers.[4]

By 1967–68, Shatila camp, established in the early 1950s by seventy-three refugee families,[5] had expanded to house nearly five thousand people. The most dramatic demographic shift occurred in 1971, when the population nearly doubled to 8,220[6] as a result of the influx of Resistance fighters and cadres in the wake of the PLO's expulsion from its headquarters in Jordan. In 1979–80, the camp was home to 8,278[7] Palestinians, and since the mid-1970s it has been home to a substantial, though unknown, number of Shi'a Lebanese fleeing war-torn and depressed southern villages.

Initially, the camps were clearly separated from the surrounding Lebanese neighborhoods, although eventually the camps bordering Beirut, like Shatila and Burj al-Barajneh in the southeast and Tal al-Za'ter in the north, merged into the sprawling urban environment to form part of the growing slum belt that by the early 1970s encircled the Lebanese capital. Over the years, the tents were gradually replaced by tight clusters of one- and two-room cement houses covered by zinc roofs. The dusty, unpaved main roads are now lined with a noisy patchwork of small shops, garages, and vegetable and fruit stands. Between 1969 and 1982, the offices and institutions of the PLO were also found here.

The exodus from Palestine and settlement in refugee camps or urban areas did not blur class differences; on the contrary, it probably exacerbated them (Sayigh 1979:119). Those Palestinians with some capital were able to buy or rent property in the towns and cities, establish new businesses, and send their children to private Lebanese schools. Those refugees provisionally settled in the camps were generally poor peasants without capital, let alone skills. The differences between camp dwellers and those settled into towns and cities were usually ones of capital, education, religion, and kin networks—the presence or absence of relatives to facilitate settlement in urban areas—and business ties. The religious composition of the camps was fairly uniform. Except for the two smalls camps of Dbayyeh in East Beirut (destroyed in 1976) and Mar Ilyas in West Beirut, they were populated by Muslim Palestinians. By and large, Christian Palestinians settled in urban areas and a large number received Lebanese citizenship and thus some sense of security. Differences in control were also evident. The camps were patrolled by the Lebanese police and residents kept under surveillance for political activism. The geographical fragmentation of urban Palestinian society in Beirut was not as conducive to control by the Intelligence Services nor was involvement in their daily lives as feasible as in the camps.

Women describe the first decade of exile in terms that evoke death and a state of mourning. The loss of country and home and a refugee status were akin to the loss of a loved one. Madame Haddad, a middle-aged woman from Jaffa, said:

> In the beginning we didn't want to go out much because we were so depressed. After a while we got more used to it. Losing Palestine, our homes, was like losing a husband or a son. Slowly, very slowly, we got used to it. In the beginning, though, we didn't want to see anybody.

Palestinians may have become "more used" to exile, but memories of Palestine remained sharp and were transmitted to the children born in exile by their parents, but particularly by their mothers and grandmothers. Women relate anecdotes of life in Palestine, painting vivid descriptions of social life there and what they had. Today young people often can discuss how much land their families owned and what was grown on it. They know many of the families of their former villages, if not by acquaintance at least by name, and are aware of village history—its land arrangements and crops, its feuds, factions, and marriage patterns.

Everyday life in the refugee camps was constantly compared to a past that had been shattered abruptly and violently. Misfortune and poverty were explained to children as a consequence of the loss of their homes and country to the Zionists. When young children asked their parents why they were so poor and unable to buy good food and clothes, they were often told: "We can't give you these things because we lost everything to the Jews."

Young adults can recall gradually becoming aware of the idea of dispossession—that everything had been forcibly taken from them and their families. Humiliated by poverty and dependency on UNRWA rations, parents would promise their children material comforts upon the return to Palestine. Youngsters began to sense the urgency of return—the need to live a normal way of life and a secure existence within their own country.

A sense of mourning over the loss of Palestine was expressed in admonitions to children to behave appropriately: "You're a refugee; you can't do this" forging a sense of shared loss. It also defined the parameters of expectation and action. In the camps, showing off "nice things" such as new clothes, shoes, school supplies, furniture, etc., was avoided. To show off new possessions sets one apart from the larger group and defies the notion of equality in suffering.[8] There was a sense that everyone in the camps suffered the disaster equally. One didn't boast of what one had now, but rather of what one had in Palestine, where differentiation was more acceptable.

The "Palestinianism" that developed in the pre-Resistance period was not yet expressed in an organizational format, but was eventually to form the basis of collective action. It was informed by sources external to the community (repression and alienation) and those internal to it (the sense of collective loss and solidarity), for all camp Palestinians underwent similar experiences of uprooting, poverty, discrimination, and the feeling of loss of control over one's destiny. The camps provided the security and comfort of being in intimate proximity with others in similar circumstances. While vulnerable to attack, they were also a source of security, a place where poverty was a way of life shared by all and a refuge from the outside world where Palestinians were "others." It was also the locus of the reproduction of Palestinian social life and the forging of national identity. Although this emergent national consciousness was still politically unorganized and had no coherent structural framework for expression or communal action, it was beginning to form the basis of social integration and cohesion in the camps.

Al-Thawrah (the Revolution) and Community Self-Reliance: 1969–1982

In the late 1960s, Palestinian society in Lebanon began to undergo a sweeping transformation. In November 1969, after a year of sporadic clashes with the Lebanese army, the Resistance's open, armed presence in Lebanon was accepted by the Beirut government in an agreement known as the "Cairo Accords." The Palestine Liberation Organization (PLO), a political body or broad national front, represents the Palestinian community in exile and under occupation. It was established in 1964 by a decree at a meeting of Arab heads of state. Fateh, the acronym for *harakat al-tahrir al-watani al-filastiniyya,* formed in the late 1950s and early 1960s. Its initial base was solidly Palestinian nationalist, and its early leading members (Yasir 'Arafat, Salah Khalaf, Khalid al-Wazir, and Khalid al-Hassan) were exiled students and professionals. On 1 January 1965, Fateh launched its campaign of armed struggle against Israel. By 1969, in the wake of the defeat of the Arab armies in the 1967 Arab-Israeli war and growing popularity and mass support for guerrilla groups and their militant actions, Fateh was able to assume predominance in and leadership of the PLO. As a broad-based nationalist organization, it appealed to a wide range of sectors of the exile population. Over the next decade, "Fateh strengthened its hold on all parts of the PLO apparatus . . ." and "expanded the PLO's hold over all aspects of Palestinian public life, knitting together the dispersed and demoralised Palestinian communities into a reformed and distinctive national group under the leadership of the PLO" (Cobban 1984:6–11).

In Lebanon the Resistance assumed authority in the refugee camps in an uneasy relationship with UNRWA. The latter continued to operate while the Resistance movement proceeded to provide internal security, a vast network of quasi-governmental social services and employment opportunities for camp residents. In this respect, the PLO became a kind of embryonic government for the refugees, providing a range of ordinary services far beyond those of a strictly military nature for which it is more commonly known.

In Lebanon, Palestinians shared a national identity and consciousness that was beginning to augment and perhaps upstage primary affiliations and loyalties such as the family, clan, village, and sect. But most dramatically it was the rise of the Resistance movement in Lebanon in the late 1960s that accorded Palestinians a new sense of identity and dignity and was to transform Palestinian national consciousness into an organized format for national liberation. In essence, the PLO refashioned the Palestinian body politic after its dismemberment in the wake of the 1948 war. Pre-1948 forms of resistance, such as the localized peasant revolt, strikes, and even the more sustained 1936–1939 revolt and strike, were of little effect in obstructing national expropriation. After nearly two decades, the exile community began to respond in a substantially different fashion. During the 1950s and 1960s, a variety of political organizations, such as Fateh and the Arab Nationalist Movement, appeared and cross-border guerrilla operations were launched.[9] However, these political movements and actions did not involve the bulk of the camp community in a direct, organized, and sustained fashion. They were not yet targets of mobilization as individuals and as a community.

The camp population was linked to the political body in a variety of ways. During the 1970s, and further propelled by the 1975–76 Lebanese civil war, the PLO developed a vast network of social and cultural institutions that provided security, quasi-governmental services, and an emergent economic sector. In the camps, the *lijan sha'biyyeh* (Popular Committees), composed of representatives from the major political factions and independents as well as camp elders and notables, for example, functioned as municipalities responsible for maintaining services such as garbage collection, electricity, sewage, and water. The Palestine Armed Struggle Command (PASC) was the local police force that kept public order. Defense of the camps from external aggression was maintained by the guerrillas of the various political groups comprising the PLO and the local camp militia. A wide-ranging infrastructural complex of health, welfare, cultural, educational, and recreational institutions and popular unions served the camp populations. PLO economic enterprises were a growing source of employment, particularly for women in the camps.

Most important for understanding social transformation and the extent to which the Resistance movement permeated everyday life, vast numbers of camp residents belonged to the political groups that constituted the PLO. The PLO as an umbrella organization includes a number of member groups. Fateh is the largest member group, and two smaller groups, the Popular Front for the Liberation of Palestine (PFLP) and the Democratic Front for the Liberation of Palestine (DFLP), serve as leftist opposition to Fateh dominance. Both these groups have their roots in the Arab Nationalist Movement in the late 1960s.[10] The General Union of Palestinian Women (GUPW), the officially recognized representative of Palestinian women, along with other unions (workers', engineers', writers', and students'), was a member of the PLO. Union membership officially unites women from all the PLO's constituent political-military organizations and groups. Accurate membership numbers are not available (principally for security reasons but also because no one really knows), but people in the camps explain it this way: "We are all in the Resistance." Indeed, it was rare to find a household without at least one member active in politics. However, such statements need to be handled with some caution and scrutiny. It says more, and less, of the actual reality. Not everyone was formally affiliated to the Resistance, but most felt their everyday life was a form of resistance and that the PLO expressed their national sentiments.

Camp Palestinians insisted on the idea of return but had little concrete political expression of how to do so. With the rise of the Resistance movement, Palestinians had a new sense of national dignity and hope. They were leaving behind nearly two decades of political passivity, reliance on charity, and faith in the elusive ability and dubious intentions of world diplomacy and international agencies such as the United Nations to secure their return. The Resistance gave political form and expression to decades of developing national consciousness and hopes for return in addition to ensuring protection from abuse. Camp Palestinians, quick to realize that it would relieve them of the repressive presence of the Lebanese authorities, gave a joyous welcome to the Resistance's entry into the camps. It was the first body in nearly twenty years to represent Palestinian national aspirations and give the exiled community an institutionalized political structure. It molded, directed, and translated national consciousness into a political strategy for liberation. Under the Resistance movement, an image, however hazy, of a future political entity was emerging in the form of a democratic, secular, independent Palestinian state. Palestinians now had a sense of control over the course and nature of their daily lives and future destiny. The critical implications of control and political autonomy were chilling, as declared by one young Palestinian man after the Resistance's departure from Beirut and the positioning of the Lebanese army around the camps in the aftermath of the 1982 Israeli siege of Beirut: "We're going to have to go back to living as we did in the fifties and sixties when they ran things and we had no voice."

In discussing the contours of Palestinian identity it is important to note that the overt expression of class tension in exile Palestinian society has been deflected by an interrelated complex of events, experiences, and social processes. National dispossession, a refugee status, and ensuing marginalization and alienation of exile and repression by the Lebanese authorities have acted in concert to forge a collective identity derived from national and cultural affiliation and experience. Rapid and extensive social mobility has also played a primary role in this process of deflection. The initial geographically bounded nature of the camps, the ubiquitous poverty, and the strong family and village ties that knit together the social fabric were instrumental in shaping Palestinian identity.

It is Palestinian national identity that assumed paramount significance in how Palestinians viewed each other, tending to obscure the political expression of class differences between camp dwellers and urbanites. In the face of repression by the host population and state Palestinians felt strong sentiments of closeness with one another. Regardless of the degree of suffering in exile, which did of course vary by class, all Palestinians were without a state of their own and constantly at the mercy of the host country's policy toward them and all felt the precariousness of their situation in Lebanon. They located themselves vis-à-vis one another by geographical and kinship origins in pre-1948 Palestine and by the experience of exile. Palestinian identity was articulated through expressions of a heritage distinct from that of other Arab regions and a historical and emotive experience that sharply distinguished them from other Arabs who were citizens of a state. As the moral nature of the national movement developed and Palestinians saw themselves as betrayed politically by the Arab states and subjected to attacks by Lebanese militias, their cultural identity increasingly took on a specifically Palestinian quality. Conceding, of course, that they are Arabs and as such share general historical and cultural features with the other inhabitants of the region, Palestinians were distinguishing themselves from the Lebanese and other

Arabs by certain moral qualities. Women, young and old alike, would swear, "By God, a Palestinian man makes the best husband," comparing him to the Lebanese, whom they consider morally corrupt and weak, with a tendency to put their own interests before those of the family. Palestinians saw themselves as honest in financial transactions, unlike the Lebanese, whom they perceived to be "devious" and "possessed of a merchant mentality." Education was a primary point of differentiation, the Palestinians insisting that they were the best-educated people in the region. The common denominator in identity was attachment to the same geopolitical entity, the insecurity of exile, the cultural identity that took shape around both, and the strong sentiments of support for the national movement.

Cultures of resistance are built upon "expressions of ethnic identity and group solidarity . . . retained in part from precolonial traditions, but they are also reshaped, altered, and created anew" and involve "a long process of redefinition of cultural identity, widening in scope from narrower village . . . to larger and larger groups, coupled with a growing awareness of the commonality of exploitative situations and of solidarity in the face of oppression" (Caulfield 1974a:203–204). It is not unusual for a community such as the Palestinians to respond to repression and exploitation by emphasizing the bounded nature of their national community and their cultural distinctiveness. A sense of separateness, a sense of national and cultural self as quite distinct from that of other Arabs, was intermingled with new forms of organization and categories of meaning to respond to more dominant and powerful structures.

A process of cultural reconstruction began to unfold. It was less an endeavor to resurrect or return to tradition[11] than one of devising new or imbuing old cultural elements with meaning derived from a new sort of experience.[12] The commonality of struggle informed new categories of meaning. The ethos, or defining quality, of the Palestinian culture of resistance was militancy or struggle (*nidal*), whose concrete expression was the PLO in all its myriad forms and armed struggle. The words *nidal* and *al-qadiyyah* (the cause) pervaded Palestinian discourse. As concepts they defined the self and were a way of categorizing segments of the community to others. During crises, staying in the camp and not fleeing attack was described as a militant act. Indeed, women referred to their whole lives as a form of struggle.

Behavior by women that would have once provoked an outcry and harsh reprisals was now reconceptualized and filtered through a nationalistic lens. Women's political involvement entailed behavior that in any other context they themselves would hardly have contemplated, let alone undertaken. Sleeping outside the home is a common and frequent example cited by women of the extent to which national political participation redefined the parameters of acceptable female behavior. Women activists had to occasionally sleep away from home, and this became more acceptable as families cited the need for their girls to help the national cause. Among both men and women, social relations were increasingly based less on kin and village ties and more on political affiliation. Politically endogamous marriages were a fairly good index of this phenomenon. The culture of resistance was a response, part of the dialectic of oppression, enabling the exile community to manage the tensions inherent in the increasingly hostile atmosphere between themselves and the host country and to overturn the political forces that initially dispossessed them.

In spite of the dominance of national sentiments in forming cultural identity, class consciousness among camp dwellers is quite apparent, although no organized arena is yet sufficiently developed for class conflict to mature and unfold. Class interest or conflict was not evident in the political divisions in the Resistance. The left-wing groups, which espouse a class analysis of the Israeli-Palestinian conflict, do not necessarily appeal to the working class and camp dwellers more than Fateh's broad national approach. But within every organization the tensions between "those who work in the offices and bureaucracy" and "those who fight" are often apparent in the guerrillas' sarcastic comments about the former. They see themselves as carrying the burden of the struggle and in doing so embody the defining qualities of struggle *(nidal)*.

Since 1948, Palestinian society has witnessed a remarkable form of social mobility, in part as a result of increased access to education. Education and the jobs that it leads to have given birth to a new middle class, whose members were prominent in the national movement bureaucracy. The immediacy of the national struggle tends to mute, but certainly not contain, other conflicts in Palestinian society, such as those of gender and class. Indeed, as we shall see throughout this book, it is the national movement and women's involvement in it that figures so prominently in the explanations concerning the origins of the debate on gender and women's feminist consciousness.

Though the camps were composed of former peasants and the majority could be considered poor, there were class disparities that were not always immediately apparent. There were, however, no major class differences that would have indicated divergent interests. An owning class whose existence as a class was predicated on the labor of another, propertyless class was absent. Yet there were variations in education, income, employment, and status. In every camp there were small groceries and repair shops, family-run affairs that hardly generated enough revenue to support a family. Office or clerical employees in the private sector, along with those employed by the UNRWA, formed a small, emergent petite bourgeoisie clearly of a higher status than workers. By far the largest sector of employed males in the camps was wage laborers in construction and seasonal agriculture, working on a daily basis.[13] The formerly self-sufficient peasants are now a wage-earning *lumpenproletariat*. During the 1970s, an important source of income was to be found in Resistance employment—either as employees or salaried full-time activists or guerrillas.

In the 1960s and 1970s, the oil boom in the Gulf and Saudi Arabia opened employment opportunities for the new generation of educated and skilled Palestinians from the camps. This gave rise to a new form of socioeconomic differentiation, the extent of which was dependent upon whether a family had someone working in the Gulf and sending home remittances and, if so, how many such relatives they had. Indeed, it was rare to find a camp family that did not have at least one relative employed in the Gulf regularly sending home remittances. These remittances visibly improved the standard of living and educational opportunities. Additional rooms were constructed to enlarge cramped homes, televisions, radios, refrigerators, stoves, and washing machines eased the margins of poverty, and the financing of private secondary and university education for sons was facilitated.

Resistance employment for women also had an effect on economic differentiation. Single women who worked often gave some of their salary to the household and kept the rest for themselves. Both remittances from the Gulf and women's economic contributions to the household budget allowed more young men to pursue higher education, creating a spiraling relationship between rising incomes and education. As sons were better educated, they also contributed a greater share of money to the household, increasing its overall standard of living.

Women in Exile

If exile had an uneven impact by class it was no less uneven by gender. For peasant women the loss of land meant an abrupt separation from their productive role in agriculture. Agricultural and domestic labor in a family-based unit of production was replaced by labor centered narrowly in the home and, conversely, by the introduction of wage labor. With men finding it difficult to procure employment adequate to feed, clothe, shelter, and educate large families, some women entered the wage labor market. They were hired as factory workers, maids, and seasonal agricultural workers by Lebanese employers eager to exploit a new supply of cheap labor. It was fairly easy to pay Palestinian women substantially less than Palestinian men. Being both refugees and illegal workers, Palestinian men and women were initially a passive labor force, posing little threat of unionism or strikes. It was not uncommon for middle-aged and older women to take up cottage industries such as sewing and embroidery to earn extra cash and to engage in small-scale trading in used clothing and dairy and vegetable products. For the first time, many women were faced with the double burden of domestic and wage labor.

Poverty, overcrowding, and unsanitary conditions in the refugee camps exacerbated women's already heavy work load of hauling water, cooking, cleaning, washing, and child care. To compound matters, the dispersal informed basic structural changes in kinship and family relations. It was often the case that extended families were broken up and larger lineages and clans were scattered to different camps or even countries. In the past, women's domestic labor had been a cooperative venture, with those who shared a household engaging in collective housework and child care. In this way women avoided being overburdened by onerous domestic duties.

The increased prevalence of neolocal residence granted women more freedom from family-imposed restrictions on their mobility, but also meant women were left alone to carry out their domestic work. The scattering of extended families, lineages, and neighborhoods broke up large domestic work groups, and women increasingly became individual household laborers. This trend was particularly evident by the time I did my research. Women, kin or friends/neighbors, still shared some cooking and child-care tasks but certainly not on a level possible in pre-1948 Palestine. Now many households were dispersed and cooperative tasks were more in the nature of helping out a friend rather than a well-defined division of labor within a household.

The loss of status that usually accompanies women's separation from an agricultural mode of production in underdeveloped nations (Boserup 1970) was not immediately apparent among refugee women. Palestinian women don't easily fit into social science categories that analyze the impact of global political-economy changes on women. Generally the incorporation of peasants into the world capitalist system refines the boundaries between public and private domains—the realms of men and women. Refugee families underwent different sorts of stresses and pressures from peasant families transformed into wage laborers in a nation-state. Camp women did not become isolated domestic laborers with a corresponding diminishment of status, as is often the case. They continued to live in a spatial universe that resembled Palestinian village society. At least some kin were close by, and in many instances cooperative

34

relations with neighbors gradually sprang up. As women became educated and entered the work force and national politics, new avenues of status were available.

The families of young girls took advantage of the free primary schooling offered by the UNRWA, forming the basis for a new generation of literate women.[14] For village girls in pre-1948 Palestine education was almost nonexistent. In the towns and cities private schools were available for the elite and emergent middle class. In exile in Lebanon, the appeal of schooling for girls gained strength for a number of reasons. The need for basic literacy was soon apparent. Girls needed to contribute to the family income, and literacy was seen as bettering their chances of earning a decent wage. Many women still cite the necessity for literacy in order to help one's children with their schoolwork and to write letters to family members abroad. In the marriage arena, a literate young girl has better chances of marrying a literate man who is able to earn an adequate salary. One hears fathers and husbands voice with frequency the need for women to be able to support themselves and their children in the event of widowhood.

Women's mobility was not necessarily suddenly and drastically restricted. The structure of the camp—its initial isolation from Lebanese population centers, its close-knit living quarters, grouping families and villages—accorded women a degree of mobility within their immediate neighborhoods, as they had in their villages. Yet for other women proximity to strange males underlay the imposition of restrictions on their movements by male kin.

Although the collective nature of loss was emphasized, it did affect the sexes differently. Women's traditional role as socializers of children was infused with new significance in the exile community, where a specifically Palestinian identity was emerging and memories of the past were highly valued. In addition, women were respected and admired for managing households in such harsh conditions. Another plausible explanation for the absence of a decline in women's status was their increasing involvement in national politics—they were valued and respected participants in strikes, demonstrations, and underground political activities that were common in the pre-Resistance 1950s and early 1960s.

When resources such as food, shelter, employment, health care, and education are scarce and access is limited, girls and women are often at a disadvantage.[15] Priority is often accorded to men and boys in such instances. In Palestinian society, such discrimination was not as prevalent as in many other third world regions, but it was sometimes a crucial factor in a girl's poor health, in her lack of educational achievement, and in the sudden rise in the school drop-out rate upon reaching puberty.

Doctors in the camp tell me that the first few years of refugee life had particularly negative effects on women's health. The overcrowded camps were excellent breeding grounds for infectious diseases, and food shortages resulted in high-levels of maternal malnutrition. Unsanitary conditions fostered high infant and maternal mortality rates. As refugees, the Palestinians were barred from access to public Lebanese medical services. To fill this vacuum, the UNRWA established rudimentary clinics, including mother- and child-care centers to serve camp women. However, the range of services was sharply limited by understaffing and underfunding.

The era of the Resistance (1969–1982) marked a significant change in women's material conditions of existence and status. The PLO strove to cut short blatant economic exploitation. Palestinian women were no longer to work as domestic servants. Indeed, women sometimes refer to the 1950s and 1960s as the time when Palestinian women worked as servants, underscoring their sense of powerlessness and shame. To meet the basic needs of refugee women, new productive opportunities were set up, and attitudes toward women working outside the home began to shift. With the intention of cutting short exploitation in the Lebanese economy, preparing women to support their families in case of widowhood, and developing Palestinian economic self-sufficiency, the PLO opened small factories and workshops to employ women. It also launched literacy campaigns and initiated vocational training programs for women in industry, nursing, sewing, and clerical work. At the same time, independent groups of women established private social service agencies, cultural associations, and educational facilities in and around the camps. These organizations coordinated networks of child-care centers and vocational training programs. The Palestine Red Crescent Society, sponsored by the PLO and with a largely local staff, provided health care for women through hospitals, clinics, home visits, health education, mother-and child-care facilities, and sanitation programs in the camps.

The meaning of work for women was transformed during this period. Women perceived work not just as a temporary necessity brought upon them by the difficulties men faced in finding employment and feeding their families. Now to work was a national endeavor and a statement of women's increased autonomy and participation in public life. These are the perceptions conveyed by women's public discourse and the discourse officially sanctioned and propagated by the national movement.

During the Resistance era, women's organizations became more self-reliant in determining their own needs and priorities. Local leaders emerged to lead activities in the camps and link the Resistance more closely to camp families. Women's organizations in the camps debated, planned, and initiated social and economic programs, and they strove to change negative attitudes toward women's capabilities and rights. New categories of action, most revolving around the political sector, opened up for women—as activists, workers, leaders, and fighters.

While the social and economic status of women improved during the Resistance era as gender boundaries were challenged and new productive and political roles were made available, a new and ominous danger faced Palestinian women. Israeli air raids and attacks by private Lebanese militias devastated some camps and gave rise to massive population shifts, with severe consequences for women.

By definition, refugee women are vulnerable to sexual attack. Protected only by kinsmen in the early refugee period, women were hardly ever objects of physical attack. Later the presence of the Resistance in the camps offered women a limited environment free from danger and a heightened mobility in surrounding neighborhoods, but the increasing violence throughout Lebanon in the 1970s and 1980s struck Palestinian women with particular ferocity.

Since the 1975–76 civil war in Lebanon, Palestinian women and children have become specific targets of attack (Kapeliouk 1984; Cutting 1988). The logic behind this gruesome strategy is to sow panic in the refugee community and precipitate a Palestinian flight to neighboring Arab countries, as well as to demoralize men serving in the military by revealing in stark grotesqueness their inability to protect their families and homes. One of the worst examples occurred during the height of the Lebanese civil war in 1976. The Phalangist militia, a right-wing, mainly Maronite Catholic group, launched a military campaign to clear East Beirut of Muslim-inhabited slums and Palestinian refugee camps. During the ensuing nine-month siege of Tal al-Za'ter camp, hundreds of women were killed attempting to bring water to their dehydrated children under heavy artillery fire and sniping. Hundreds more were indiscriminately slaughtered when the camp was overrun. During the Israeli-sponsored massacre in Sabra-Shatila camps in September 1982, women and children were deliberate targets of murder and mutilation (Kapeliouk 1984).

With this background in mind, we can now look at the early years of the women's movement. Its development was fairly isomorphic with the historical, political, and social development of the Palestinian national movement as a whole.

2

The Palestinian Women's Movement: Organization and Representation

Initially scholars of the Palestine question focused their research and writings on the historical and political dimensions of the loss of Palestine and the creation of Israel (Sayigh 1987:15). There was a dearth of interest in social history, the groups through which it studies society and history —peasants, workers, and women, among others—and its methodologies. The discourses produced by these social groups and their version of history, what Foucault terms "subjugated knowledges," were perceived as somehow less truthful and legitimate than institutionalized knowledge and thus as falling outside the canons of scientific knowledge (Foucault 1977:81–84). The research, writing, and presentation of Palestinian women's history is characterized by "fragmentation" (Sayigh 1987:13) attributable to a conception of knowledge in which alternative discourses possessed little relevance or standing in the world of "science."

Usually illiterate and distant from the institutional expressions of scientific knowledge, these groups leave less record of their achievements; indeed, they are not seen as actors or participants on the stage of history but as, by and large, passive bystanders or, more generously perhaps, as recipients of social change, certainly not as pivotal in the momentum of history as the urban literati with their written records (Foucault 1977:81; Khalidi 1988:207–209).[1] Most early women activists were literate, and some did leave record of their undertakings (Mogannam 1937). However, the written sources of women's history are scattered in several countries, many are in private collections that are difficult to locate, if not unknown to the interested researcher, and war has led to the destruction of some sources (Sayigh 1987:20).

In examining women's history in the context of "subjugated knowledges," younger women activists until very recently had largely discounted the early history of the women's movement, consigning it to a few references in their popular literature. As one consequence, contemporary activists draw a distinct line between their activism and that of women in the pre-1948 period (Sayigh 1987:18). They perceive their own actions as innovative, radical, and a break with tradition. One young militant scornfully commented, "Those women just used to meet to drink tea, discuss clothes and their charitable projects for the poor."

Palestinian women have been somewhat hesitant to give written expression to their collective and individual experiences of the past fifty years. Until recently few autobiographies, semifictional novels or essays presented intimate portraits of immediate experiences of the forces, both internal and external, that shaped their lives (see Al-Hamdani 1987; Khaled 1973; Khalifeh 1985; Boulatta 1978; and Tawil 1980). In part, this is related to the state of Palestinian literature, in which the novel is a relatively recent phenomenon. But by and large, the embeddedness of women's lives in larger family structures and networks, whose distance from the political was not pronounced, meant that they more easily located their own situation, as individuals and as a collectivity, within a broader political framework. The multiple forms of domination in their lives were not culled one from the other. Women did not endow their situation with qualities distinct from those shaping the national situation.

Most significant for women, contemporary alternative discourses, such as those given expression in writings on or by women, challenge the cultural and ideological dominance of the prevailing institutionalized "scientific" discourse and expose how it reproduces and upholds specific power arrangements in society (see al'Amed 1981; Sayigh n.d.). The lacuna in knowledge of pre-1948 women's history should be situated in this light.

To undertake comprehensive research on women's history of political activism in the pre-1948 period is a daunting task requiring extended research excursions to various countries to seek out private papers, conduct interviews with surviving women, and carry out archival research in libraries and research institutions. Secondary sources offer little information, since few exist and their authors faced many of the obstacles mentioned above. This chapter is an overview of the period in question cast in an analytical framework that explores the relations between nationalism and feminism. Sources include interviews with women active at the time and published materials. The contemporary period (1968–69 to 1982) will be taken up in chapter 5.

The origin of the Palestinian women's movement, its social bases, and its development, both theoretical and in terms of praxis, are located in the historical and social specificity of early twentieth century Palestine. Like women's movements in other third world areas, its history is embedded in the Palestinian experience of response to specific historical and political events such as the British Mandate, the imposition of Zionism in Palestine and its eventual hegemony, dispossession, and the emergence of a national movement that attempted, ultimately in vain, to assert the indigenous population's historic right to Palestine. It would be incorrect, however, to assume that the women's movement was simply a response to these events. Its contours were nuanced by the impact of these events on the lives of women and their response to them as crystallized in the cultural milieu of early to mid-twentieth-century Palestine. In short, the women's movement is intimately framed by global historical time, the determining force of specifically Palestinian sociocultural forms, and the transformative social practices of women themselves.

A specifically female perspective was evident in women's activism that allows it to be subsumed under the category of feminism. Undoubtedly a nationalist political framework and continuous conflict have been prominent forces shaping its growth, stances, successes, and failures. Several characteristics define the Palestinian women's movement from its origins through the rise of the Resistance: a tension between feminist and national demands, secularism, a decentralized structure, a largely urban character, an upper- and middle-class leadership and membership, and a close alignment with the national political movement. Like the broader national movement, the women's movement, since its inception, has been distinctly secular in ideology and membership. The Palestinian Christian minority (approximately 15 percent) was involved in both the national movement and the women's movement. Some of the qualities that shaped the contours of the early women's movement—its nationalist affiliations and its class bias—have acted over a fifty-year span to circumscribe its boundaries, range of action, and ideological development.

Intermittent but protracted conflict and the nationalistic character of the Resistance movement have more often than not overridden attempts by the women's movement to bring to the political forefront specifically women's issues, tending along the way to deflect a momentum toward a feminist consciousness. Women's organizations were part of the emergence of a very nascent civil society, in this case organizations that crosscut sect, kin, and regional affiliation but did remain largely class bound. A major question that arises concerns whether or not women's participation in civil society offers any guarantee of emancipation in the event of statehood. This question will be dealt with more extensively in chapter 5.

Alongside the prominence of the national movement, feminist currents were coursing through the region (Shaarawi 1987; Badran 1988; Bayat-Philipp 1978; Philipp 1978; Marsot 1978). While national movements may be the political backdrop against which women's movements emerge, that they also constrain their scope of development and action is equally evident. The dynamics of interaction and articulation seems a more appropriate and ultimately useful manner of approaching the relationship between nationalism and the women's movement than counterposing them. Badran astutely reminds us that in asking whether women should put women's issues before national liberation issues we are forcing an "either/or position" (Badran 1988:16). The question we need to explore is whether Palestinian women in participating in the national struggle were also waging a struggle for their own rights. What kinds of political consciousness propelled these early activists into the political arena? Did their perception of the national struggle and its hoped for outcome—Palestinian independence—contain a women's agenda? Did women feel their position in society would improve after the achievement of national goals? Egyptian women active in the late nineteenth and early twentieth centuries "refused to be maneuvered into an either/or position" and instead *"generated a construct of nationalism in which women's liberation was embedded* and fought *concurrently* as feminists and nationalists" (ibid.).

The sociopolitical and ideological climate in which the women's emancipation movement arose in the late nineteenth- and early twentieth-century Arab world was engendered by the interrelated political currents of nationalism and the quest for independence and reform. As attested to by the appearance of numerous books and articles on women and a plethora of women's magazines, the issue of women's position in society was a much debated and controversial topic in nationalist and reformist circles in Syria, Lebanon, and Egypt, the first Arab country to foster a women's movement and achieve independence.

The desire for independence and social development was the impetus for an incipient, indigenous Arab feminism that emerged coterminously with the national movement but that certainly, at this early stage, had its own character and dynamic.[2] Led by middle and upper class urban women, the early women's movement flourished in an era that increasingly looked with favor upon secular education for boys and increased access to education by girls. The reforms in the status of women within an Islamic framework suggested by Muhammad ʿAbduh, Saʿd Zaghlul, and Qasim Amin were designed to present an enlightened and liberal Islam as a way to meet the challenge posed by Western hegemony (Badran 1988:18; Haddad 1980:159). This liberal atmosphere, along with British occupation and an awareness of the necessity of elite-peasant cooperation to confront Zionism and for all sectors of society to be politically engaged, was the climate in which Palestinian women's organizations developed.

Equality in Repression: Nationalist Roots

Palestinian women perceived themselves as victims of Zionism not as women, a separate social category, but as Palestinians who felt their national identity and survival in their homes threatened by British occupation and a hardly disguised Zionist claim to their country. In conformity with gender ideologies that prescribed separate social activities for men and women, expressed in norms of seclusion, women undertook to organize separately from men, but not from the larger national movement in terms of goals and issues. They claimed public space for themselves but maintained in general form the norms of segregation; there was no dramatic, public ritual of lifting of the veil as occurred in Egypt.

Early accounts of women's political participation and organizations are scarce and often present contradictory information. From the literature and discussions with activist women an overview of the situation can be sketched. Four historical periods distinguish the women's movement, each framed by a specific set of historical circumstances and the nature of relations to the national movement. The 1920–1929 period is noteworthy for the initial emergence of the women's movement in the context of growing opposition to Zionism and the British Mandate. Between 1936–1939, a period of revolt in Palestine, women's organizations displayed mounting militancy and gained experience in militant politics, preparing them for the battles of 1947–48. From 1948–1965, the women's movement was fragmented as the Palestinians dispersed throughout the Arab world and beyond and was subjected to restrictions by Arab governments. Eventually, between 1965–1982, a centralized women's movement led by the middle class emerged. It was geared to preparing women for national struggle and was formally integrated into the national movement.

The earliest mention of women's participation in national politics is references in the PLO literature[3] to demonstrations in Haifa, Jaffa, and Jerusalem in 1917, a year of large-scale manifestations of widespread discontent with Zionist immigration and British occupation.

Peasants were the first to sense the potential dangers of a form of colonialism based on colonization of the land and not the people. As the first victims of land takeovers, they reacted violently only a few years after the first *aliyah*[4] of 1882.[5] Little mention is made in the literature of the specific role of women, though peasant women later played a vital support role in the rebellion of 1936–1939.

1920–1929: Striking Out on Their Own

In January (or February) 1920,[6] the largest demonstration to date, 40,000 people, some of them women, took place in Jerusalem. Afterward a group of women formed part of a delegation to meet the British High Commissioner, demanding abrogation of the Balfour Declaration and cessation of the mistreatment and torture of prisoners by the Mandatory authorities.

Women's organizations' claiming of public space and their ideological development closely parallel the incidence of British and Zionist policy and violence toward the Palestinian population on the one hand and both peaceful and militant response by the latter on the other. In previous years, urban elite women had been active in charitable associations that also promoted education for girls (see Mogannam 1937 and Haddad 1980). They increasingly expanded the content of their work to encompass political as well as social endeavors and extended the boundaries of space for protest into the public realm and toward the occupying power as the threat to their national position became clearer. A growing discontent with Zionist and British policy and actions in their country was evident in increased organizing and activities of the women's associations. Outbreaks of communal violence in 1921 and 1929–30 were pivotal in giving birth to new women's organizations. On 1 May 1921 there were riots and indiscriminate killings by both Palestinians and Jews in the port city of Jaffa. A small Zionist march through Jaffa and ensuing clashes between rival Zionist groups ignited the conflict. The root cause, however, was considerably more complex. Palestinians were by now convinced that the Zionists intended to take over Palestine economically, politically, socially, and demographically.

In Jerusalem in 1921, a group of urban, educated, and upper class women, led by Milia al-Sakakini and Zlikhah Ishaq al-Shahabi formed the Palestine Women's Union (PWU), the first women's political organization, which activists today refer to as the precursor of the current GUPW. The PWU's interests were in welfare activities designed to improve the standard of living of the poor and to organize women around national activities.

One of the few books on this period, *The Arab Woman and the Palestine Problem,* by Matiel Mogannam, herself an activist, begins discussion of women's political role with the events of 1929, when the First Arab Women's Congress of Palestine was held in Jerusalem to consolidate the PWU.[7] Between two to three hundred delegates attended, bringing together representatives of the various women's societies, associations, and organizations from locales scattered throughout Palestine. In an interview with the author in 1985, she recounted how the 1929 congress was initiated:

> You see, there were a lot of disturbances going on in Jerusalem and in Haifa and all over. As everyone knows, at that time the Muslim women would not do anything. They were veiled. But there are times when you cannot do anything except just go out and do something. We had to do something to help the men. So we decided, a few women together, to hold a conference of all Arab women and have a demonstration and go to the High Commissioner and protest what the Jews are doing and everything that is going on. That's how it started.

The flurry of women's organizing following violent outbreaks was intended to meet the social needs of the population and to protest a political and economic situation in which peasants were being forced off the lands they worked. There was minimal industrial development to absorb labor, and the incipient industrial sector was designed to employ largely Jewish labor. The effects of such a process of changing relations of production and reproduction on peasant women cannot be minimized. With the loss of land, women likewise lost a significant aspect of their productive role in the larger agricultural household unit. Isolation increased with migration, as did the loss of productive work outside the now narrowly defined domestic sector, which was no longer the main unit of production and consumption.

During the previous decade, in a charitable spirit and with an awareness of the importance of socioeconomic development to face the challenge of colonization, elite women had organized a number of benevolent associations. These were intended to assist the poor through relief, infant- and child-care instruction, and education for girls. Groups of women formed associations, either religious or secular, to promote education for girls and to tend to the needs of the poorer members of their religious communities or, in the case of secular associations, assist the poor in their neighborhoods. With growing peasant landlessness and poverty, the women's societies faced an increasingly daunting task.

These associations and organizations evinced little conscious interest in confronting—with a view to changing—the gender status quo. Little effort was directed toward discussion of changing male-female or familial relations. However, the issue of women's participation in the public realm was directly confronted in practice. The compulsion to act as involved citizens in the public arena was an endeavor to recast women's social position. At the time, Palestinian women were acutely aware of the organic links binding their movement to the national movement and located their own situation as women squarely in the prevailing political situation. Accordingly, they were cognizant of the limitations they faced if they were to attempt to formulate and demand reforms in women's legal status while under Mandatory rule. Mogannam stated in reference to the Egyptian women's movement, concerned as it was with women's rights, particularly legal ones.

> . . . such measures of reform can only be introduced by National Governments, or by persons deriving their authority from the people. A Mandatory Power finds itself unable to embark on any scheme of reform which in its opinion may arouse the least religious susceptibility of any community . . . If Palestine had a legislative council elected by the people, it could introduce any such reformatory measures without making itself liable to or risking any criticism or attack . . . It is therefore difficult for any woman's organization in Palestine or Syria to obtain any legislative sanction for matters of which the country may be in need . . . In Palestine, however, owing to the prevalent peculiar circumstances . . . Arab women's activities were developed into a widespread movement of a general political character, under the auspices of a woman's executive (1937:53–55).

Early Organization

Without more extensive research it is difficult to determine with precision the nature of the relations between the national movement and the women's movement. Mogannam commented: "We always combined forces with them, that is with the men on the Executive Committee. For instance, if we were to send a memorandum to His Majesty the King of Britain, we wouldn't do it without having the Executive Committee look it over to see if it is all right."

She also noted that the men encouraged the women in their protests and charitable work but did not direct their actions. Moreover, the women were financially independent of the national movement, raising money through bazaars and festivals and collecting donations from religious institutions to pay for their expenses.

The strengthening and consolidation of the women's movement got under way in 1929, another landmark year in Palestine, noteworthy for the level of violence. Zionist state formation was no longer in an embryonic stage. It was openly and actively taking shape and becoming entrenched. Immigration was reaching record levels, and the Palestinians were becoming alarmed by "unfolding evidence of the fully fledged statehood they planned: their 'conquest' of land and labour, their insistence on Hebrew, their separate schools and hospitals, their self-segregation—residential, economic, social and cultural—and their expulsion of the Arabs from every institution they established" (Hirst 1977:63).

Landlessness among the peasants and the ensuing process of urbanization and *lumpenproletarianization* were precipitating factors in the calamitous events of 1929. Pursuant to the 1929 riots and killings, numerous Palestinian men were jailed in British prisons and sentenced to death. Living conditions among their families were appalling; having lost their chief breadwinners, they were in dire financial straits. Numerous homes were destroyed in a policy of collective punishment, and in some families children became orphans.

The women's associations and societies, Muslim, Christian, and secular-nationalist, that gathered in Jerusalem on 26 October 1929 for the First Palestine Arab Women's Congress found themselves confronted with the social and political problems resulting from the upheavals of 1929. Mogannam referred to the effects of this period on women as "the greatest change in the life of the Arab woman in Palestine and in the concentration of their forces" (1937:69). She relates that women leaders thought it necessary to hold a general women's congress to consolidate diverse efforts (ibid.:70). Women were clearly organizing around national issues: the Balfour Declaration, Zionist immigration, land sales, the economy, and national independence. The main topics on the agenda were the current political and social situation and the responsibility of the Mandatory Power. In pursuit of its goal of organizing women to confront Zionist immigration and the British Mandate, the congress called for a "national movement of consolidated action" by all women's groups. The congress passed three resolutions; the first condemned the Balfour Declaration as indicating the destruction of the Arab nature of Palestine and called upon its inhabitants to work for its abrogation, the second called for independence for Palestine and declared support for the national movement, and the third called for efforts to support independence in trade and commerce and a cessation of land sales to Zionists.

As women's organizations acquired a more overt political tone and intent, cultural norms governing women's access to public space and comportment were being held up to scrutiny. Initially, Mogannam relates, the women desired to present their memorandum to the wife of the Chancellor, "as Moslem members of the delegation could not properly appear before the High Commissioner" (ibid.:73–74). Since the Chancellor's wife was unable to receive a delegation with political intent, the women's delegation "had no other alternative but to wait upon the High Commissioner at Government House, and to ignore all traditional restrictions" (ibid.:74). In discussing this incident, Mogannam relates that she spoke with the governor of Jerusalem about holding a demonstration and he expressed his disapproval, anticipating that men would join in and a riot would ensue. When the women insisted he compromised: " 'Alright, you can have a demonstration, but you cannot walk. You must go in cars.' "

Returning to the congress, still in session, the women organized a procession of cars, 120 to be exact, to depart from the meeting place and pass through the streets of Jerusalem, stopping at foreign consulates to present their resolutions (ibid.:75–76). The governor had also warned them not to make speeches and to stay in their cars. The women followed his orders but instructed their drivers to blow their horns. "They couldn't do anything," Mogannam laughed. "We didn't make speeches. We only tooted our horns."

Before adjourning, the congress also pledged to support the Arab Executive Committee[8] and they elected a fourteen-member Executive Committee. They resolved to establish women's societies in all cities and major towns of Palestine and, where benevolent organizations already existed, to coordinate their activities (ibid.:77).

The congress organized for both political and social work to confront a national crisis, and as women do today, they sought to organize relief services. Mogannam, outlining some of the charitable activities of the congress, notes that it established the Arab Women's Society of Jerusalem in 1930, whose aim was to "assist the Arab woman in her endeavours to improve her standing, to help the poor and distressed, and to encourage and promote Arab national enterprises" (ibid.:55). Their first project was to open an infant welfare center in 1931, and eventually, as a result of their expanding awareness of poverty as a cause of poor infant health, they undertook home visits to give mothers health education and to distribute food, money, and clothing.

In their many appeals to the British Mandatory authorities and government in England the women stressed their humanitarian perspective on the violence racking Palestine, underscoring their particularly feminine perspective of conflict and their role in its resolution. Indeed, while the women were also avid nationalists, this public humanitarian stance, real though it was, also was an indication of their astute awareness of how they were perceived by the occupying power.

The leadership of the women's movement was concentrated in urban areas, particularly Jerusalem, but efforts were initiated to encourage formation of women's societies in smaller towns like ʿAkka, Nazareth, Ramallah, Tulkarem, and Safad (Ibid.:77). Mogannam relates that to foster women's societies, members of the Executive Committee would visit villages and towns in groups of five or six in cars with their drivers. They lodged with local families and never traveled alone. To initiate new organizations, they would ask the *mukhtar* (mayor) to suggest names of women able to manage an organization. They then visited them to ask them to start organizations. Relations between the branches and the center were fairly decentralized, with local branches making their own decisions as to their course of action. Relations with the center were maintained through an annual meeting to which each affiliated society or association would send its delegates. Relations were also maintained by occasional visits from the Jerusalem-based leaders.

These leading women were, for the most part, from elite urban families, and their husbands were often involved in national politics during the Mandate period. In spite of the intense rivalry and feuding between the two dominant political factions of the national movement (associated with the Husayni and Nashashibi families) women from these as well as other leading families worked together.[9] The Chair of the Arab Women's Society, established in Jerusalem in 1930 from a resolution of the First Arab Women's Congress, was held by Madame Jamal Husayni. The fourteen-member Arab Women's Executive Committee (AWE) elected at the First Arab Women's Congress crosscut political factions and their associated family blocs and religious lines. Its president was Madame Khalidi, the secretary-general was Matiel Mogannam (a Christian and member of a family allied to the Nashashbis), and the treasurer was Miss Shahinda Duzdar (Muslim) (Mogannam 1937:76). Nine of the women on the Executive Committee[10] had husbands on the Arab Executive Committee, many of whom were instrumental in the formation of rival political parties (the Husaynis, Nashashibi, Mogannam, ʿAbd al-Hadi, ʿAlami, and Khalidi).

A variety of explanations are possible to explain the seemingly curious phenomenon of women of rival family and political blocs organizing and working together. In a discussion I had with Mogannam's daughter Layla, she approached it this way:

> During this period most of the women just didn't compete with each other. This was the only intellectual activity they really had. So they felt they had just better do a good job together. It was almost like a monarchy. There were two or three women up there, that were acknowledged. Everybody wanted to help and they knew there were two or three leaders. Today . . . women have a different role and see themselves differently. During my mother's time they didn't have those ambitions for position.

Why would elite politically active men not oppose their female relatives' working in such organizations, considering the proximity to rival women? Perhaps these women and their charitable and political endeavors weren't taken seriously by their male relatives. If such proximity to rivals was considered threatening to a family bloc's political maneuvering, most likely their women would withdraw. A more plausible explanation is that male political elites tolerated and perhaps even encouraged such participation by their wives and daughters in order to maintain crucial social relations with rivals. Preservation of social relations by women of rival factions may serve as a conduit of information and may even tone down potentially volatile outbreaks.[11] Visiting, mutual aid, and in this case charitable and political work reproduced social networks, keeping open lines of communication with rival blocs. Rival blocs may be feuding and vying for power one day, and the next they may be allies.[12] Noteworthy in this respect are the intermarriages between member families of the Higher Arab Council (Nashif 1977:116). Mrs. Jamal Husayni was the sister of Musa 'Alami; her husband and brother were political rivals on the Arab Executive Committee. Her brother's wife served on the Women's Executive Committee. It is likely that the complex and overlapping agnatic and consanguineous relations between these women ensured a continuity of social relations regardless of male political rivalry.

Recasting Tradition

Two events stand out in the history of the women's movement, one for its rearrangement of religious tradition, stating the nonsectarian character of the women's and national movements. The second is noteworthy for its symbolic import in recasting the ideal of maternal sacrifice in national and secular, rather than Islamic, terms.

During a 1933[13] visit to Palestine by Lord Allenby (Commander in Chief of the Allied Forces of Palestine during World War I) and Lord Swinton, then Secretary of State for the Colonies, the Arab Women's Executive Committee organized a march to the Omar Mosque and the Church of the Holy Sepulchre. On Friday, 15 April, for the first time in history, a Muslim woman, Madame ʿAwni ʿAbd al-Hadi (wife of the head of the Independence Party and relative of the current president of the GUPW), gave a speech in the Holy Sepulchre. M. Mogannam, a Christian and general secretary of the AWE (whose husband was secretary of the Arab Executive Committee and later secretary of the National Defence Party), gave a speech at the Dome of the Rock (ibid.:97–100). Both called attention to the potential replacement of the indigenous Arab population of Palestine by Jewish immigrants and the sense of betrayal felt toward the British. In a portentous vision of the future, Mogannam stated that "independence is taken and not granted" and warned of violent collective action to achieve it. Women were expressing themselves as citizens—nationalists and patriots. They claimed traditionally male public space as their own. Not only was this public space male; it was religious, a fundamental division in the society. By consciously and purposely desectarianizing and temporarily feminizing this sacred space women were publicly proclaiming their identity and loyalties as nationalists. A national context gave their actions legitimacy. Social situations that give rise to a suspension of norms are an opportune time to cast aside behavioral proscriptions.

The second event was noteworthy for its symbolic recasting of motherhood in a national context. In the initial stages of Zionist colonization, peasant women were more immediately affected by Zionist intentions than were urban bourgeois women. They were victims of the process of depriving Arabs of access to land and the ensuing process of urbanization, which meant the loss of women's agricultural labor and thus their individual source of income and status and the alienation of urban life, removed as it is from the village community. As a result of the 1929 riots and killings, many peasant men were sentenced to death by hanging. Tuesdays became known as "Black Tuesday," the day when death sentences were carried out at the old prison in ʿAkka.

At the execution, in a highly emotional and politically charged ritual, peasant women would gather at the ʿAkka prison and ululate as their sons were hanged. Mourning behavior was being suffused with national meaning, an innovation in the symbolic repertoire that had a precedent in the behavior of the poet al-Khansa, who straddled *al-Jahiliyyah*[14] and the era of Islam and was well known for her avid loyalty to and sacrifice for the religious community. When told of the death of her four sons in the battle of Qadisa, she proudly retorted, "They have honoured me with their death" (Mogannam 1937:22).

After the 1930 execution of Muhammad Jamjum of Hebron, condemned to death for his participation in the 1929 riots, people gathered at his mother's house to pay condolences. She is reported to have refused to receive them, calling out from her home, "Why do you cry? I am proud of my son who achieved great honour through martyrdom" (Abu Ali 1975). The story of his mother's action acquired a positive moral value, becoming a model of sorts, for the militant mother in the 1930s and 1940s. Other women followed her example, refusing to grant recognition to the bodies of fighters shown them for identification, for village-level collective punishment was the British Mandatory authorities' response to identification of dead or captured *fida'iyyin*.

In a spirit of cooperation between the urban bourgeoisie and the peasantry, women's societies actively assisted the families of prisoners and martyrs, setting up schools for orphans and collecting and distributing money and clothes to them. Their memoranda to the Mandatory authorities repeatedly asked for leniency for those prisoners condemned to death. In addition they set up facilities to care for the prisoners' families during their visits to the ʿAkka prison (Jamal 1981:32).

In the early 1930s, the AWE persisted in the path of passive resistance, involving itself in a number of issues related to the national question and calling attention to impending national disaster. They drafted a memorandum to the government on the deplorable situation of the *fallahin* (peasants), who, unable to repay loans, were rapidly falling into debt and being forced to sell their land. They were also active in opposing the now openly armed Jewish paramilitary groups and Zionist arms smuggling, sending a delegation to the High Commissioner to make known their displeasure and fear of such ominous happenings (Mogannam 1937:80).

As women claimed public space to air their grievances, some of them met with violence. With growing anti-Semitism and attacks on Jewish communities in Europe, Jewish immigration to Palestine in 1932 alone exceeded 30,000 entrants (ibid.:225). To register protest over uncontrolled immigration, the Arab Executive Committee called for a strike and demonstrations in Jerusalem on 13 October 1933. During the remainder of the month, demonstrations in the larger Palestinian towns and in Jerusalem were met by police who charged the demonstrators. Prominent women, who formed the rear of the demonstration, were among the injured.

Later in the month in Jaffa, local women activists organized themselves in a procession and in a spirit of national cooperation and solidarity. were joined by a group of women from the Jerusalem AWE (ibid.:227–228).

This gesture of solidarity suggests the extent to which, in a society long known for its regionalism, the national interest was bringing together women to organize and protest assaults on the larger community.

Women were cautious about the extent and nature of their political participation, yet it continued, as it does today, to consciously deviate from established norms of female comportment without, however, subjecting them too openly to inquiry. To do so might bring a backlash. Women's organizations sent a delegation to meet the High Commissioner on 30 October 1933 to protest police brutality at the October demonstrations. They told him, "The tragic events of the last few days have compelled us to deviate from the usual Arab tradition and appear before your Excellency in the interest of our men and children, who are being murdered . . ." (ibid.:230).

But such passive resistance was not to last long. A decade of relatively peaceful protest by women and men—demonstrations, petitions, appeals, etc.—had little tangible effect on curbing levels of Jewish immigration or land acquisition. Sensing approaching disaster, Palestinian peasants resorted to armed rebellion.

Armed Revolt: 1936–1939

During this period poorer, less educated rural women became involved in the national endeavor, particularly in the armed rebellion in the countryside. Although their involvement was still exceptional, the precedent of women in combat was established. As a whole, the latter part of the 1930s marks a new approach in the Palestinian response to British occupation and increasing Zionist hegemony in Palestine. In its initial stages during the spring and summer of 1936, a six-month strike "represented the height of unity achieved by Palestinian Arabs" (Miller 1985:123). The revolt, however, was unable to surmount class, regional, village, and clan cleavages to mobilize all sectors of Palestinian society around a unified response to Zionism. Indeed, the revolt was a "a simultaneous battle to determine the nature of Palestinian Arab relationships within the country as well as with outsiders" (ibid.). The revolt actually took on aspects of class tension as peasants attacked land agents and some elite figures who were deemed collaborators for their relationships with the Mandatory authorities and their lack of commitment to the revolt (ibid.:124; Smith 1984:64; Antonious 1965:406–407). Indeed, its class character prompted some national leaders to actively work against the revolt. Realizing their interests were at stake, Smith argues that national leaders tried to prevent strikes and the use of weapons and in some cases passed on information about rebellion activities to the British authorities (Smith 1984:66–68).

Jewish immigration was again hitting record levels, and 22 percent of peasants were landless. Proletarianization was being thwarted by a Zionist labor policy that paid Arab workers substantially less than Jewish workers and an exclusivist Jewish-only hiring policy (Warriner 1948:61–62). Massive unemployment among the Arabs was the result. The origins of the predominantly peasant revolt of 1936 lay in the contradictions inherent in Palestine's transformation from an Arab and largely agricultural society into an industrial, Zionist one, exemplified by the continuing alienation of peasants from the land and concomitant *lumpenproletarianization* and unemployment under an increasingly Jewish-dominated economy (see Antonious 1965:405). The outbreak of the revolt can also be attributed to the peasantry's growing awareness of British support for partition and their continuing alienation from the land (ibid.:408).

The revolt broke out in April 1936, led by groups of localized peasant *fida'iyyin*. Based in mountain redoubts, they would take over towns and villages, striking at the British presence. The six-month nationwide strike, which began in April 1936, marked the first stage of the revolt; the years 1937–1939 were the second stage. By 1939, the militarily superior British were able to crush the revolt.

Though the leadership of the national movement was lukewarm to the revolt, their kinswomen agitated for strikes, demonstrations, and boycotts of Zionist products. Peasant women were openly involved in political acts on a more active and dangerous scale than their appearances in demonstrations. The activities of urban elite women were expanding, but the two classes of women followed no discernible pattern of cooperation. A microcosm of larger Palestinian society, women remained divided by regional and class cleavages. As participants in sustaining an armed revolt, they were required to perform more dangerous and life-threatening actions that took them into the public realm. Nevertheless, they remained a separate organizational element.

In part, separate organizing frameworks can be related to cultural rules prescribing sexual segregation. The recollections of Madame Fatmi illustrate the perception of the dangers of too overtly confronting these rules and how women behaved so as to appear to be upholding them while carrying on with their work. As president of the local women's association in her town during the 1948 battles, she converted her spacious home into a hospital. The day it opened, 'Abd al-Qadir al-Husayni, a prominent military leader, paid a visit. Norms of segregation prevented her from receiving him: "I couldn't greet him myself so I quickly dressed my ten-year-old daughter as a nurse and had her greet him. If I welcomed him no one would work with us, accusing us of just wanting to be fashionable like the ladies of Lebanon." Behavior (particularly individual behavior that bordered on the "feminist") that suggested autonomy reflected in decisions to openly question and defy the cultural order was strongly frowned upon, perhaps out of a sense that women's individual pursuits threaten group solidarity in face of external challenges. Women were quick to recognize and avoid the appearance of behavior deviating sharply from that mandated by gender constructs, realizing that it posed a challenge to male control of women and the cultural system underpinning it that female members of society also upheld. Political and social isolation, forms of control exercised over women, can result from such trespassing. Even though they were organizing separately, women perceived the crisis and struggle in much the same terms as men. Women felt the Zionist threat as Palestinians, as members of a community under political and cultural assault, and as members of classes with specific interests. Though women and men from similar classes had similar interests in the political situation in Palestine, they organized separately. Aside from the fact that their work was coordinated and certainly did not conflict, women served as links between classes. Elite women in their charitable endeavors directed toward the needy crosscut class cleavages in the line of patriotism and in doing so spread resources and initiated and maintained relations among vastly different sectors of society.

During the revolt, urban elite women continued their social work, but it now extended to more directly assisting those fighting in the rural areas. Undoubtedly these women drew little formal distinction between social and political work: "Social work was a cover for political work," Madame Fatmi informed me. These women organized medical care for the wounded and taught first aid; they collected money, sometimes selling their jewelry to purchase arms and ammunition; they knitted sweaters for the fighters and provided financial assistance to the families of dead fighters and detainees. Though few in number, some occasionally undertook dangerous missions, smuggling weapons past checkpoints, hiding fighters or wanted men, and carrying messages. In the cities women persisted in political work, attending demonstrations, distributing leaflets, and sending telegrams of protest to the Mandatory authorities and agitating to sustain support for the boycott. Six hundred schoolgirls organized students to participate in the six-month general strike and boycott, in addition to organizing a demonstration on 6 May at which women were present in large numbers.

Whereas the organized elite women were active in passive forms of resistance and in a support capacity, peasant women were more actively involved, probably because it was their communities that were coming under direct physical attack. Peasant women were prompted into action largely by a policy of collective punishment that destroyed homes of suspected activists. This intrusion into domestic space, which dissolved the appearance of public/private boundaries, compelled them to support the revolt. Also, it enhanced feelings of national belonging and affiliation among Palestinians, since all were made to suffer for the actions of a few.

Village women suffered the brunt of reprisals and collective punishment. Now elderly peasant women recall men going off to fight and the harassment they faced from British soldiers. The policy of collective punishment[15] prevailed throughout the revolt. Searching for fighters, British soldiers would enter a village and proceed to ransack it. Furniture was smashed; large storage bins of oil, dried legumes, and grains would be turned over, spilling onto the floor their contents, which were then mixed together with broken glass and olive oil. For peasants who depended on their stockpile of foodstuffs for subsistence, such pillaging meant the likelihood of a year of hunger and hardship. Homes of suspected activists were dynamited, leaving entire families homeless. Large fines, to be paid in cash and kind, were imposed upon the villages (Newton 1971:357–366).

In stalwartly facing the soldiers, peasant women relied on secrecy, a fundamental principle of clan solidarity. While clan secrecy protected a family's reputation, village secrecy protected the village from external threat. Women's secrecy took on patriotic connotations. Following armed clashes, the bodies of fighters were brought to nearby villages for identification. Women, like Um Jamjum, would examine the bodies of their dead husbands, sons, and brothers and withhold recognition to avoid reprisals against their families and collective punishment of their villages. One woman recalls that a woman said of her dead son, "This one well resembles my son. If it were him, I would have chanted in rejoice" (Jamal 1981:32). Also the fear of dispossession as a result of land sales and evictions gave them a stake in asserting Palestinian political autonomy vis-à-vis the British and the Zionists.

In struggling to protect their villages and stay on the land, women participated in the rural armed campaign as supporters, though some did take up arms. A few fought and died, like Fatmeh Ghazzal, killed in battle June 26, 1936 in Wadi Azzam. She is the first known Palestinian woman killed in combat.

An urban middle-class woman, active in Haifa during the 1930s and 1940s, Um Samir (Ruqqayyah Khuri) bridged the gap between the activities of urban elite and the peasant women. She was greatly influenced by Shaykh 'Izzidin al-Qassam, the leader of the nascent revolt, who was killed in 1935. She notes that al-Qassam gave political and religious

55

education to young girls in Haifa and encouraged the participation of peasants, both men and women, in the struggle (Sayigh 1987:26–27). Aside from establishing literacy classes for women, he set up the Rafiqat al-Qassam (the Comrades of Qassam), a women's group, and for the first time women begin to receive some training in the use of weapons (ibid.). Though married at eighteen years of age, Um Samir continued to play a role in the revolt and later in the war of 1948. She worked with her husband to transfer arms to the peasants and helped to treat wounded fighters (ibid.).

It can hardly be said that national unity was achieved during the revolt. Cooperation between AWE members and peasant women occurred when the former handed over weapons, ammunition, and money to peasant women for delivery to the fighters. Um Samir mentions that many of the masses of women joined the Arab Women's Association and that cooperation reached high levels during periods of uprisings (ibid.:29). The elite women also set up social services for peasant victims of the revolt. Yet perceptions of the revolt differed. To elite women, their class was in the forefront of the struggle and peasant women in cooperating with them were aiding them in the struggle. As one woman told me, "'The peasant women used to *help us* by smuggling weapons and carrying food to the mountains for the fighters." This was a lucid expression of the elite's sense of hegemony over the political process and perception of the struggle for independence as largely their own, since they assumed they would lead the country if independence were achieved.

Crushed in 1939 by the British, the revolt had little outwardly discernible effect on gender constructs or ideology or women's rights. However, the seeds of their future organizations had been planted, role models had been established, and in the name of nationalism public challenges to the established order of sex segregation and norms of women's public comportment had been registered. The traditional sexual division of labor formed the basis for the organization of tasks, yet it was precisely at this point that the sexual division of labor began to display minor cracks, as women entered the public political arena. Early women's organizations and their public political participation set a precedent. Initially women's political work was tolerated because of its origins in women's charitable and welfare activities and because it did not substantially challenge the structure or ideology of gender but was done in the name of nationalism.

Women were organized around the national question rather than women's issues. Specifically women's issues, aside from calls for education for girls, were not on the agenda. Unlike their Egyptian counterparts whom Badran calls "nationalist feminists," the Palestinian women's movement can hardly be said to have *directly* addressed the issue of the rights of women. Palestinian women were certainly cognizant of feminist currents in the Arab world. But they themselves were quite clear about the nature of the tasks facing them and the place of social reforms. One prominent woman, active in the 1936 and 1948 conflicts, told me, "We never thought we women had any problems. We were working in a revolution for the rights of men who had none. Our main concern was politics—the Palestine problem—though we did encourage and initiate education for girls."

Mogannam's daughter Layla attributed a more feminist bent among some Palestinian women to foreign influence, particularly Egyptian. Noting that conditions in Egypt at the time granted women more leeway in pressing feminist issues, she declared that Palestinian women couldn't focus on feminist demands, given the dire political situation in the country. But as these women were well aware, being involved in national politics was a form of action that ultimately served to initiate the process of transformation in women's position. She stated adamantly, "The fact that women at that time were so sheltered, the fact that they were covered and yet they would travel alone to Cairo and would go all over the country and talk on issues that were not just charitable—it was real action instead of just talk." Interviews with Um Samir shed light on such a process of action and transformation. Political actions took her far from home among strange men and involved her in activities such as making bombs and transporting grenades and arms, activities unusual for women at that time. The nationalist context of such actions served to accord them legitimacy. Um Samir said, ". . . as long as we were involved in the struggle no one ever criticized us, although we were in our teens and roamed around quite freely" (Antonious 1979:36). It was only much later with the establishment of a desegregated national movement in the 1960s that women begin to agitate for their rights, spurred on by their desire to participate in the revolution not in a support capacity but as patriots and militants equal to men.

What was new about women's organizations and activities during 1921–1939 was that social work had become political work and for the first time women left the confines of the home to work for their country, an activity that, because of its national framework, was fast becoming a legitimate undertaking. Women's social work did not operate in a political vacuum. In itself, social work was a form of political activity, a response to assaults on the community and an attempt to develop human resources and potential for the protracted process of achieving national independence.

Al-Nakbah: 1948 [16]

Its foundations laid in the 1920s and 1930s, the women's movement underwent relatively little change in structure or ideology until the rise of the Resistance in the mid-1960s, when the political and social transformation of Palestinian society began under Resistance auspices. This was also the time when women took up military training in a sustained fashion.

With the British having crushed the nascent armed resistance, the Zionists prepared for statehood and their concomitant goal of reducing the native population (see Khalidi 1961). The Palestinians were aware that a struggle was brewing for control of Palestine, but they could not know that the native population was to be reduced so drastically.

During the 1930s and 1940s pan-Arab women's ties were extended. In 1938 four Palestinian delegates attended a conference of Arab women in Cairo held under the auspices of Huda Sha'rawi, where the situation in Palestine was high on the agenda (Shaarawi 1987:135). In 1944, the PWU changed its name to the Palestinian Arab Women's Union. Huda Sha'rawi attended a union conference in Jerusalem, and in 1947 a group of Egyptian feminists attended one of the last meetings of the union before the war and pledged their assistance in the coming battles. In a display of solidarity, Egyptian and Palestinian women marched in a demonstration and presented a petition to the British governor. In light of the adoption of a resolution calling for women to prepare for war and their role in it, they begin to prepare local hospitals and to teach first aid and basic nursing. Once again women collected money to buy ammunition and weapons.

In Jaffa in 1947, a secret women's organization, Zahrat Al-uqhuwan (Chrysanthemum Flowers), formed to furnish supplies and aid to the fighters. Other activities included digging trenches, smuggling weapons, and at times manning the barricades. Accounts differ as to whether or not the Al-uqhuwan were directly involved in combat. Haddad states that they wanted to fight but were not allowed to, though some did fight in Nablus with the Syrians (Haddad 1980:168). Sayigh refers to them as a paramilitary group that saw combat action (1987:30). A number of women were killed in action during the 1947–48 battles, and they are remembered today as some of the first women martyrs for the homeland. [17] Abu Ali (1975) writes that the women of Jenin fought with the men of the town and the Iraqi forces stationed there when the Haganah forces attacked the town.

While women's organizations concentrated their efforts on social work and preparation for the coming battles, something fundamental to women's position was changing and women found themselves fairly powerless to confront it. Prior to this time, they were victims of conflict as Palestinians and, for peasant women, as members of a historically victimized and voiceless class. As conflict spread and intensified, women were becoming victims of war precisely because they were women, the crucial repositories of family honor, strictly controlled by men, yet holding the fragile reins of their families' individual and collective social standing.

During the 1940s, popular Palestinian thinking contends, women were targets of the campaign to rid Palestine of its native inhabitants. In fact, it asserts attacks on women were carried out with the full knowledge and anticipation that Arab notions of honor would incite Palestinians to remove their families from the path of danger.[18]

Norms of *'ard* (honor) circumscribed the behavior of men toward women, and any man who harmed or molested a woman knew that revenge against him and his kin would be called for and that he would likely face ostracism by his fellow warriors and punishment. European Jews, alien to Arab and Palestinian culture, were not perceived as bound by such codes. Indeed, they exploited notions of *'ard* (honor), fully cognizant of the reaction of the Palestinian population—flight rather than dishonor and shame.[19] Dayr Yasin, a small, peaceful village on the road between Tel Aviv and Jerusalem, is a name gruesomely familiar to all Palestinians. A nonfighting village, it was attacked by units of the Irgun and Stern groups[20] commanded by Menachem Begin, head of the former, on 9 April 1948. The attack on the village was part of a military scheme to keep open the supply route from Tel Aviv to the Jewish sector of Jerusalem. The larger Zionist objective was to secure the hilly area between the coast and Jerusalem. Morris contends this operation "probably had the most lasting effect of any single event of the war in precipitating the flight of Arab villagers from Palestine" (1987:113). Some 250 of its inhabitants, men, women, and children, were slaughtered (ibid.). Young girls and women were raped and butchered; pregnant women were found disembowelled. The survivors were paraded naked in open trucks through the streets of Jerusalem, where they were spat upon and taunted. The effect of what transpired at Dayr Yasin was to spread panic throughout Palestine and, along with forcible expulsion, ensured the desired flight of large numbers of Palestinians (see de Reynier 1971:761–766; Morris 1987:113–115; and Kimche 1971:775–778).

The battle for Haifa, the major northern port city of Palestine, was launched by the Haganah on April 21, 1948. The city fell into Zionist hands quickly, and Palestinian refugees streamed north to 'Akka and to Lebanon.[21] With the fall of Haifa, 'Akka, to the north, became a "major refugee way-station and absorption centre" (Morris 1987:107). Women's organizations received refugees for three continuous days. They organized committees to care for the injured and those separated from their families, especially children, and to collect and distribute food.

Organizing in Exile: The 1950s

With the dispersal of the Palestinians and the establishment of the state of Israel, Palestinian society fragmented and many of its sociopolitical institutions nearly ceased to exist until the rise of the PLO in 1964 and the process of social reconstruction got under way.[22] Politically, the tradition of women organizing around charitable issues continued but was eventually to be eclipsed by the entry of peasant, now camp, women and women of an emergent middle class into a political arena previously dominated by men of the landed, mercantile, and clerical elite and the intelligentsia. The political arena was beginning to face a challenge by the middle class and, to a lesser extent, by the poorer peasant strata, a trend that reached its apogee in the 1970s when a considerable proportion of political positions were filled by men and women of the middle class.

During the 1950s and early 1960s, women's organizations, though scattered, persisted in social and political work until a Resistance-affiliated women's organization co-opted them and laid official claim to represent all Palestinian women.

As for women's political affiliations during this era, the appearance of pan-Arab nationalist organizations—al-ba'th, the Arab National Movement, the Nasserites—and the Communist parties—drew younger middle and lower class Palestinian men to their ranks and a smaller number of women. Commensurate with the often close affinity between kinship and political affiliation among Arab women, these women were usually relatives of male members or students. None of these parties was particularly concerned with mobilizing or addressing the specific problems of women or even in women as a political question (Abu Ali 1975). Some middle-class and camp women were entering political parties, portending the future trend of Palestinian women in mass-based organizations. The elite women who settled in Lebanon and Jordan soon resumed their organizational work.[23]

There was a paucity of social services to cope with the scope of relief and emergency welfare requirements imposed by the national disaster and the ensuing social chaos of 1948. Women's charitable organizations sprang up to meet the social needs of the refugee population.[24] Hind al-Husayni, for instance, formed a charitable association of elite women to build the Arab Children's Home in Jerusalem to care for the Dayr Yasin orphans. In the aftermath of the war, societies, both old and new, helped the Red Cross in welfare and relief work until the UNRWA was established. The remnants of the PWU and the AWE, first established in 1921 and 1929, reorganized in Lebanon, Syria, Gaza, and Jerusalem. In Jordan, which annexed the West Bank in 1950, political work was not tolerated. The word "Palestinian" was deleted from the Palestinian Arab Women's Union, and their work was confined to relief and welfare (Brand 1988:196). Similar organizing was undertaken by Palestinian women in Lebanon. Madame Fatmeh related how the union reorganized in Lebanon:

> I was so broken down and dispirited at first that I didn't want to see anyone or go out.[25] Following the disaster, both the Lebanese Women's Union and the Red Cross looked after the refugees and did social work with them. I thought this wasn't right. Many of the Palestinians who came here were rich and had previously been active. So I said, "Why don't we do something?" I called a meeting and we formed a Palestin Committee. We began by working in the camps alongside the Red Cross and Lebanese relief organizations. For about two years we worked in this way, and then we thought we should reorganize the Palestine (Arab) Women's Union. We put an appeal on the radio for Palestinian women to form a union. We were able to gather women from all the cities of Palestine who had previously worked in the union, and we elected an Executive Committee. We maintained contact with the union in Jerusalem; we were the Lebanese branch of the Palestine (Arab) Women's Union and Zlikhah al-Shahabi was still its president at that time. We called ourselves the Palestine (Arab) Women's League.

The link between women's organizations and the national crisis continued as the union engaged in social work in the refugee camps in Lebanon. The class character of the league was not so different from that in the pre-1948 period. More than ever before, peasant women, now the inhabitants of refugee camps, were the recipients of the elite's charity and they remained organizationally marginal. Indeed, the same spirit of charitable work prevailed—"they received us so well"—a sort of paternalistic (or perhaps maternalistic) continuation of the old, no longer so relevant, patron-client ties. But now the peasants had little to offer in return; political alliances counted for little, and peasants no longer were locked into a sharecropping relationship with landowners. Possibly they could offer support to one faction or another in any upcoming political organizing. These elite women were motivated both by nationalism and a sentiment of collective loss that at some points transcended class boundaries, though it continued to be expressed in a form of noblesse oblige.

In Lebanon, the league directed its energies toward two activities: relief for refugees and representing Palestine at international conferences. The deplorable conditions in the refugee camps and the absence of a state infrastructure left the provisioning of social services to benevolent groups and the UNRWA. Madame Fatmeh, instrumental in reorganizing the league/union in Lebanon, described their early activities:

> We were assisting the UNRWA in social work in the camps and we ourselves used to visit families there, taking them money, medicine, clothing, etc., and we tried to help them in arranging education for their children. They were very happy to see us and received us so well. At that time TB was widespread. In a desire to help well children, as well as those with TB, we opened the Suk al-Gharb school and arranged to place the sick children in hospitals. We had to work to convince the parents to let us place the sick children in hospitals—they were quite opposed to it. We began organizing to build a TB hospital for Palestinians, since all that was available was a miserable tent hospital in Miyyeh-Miyyeh camp near Saida. We sponsored patients for treatment, paying for their care and looking after their families.

The league was active on the international level representing Palestinian women abroad. Indeed, this remains one of the essential tasks of the current GUPW. Delegations represented Palestinians at conferences for the International Alliance of Women and the Women's Peace and Freedom League. Madame Fatmeh, for instance, represented Palestinian women at a 1953 UNESCO conference:

> In our 1950 conference here in Beirut, Zlikhah al-Shahabi, as president of the union, should have spoken in the name of Palestinian women, but King ʿAbdullah forbid her to do so. She and the union in Jerusalem could only speak in the name of Jordan. Because of this restriction on any form of Palestinian national expression, the Lebanon branch represented Palestinian women in international forums and in the Arab League.

Women were gaining new and firsthand experience in the world of formal politics. Representing Palestine at international conferences required more than simply attending and delivering speeches. They were learning the ropes—how to rally political support for their cause and attain political positions. One delegate to a conference said:

> In the early 1950s, I attended the conference for the International Alliance for Women, held in Ceylon. An Israeli woman was on the

executive committee. We gained membership for the union, and I was to try to get on the executive committee. I knew there would be a lot of Zionist opposition. I was only twenty-six years old then and quite new at this kind of political activity. But I caucused the Islamic and Arab delegates for support and eventually I made it on the committee.

The PWU/league continued operating in Lebanon until the late 1960s, and though currently all activities are suspended, it is still a registered organization with a president. The eventual usurping of the functions and legitimacy of the league, and the class of women affiliated with it, were inevitable given the formation of the PLO in 1964 and the establishment of the GUPW in 1965. Conflict, expressed in class and generational tensions, between the old and new unions centered around the question of who would legitimately represent Palestinian women and control the resources and gain the prestige commensurate with such a position.

Integration and Transformation

The mid- to late 1960s marked a turning point for women and their movement. The emergence of the PLO and the GUPW presented women a unified format within which to organize, promote women's development, and support the national cause. Yet from its inception, this unified women's organization was linked closely in an official manner to the larger structure of national representation, a linkage with serious implications for its autonomy, internal development, and day-to-day operations.

Sources of data on the GUPW include interviews with several of its executive committee members, members, former members, and secondary sources. The GUPW is the second largest popular organization in the PLO and claims to represent the bulk of Palestinian women. With eleven branches, and offices in every camp in Lebanon, the GUPW had 22,878 registered members in Lebanon in 1982; about 540 of these were active members, i.e., women who were working on projects in the camps or in the union's offices or who worked to mobilize other women. The figure of 22,878 indicates those registered to vote in union elections; prior to each election there is a concerted door-to-door campaign in the camps by union activists to register women to vote.

Soon after its formation in 1965, the GUPW became a component unit in the PLO, signaling a fundamental transition in the women's movement as a whole. Initially the impetus for the formation of the union came from women who were scattered in various Arab capitals working in small women's associations or societies and from women active in remnants of the Arab Women's Union of the 1920s and 1930s. Representatives of Palestinian women's organizations assembled after a call was issued by Arab Women's Union president Zlikhah al-Shahabi. They met in February 1965 in Jerusalem in the offices of the Arab Women's Union. From this meeting a preparatory committee was fashioned of representatives from Egypt, Gaza, Jordan, Kuwait, and Syria. They met on March 18 in Jerusalem to discuss the convening of a conference on Palestinian women. Elections designated Zlikhah al-Shahabi as president and Samirah Abu Ghazalah as secretary. It was decided to meet in Jerusalem in July 1965 and form a unified organization, the GUPW. The PLO's Department of Popular Organizations (DPO) helped to coordinate the conference. At the conference, women asked for recognition of the union as the official, legitimate representative of Palestinian women, that the union become a popular organization in the PLO, and that representation in political bodies and forums be guaranteed to the union (Brand 1988: 197–198).

With its integration into the PLO later in the year, the impetus began to come from above and brought with it the priorities and factionalism of the larger political body, thus constraining its autonomy to develop according to its own momentum. Henceforth the direction, composition, and development of the women's movement were intimately linked to that of the larger national movement.

Union leadership has remained remarkably intact since 1974. A transition in the late 1960s involved the takeover of the union's Lebanon branch by younger, more militant Fateh women. The GUPW that emerged from the first meeting in Jerusalem in 1965 can be seen as a continuation of the union that started in the 1920s. In Beirut, some members of the (Palestinian) Arab Women's Union or PWU had continued their work during the 1950s and early 1960s and then joined the GUPW. From well-known upper and upper middle class families, they belonged to no particular political organization. Several young, middle-class Fateh women joined this union on orders from their political superiors. The intent to transform it into a Fateh-dominated group succeeded when they finally took over the reins of power and removed the president from her position. In addition they took over the operations of its charitable institutions, later incorporating them into GUPW activities. They were not able to assume control over its financial assets, which in 1982 were still locked in a Beirut bank. This transition in leadership signaled the end of the reign of the elitist women over the movement.

Since its inception, the GUPW has represented Palestinian women in international conferences, still considered one of its primary and most important political tasks. Gaining international recognition and legitimacy has been a cornerstone of PLO policy since the mid-1970s, with the shift to diplomacy as a main strategy for achieving national independence.

On the ideological level, the Resistance never did adopt a decisive stance on the question of gender equality. The campaign for women's participation was forced upon the leadership by women themselves. On such a sensitive and potentially volatile issue, one that strikes a deep cultural chord, the ideologically disunited and organizationally disparate national movement could not pronounce itself.

In very broad form, however, one can distinguish the positions of the different political organizations derived from Fateh's nationalist stance and from the PFLP's (and DFLP's) class-based approach. Fateh assigned the gender question a secondary status vis-à-vis the national question. Women were to participate in the national struggle, but the emphasis was on national struggle to confront externally imposed forms of repression and domination, not on social transformation and internal forms of domination. The GUPW, dominated by Fateh women who set policy and allocated resources for projects, echoed this view. Yet as will be discussed in chapter 5, Fateh's women leaders exhibit a wide range of views on gender issues. Alternative voices deny a complete hegemony of official Fateh discourse on gender.

By the late 1970s, the PFLP's class analysis was extended to encompass the question of gender. Based on a reading of Engels' *Origin of the Family, Private Property and the State,* women's subordination was explained as a function of the historic emergence of private property and concomitant class formation.

Regional feminist currents and a general interest in social reforms, in conjunction with the colonial threat and Palestinian nationalism, served as the initial catalyst for women to begin a fifty-year history of participation in the national political arena. The early activists set the precedent for subsequent political organizing. They inaugurated the process of accumulating experience and skills in political work that was transmitted to a younger generation. Moreover, they broke the first crucial boundaries of the normative gender order. In addition, the organizational and administrative skills they acquired in carrying out charitable and political work were cultivated and matured. Peasant and urban middle and lower middle class women conferred legitimacy on the phenomenon of women on the battlefield.

In sum, the initial organized women's movement was a specifically female response to national threat by a specific sector of the population —urban upper-class women related through kinship ties to the leadership of the national movement. Their privileged class position facilitated their activism; the availability of servants freed them from domestic duties, according them the time to pursue politics. As literate and educated women, they were able to engage in dialogue with foreign officials, linguistic skills that today help to advance women politically in a national movement where foreign diplomacy is vital.

Rural women were motivated to action by a different set of circumstances. Compelled by the need to defend their villages and retain access to the land, they acted in response to evictions and attack. During uprisings they acted in a sustained fashion beyond the village to support peasant fighters. They shared in the battles with their male kin, provisioning them with food, water, arms and ammunition, and medicine. It was often women who confronted the British forces entering their villages, upholding community defenses by subterfuge.

Before the exodus from Palestine, women perceived the national crisis in generally the same terms as men. While assuming that independence and autonomous socioeconomic development would improve life for all Palestinians, they did expect that independence would provide the national legal infrastructure and climate of legitimacy for reforms in women's status, particularly in the areas of education and legal rights. While the early women's movement did not propose fundamentally new definitions of women as social beings, their new public roles signaled the beginning of the process of realigning gender relations.

With formal integration into the national movement, the women's movement's potential for autonomous development was circumscribed. Such a linkage brought greater access to national resources and positions of power and conferred some legitimacy on female activism. However, the linkage also gave the national movement the opportunity and platform to extend and make official its vision of and discourse on gender.

Having reviewed the history of the women's movement, we can now turn to the situation of Palestinian women in Lebanon in the Resistance era.

3

Ideas and Action: Political Consciousness

■

This chapter explores the various foundations and dimensions of women's political consciousness—nationalist, class, and female/feminist. These forms of consciousness and their expressions are framed in the specific sociopolitical and historical context of the relationship with the host country, the emergence of the Resistance, and the location of gender in the Palestinian cultural complex.

Consciousness and Action

Since the rise of the Palestinian Resistance movement in the late 1960s, Palestinian discourse has been laced with terms such as *struggle, revolution, resistance, armed struggle, mobilization, activists,* and *political consciousness,* just to mention some of the more common ones. The last term, and its relation to action, is the topic of this chapter. It would be prudent to define the concept as it is used in the Palestinian lexicon and its social context. First, political consciousness *(wa'i siyasi)* indicates an awareness of one's position, as an individual or as a collectivity, in the prevailing global and local power structures and an understanding of the actions necessary to transform them. Second, it refers to a sense of identification with others in the same position, manifested in a sense of communal solidarity. Last, political consciousness should logically lead to and inform social practice; otherwise it remains unactivated, uncommitted, and thus underdeveloped.

What are some of the specific qualities that index political consciousness? Being well versed in political theory and using a political discourse to conceptualize and make sense of the world is evidence. It refers to someone who keeps abreast of developments in the regional and international political arenas; it indicates a clear knowledge of who is the enemy and why and what is the nature of the struggle, both politically and militarily, to create a new power order, and it should include a social practice that confirms one's ideology. Knowledge of one's society, its social composition, particularly the distribution and meaning of power, the cultural system, and how the particular social formation affects the course of national liberation is indeed the high mark of political consciousness. In the Palestinian lexicon, with few exceptions, political consciousness as well as "politically correct" notions of power refer to external phenomena. It is about national domination. It includes in muted form reference to women's experience of gender subordination, at once decidedly internal and external. Forms of power are recognized as multiple and diffuse, but they are ordered hierarchically in terms of prestige and priority of struggle. While identifying the multiplicity of power, Palestinian political discourse locates imperialism, and its local variant Zionism, as the central form and operation of power in Palestinian daily life.

Political consciousness is also embodied in an ability to remain steadfast in the face of political and military adversity. One of the more dynamic aspects of political consciousness in the Palestinian context is its universal qualities, which take on added significance in a social environment where village, sect, and family are sources of primary affiliation, identification, and loyalty. Political consciousness unites people by ideas and practice and the social relations these give rise to, rather than primary affiliations, and thus has the potential to constitute a serious challenge to the centrality of primary affiliations.

Political consciousness is a term frequently used by militant women to order and rank others. Activist and ordinary women perceive each other through a political filtering lens. Activist women see ordinary women as material for mobilization or, at the least, in need of consciousness raising, while ordinary women perceive that activists operate in a realm somewhat unknown and alien to the traditional sphere and its tasks. Militant women's use of the term to describe others indicates that one either possesses it or doesn't, i.e., is in the "prepolitical" stage or is in the process of acquiring it. The latter process, awakening the political consciousness of the masses of people, is one of the defining goals of all militants, and the Women's Union has assumed the task of politically educating women.

There are, nevertheless, men and women active in politics or military affairs who are considered politically unconscious *(ghayr waʿin siyasiyyan)*. Rula, a young full-time fighter based in a guerrilla unit in the south, was illiterate and had a very rudimentary understanding of the political theory of her organization, Zionism, or the history of the Resistance movement. She was mobilized during the civil war when Tal al-Zaʿter camp[1] was under siege for nearly nine months. She had been badly wounded and taken prisoner during the civil war. Though some of her fellow fighters attempted to teach her to read and write, she never did learn. Last I heard she had found work as a governess with a well-to-do family in the Gulf and had severed her affiliation with the Resistance. Rula's actions seem to have been inspired by an immediate, personal experience of crisis and community mobilization for survival rather than by a well-defined political ideology.

Does political consciousness have a different meaning and social context for women than men? Women often comment that political consciousness is more intense and socially meaningful for women. Being politically conscious can indicate a profound distaste for current social constructs and a commitment to creating new ones. Active involvement in the process of reconstructing society implies a questioning of the gender order and domesticity as a primary locus of loyalty and identification. Like education, political consciousness has shaped a new sense of self-worth and pride. But is this perception of political consciousness and its manifestation in action as more meaningful for women valid? Convention holds that unmarried activists are likely to engage in disreputable behavior as a consequence of activism, which gives them fairly free access to men. Amal, an unmarried activist, used to say of herself, "For a girl like me there's no going back." What she means is that girls[2] who have managed to remain active in spite of their families' opposition and who have broken the reins of family control cannot return to a state of existence where others make decisions for them. Formal political participation, in a traditionally nonfemale arena, implies a challenge to what is, in effect, proper female comportment. For men, activism carries no such affront to cultural definitions of maleness. Yet as we will see later, marriage often serves as a deterrent to women's political involvement. The drop-out rate correlates closely with marriage, and few married women join organizations. For women who drop out with marriage activism may be a temporary interlude that poses little threat to domesticity. For women who remain active after marriage, usually the cadres, activism is more socially meaningful, indicating a measure of freedom from family control and independent decision making.

This chapter and the next examine the development of women's political consciousness in its national, class, and female-feminist dimensions and political mobilization, distinct yet intimately intertwined processes. Political consciousness remains an individual property, weak, uninspired, and uncommitted unless it is activated, articulated, and given organizational format through the processes of mobilization and membership in a political organization. Rather than a quantum step in time, women's political consciousness is a drawn out social process informed by the individual's particularly unique experience of the objective circumstances shaping social life as they interact with local sociocultural structures and forces.

In Palestinian political discourse we encounter the frequent use of *political consciousness* and *mobilization,* terms that refer ultimately to ideas and action. The relationship between ideas and action, specifically political consciousness and practice, is a central concern of this study. The essential question is what motivates women to act, particularly if we are concerned to move beyond an objectified vision of women that categorizes them as simply respondents (or objects of larger structural processes) to movement in the political economy, for, indeed, hegemonic culture and social structures equally nuance action. If, as I believe, ideas and experience can occasion innovative action leading to social transformation, a practice-centered view of history and society emerges, where women are creative forces in its making. The ideas that compel action in this specific case are those that constitute political consciousness. Among women, this consciousness is derived from the experience of powerlessness on a communal and individual basis and from an inability to live daily life according to the norms that society has set for the operation of domesticity. The kinds of ideas that developed from these experiences have colored women's view of history and society and the role they envision for themselves and indeed are adopting.

The experience of conflict and powerlessness has not given rise to uniform ideas or forms of action. Indeed, the variation in ideas and action lends credibility to the perspective adopted here that the interplay between women's response to the forces, external and internal, that shape their individual realities and the cultural forms that mediate and nuance that process of influence and response accords women a place as creative actors in the historical and political process unfolding in their midst. The social composition and ideological positions of the Resistance, as well as its cultural content, embody the variable relations of women's ideas and action to the political process.

Palestinian women's political consciousness has multiple dimensions. The question of female consciousness is explored in greater detail later in this chapter, but for now it is important to set forth the theoretical parameters guiding the vision of women's ideas and action propounded here. Female consciousness is women's awareness of their rights within the prevailing division of labor and dominant ideology (Kaplan 1981). It informs a sense of solidarity revolving around women's shared domain, tasks, and status. Unlike feminist consciousness, which is women's awareness of their subordinate position within a cultural and power system and the articulation of a specifically female perspective of the social process, female consciousness is usually accompanied by a demand by women for what they perceive to be their due rights in the prevailing system.

The neighborhood-based actions of housewives in the camps when their communities are under assault—their readiness to risk life and limb —are a barometer of "female consciousness."[3] Compelled to act by a community-shattering crisis that impeded their ability to carry out the tasks associated with domesticity, camp women's consciousness can be characterized in terms of a "moral economy of domesticity" (Piven 1985:270).[4] Both female consciousness and the moral economy of domesticity point to a female view of events and their place in history predicated on a division of labor that assigns women domestic maintenance and nurturing tasks.

Female consciousness is an index of the extent to which domination is as much cultural as political or material. Bourdieu notes: "When . . . the established cosmological and political order is perceived not as arbitrary, i.e., as one possible order among others, but as a self-evident and natural order which goes without saying and therefore goes unquestioned, the agents' aspirations have the same limits as the objective conditions of which they are the product" (1977:116).

Yet studies of women's political behavior illustrate that female consciousness can achieve a revolutionary momentum under certain circumstances, as when civil violence transcends domestic boundaries and undermines the survival of the community.[5] Among some sectors of Palestinian women, political actions motivated by female consciousness confronted a system of external domination and in doing so led to a confrontation with and ultimately a questioning of internal forms of domination. Such were the foundations of a nascent consciousness of gender subordination as a structure of power that may overlap with other forms of power but one that was also possessed of its own momemtum and logic.

National and class consciousness are certainly critical components in motivating political actions. I argue that forms of consciousness cannot be separated into distinct categories for analytical purposes. Nor can they separately constitute the impetus underlying action. Each form of consciousness serves as a filtering lens, as a mediating factor, for the others. Female consciousness was a significant factor in the development of national consciousness, and it was instrumental in shaping reactions to national crisis and the actions taken to cope with it. Moreover, it played a role in shaping class consciousness and served as the point of transition to feminist consciousness. Different forms of consciousness and their interrelations point to variable forms of power and their overlap.

Women cannot be isolated as a separate category of social being, nor can they be discussed as a whole without regard for variation in experiences and ideas. Nevertheless, their experiences of exile, national discrimination, and political transformation did differ in fundamental ways from those of men. In addition to the external dynamic of national discrimination, women were subjected to an internal form of domination located in familial control and authority over women. A specifically Palestinian feminist perspective emerged in the context of a contradiction between women's national consciousness and a structurally grounded and culturally-sanctioned limit on female autonomy that prevented women from a practice of the former.

The Multiplicity of Experience

We used to live in Nabatiyyeh camp in South Lebanon until it became unbearable because of the constant Israeli shelling. Then we moved to Tal al-Za'ter camp in Beirut to be more secure and to find jobs. There were few work opportunities in Nabatiyyeh. But in Tal al-Za'ter, the police would come and tell newcomers to return to the south. They would take our household possessions, put them in trucks, and order us out. We would plead with them, "In the south there is no work. We have children. We need to feed and clothe them." They would shout at us to shut up and then beat up some of our people. But we resisted and managed to stay in the camp.

My mother used to work as a maid in rich Lebanese homes. She also collected herbs to sell at the market. At sixteen I started to work in the factories near the camp. In the factory where I worked there were few Palestinians. We Palestinian women didn't earn as much as Lebanese workers. We were paid about 6L.L. [U.S. $2.00] a day while the Lebanese were paid 9L.L [U.S. $3.00] a day. Lebanese workers could take a day off if they were sick, whereas Palestinians could do so only under the threat of being fired.

The Communist Party of Lebanon had a strong presence in the factory. During the many strikes and demonstrations the army would come and shoot at the workers. Once I was arrested along with some other workers and we spent a few days in jail. There was so much persecution! In a factory you might have a shock, but they won't send you home or to the hospital. Once a worker lost his fingers while working with a machine. The boss kicked him out. If somebody was sick the employer would tell him, "You're an animal and a liar; you're not sick." He used to beat the workers, too. We worked very hard— eight hours and often four hours of mandatory overtime. We stood all day in the heat, and the work was very tough because it was automated. If production was low your pay would be reduced.

After I had been working for nine months in one factory they suddenly told me, "You're not getting a wage increase nor are you entitled to an annual vacation." I asked why and the boss said, "Because you are a Palestinian." I said, "Because I'm a Palestinian?" He said, "Yes." Again I said, "Why? I work like the Lebanese. I even do better than some. At least I know something about the factory, while some of them are new and I'm training them." He said, "No, you still aren't allowed any increase or vacation." Then I said, "I don't want any money. I don't want an annual vacation. I don't want to work here anymore." He said sarcastically, "As you like; *maᶜ al-salameh*" [go in safety or peace]."

Once my mother was putting a nail in the house. It was raining, and there was a leak in the house that she was trying to repair. The Lebanese police came and told her it was forbidden. She replied that she was just making repairs. They shouted, "No, you can't make any repairs—it's illegal," and they fined her.

When I was little I did not go to school, so I'm illiterate. My father was sick, and my mother had to work. She used to pick wild greens and sell them at the market, so I had to stay home to take care of my younger sister. My mother used to go long distances in search of herbs. I was seven years old when I started working. I had to because we had no money.

The siege of Tal al-Zaᶜter camp by the Phalangists[6] in 1976 was very difficult. We couldn't get water or food, and children were dehydrated. But women would go out of the shelters to get water. Ten women would go out for water; only two or three would come back. They died—there was no solution: either their children died of thirst or their mothers died under the shells and bullets. Women couldn't bear to see their children die of thirst. They would leave their children crying and go running under the shelling to bring them water. Some never came back with the water. One woman was killed in front of me. She was balancing a bucket on her head when a bullet hit her. She didn't fall down directly. Still holding the water container with one hand, the other hand on her chest where the bullet had entered, she slowly sank down. There was no choice: either children died of thirst or their mothers died trying to get water. So many children left the camp without mothers and fathers. Many, many people died.

The day most people died was when we left the camp through Dikwaneh.[7] Many people died—girls, boys, little children. It is very difficult for me to reflect back on these things. I can't imagine going through the same tragedy again.

In Dikwaneh, a young fellow of about sixteen was walking next to me. He was carrying two little children in his arms. These children were clutching him tightly. A Phalangist came up to him and tried to take the children. They refused—he refused. They all clutched each other so the Phalangist couldn't separate them. So the Phalangist put his rifle right between the boy's eyes and shot him. They all fell to the ground in a heap. I saw it; it was very close to me. It was something like Hitler's war but even worse.

As far as a Palestinian woman is concerned, she is not discriminated against in Palestinian society or at home. At first girls were not allowed to work in the clinic or to go outside with boys or to go out in general. But due to what we've seen in Tal al-Za'ter, no mother would tell her daughter, "You're not allowed to go to the clinic." She would tell her to go and not to stay in the shelter—"You have to go to the clinic and work, to see if there are wounded, help them, check if people need food, cook for them." Even the older women started to go to the clinic. They would go and check if they were needed. Now Palestinian girls are not discriminated against. Now girls work in agriculture, they work at home and in the offices—they cook and clean or make coffee, and then when they return home there is no one to tell them they are forbidden to work or to go out. Now a girl knows what she should do. She is doing the right thing. She is being of benefit to the revolution, to her people.

Haifa
Damur, Lebanon

I met Haifa while on an extended stay at Damur,[8] a small coastal town south of Beirut where hundreds of female-headed families provisionally settled after the fall of Tal al-Zaʿter. Though not politically active when we met, Haifa had been during the early 1970s and remained a supporter or friend of her former organization. Illiterate and extremely articulate, she tells a story representative of what many camp women experienced in the late 1970s and the early 1980s. Her story, moreover, shows the relations between the multiple kinds of domination experienced by these women. Exploitation in the workplace, for instance, is not solely a consequence of class position. It must be located within a context of national status and gender relations as well.

Haifa was acutely aware of discriminatory experiences as a poor Palestinian woman. Her vivid recall during our discussions brought to the fore what these different levels of domination meant to her and how she ordered them. She is not unusual in minimizing gender inequality—many camp women do so, stressing the improved condition of women since the Revolution. Or, like Haifa, they do not perceive it as a particularly salient issue, since they themselves have little desire to radically alter the existing structure of gender relations.[9] Her comment that women "are not discriminated against" can be taken as an expression of female consciousness. Like Haifa, many women participated in the defense of Tal al-Zaʿter and considered it their natural right to defend their community against aggression even if it meant risking their own lives to tend to the needs of others. Their mothers judged their actions natural and legitimate and even encouraged their daughters to perform acts that would not normally be within the bounds of acceptable behavior, such as sleeping away from home and mingling with young men. Haifa pinpointed the Resistance presence in everyday camp life and threats to the survival of the community as the reasons for women no longer being discriminated against. Sharing in the defense of the community is considered a form of liberation. Haifa's words echo a common sentiment, especially among older uneducated women, young or old, who are self-consciously nationalistic and sustain the community during times of crisis.

An atmosphere of crisis and uncertainty had entered the camp home. Calm and security were violated by a military conflict that pitted the Lebanese army and private militias against the camps in 1973 and 1975–76 and continued intermittently until the Israeli invasion of 1982.[10] No longer a sanctuary from the turmoil of political life, the camp home was caught in the cross fire, increasingly becoming a target. Thus Palestinian women seldom felt removed or distant from political conflict, for its most visible and destructive elements entered their homes. Crisis, repression, and revolution acted in concert to shape the contours of women's political consciousness and actions. In Haifa's case the violation of domestic boundaries—the migrations accompanied by hostility, the intrusion of strangers into domestic affairs, a mother working as a domestic for others in order to feed her own children—exploitation in the workplace, war, and the destruction of a community compelled her to take political action. The specificity of her actions—initially a member, then a friend of the Resistance, during crises she volunteers in the clinic—was colored by her culturally approved vision of women's role in the Revolution.

National Consciousness

Exile in a frequently hostile environment has ensured that few Palestinian camp women escape repressive experiences. A crisis-ridden life in exile on the one hand and the pervasiveness of the national movement in all aspects of daily life on the other make the distinction between politically active and ordinary women a tenuous, yet conversely at some points very real, one. The majority of camp women are not politically active in the formal sense of being members of an organization, but few are unaware of the external forces directly and indirectly impinging on their everyday lives. Most significantly, however, these women define themselves as "strugglers" and are self-proclaimed nationalists. Militancy is a popular and pervasive idiom in the discourse of everyday life, including women's.

Palestinians overwhelmingly agree on the prominence of their national situation, intertwined with class position where appropriate, as being instrumental in the formation of their political consciousness. When I asked women to trace the evolution of their political consciousness and involvement they invariably retreated in time, recalling childhood stories of repression by Lebanese representatives of the state and humiliation by civilians, the feeling of being outsiders, of not belonging, of having no secure refuge, of being at the mercy of external factors over which they had little control, and of poverty. The Resistance movement endowed them with a sense of dignity and empowerment. They were protected from external aggression and achieved some control over their daily lives.

Repression

One day my father didn't come home from work. We were waiting at home with our mother when the Lebanese police came and kicked in the door. They tore up the mattresses and pulled down all the food, spilling the rice, lentils, and chick-peas, mixing them with olive oil.

They said they were looking for weapons, and seeing a large bin of flour, they asked my mother what was in it. She said, "It's only flour." As one of the policemen bent over to look in the bin, his hat fell into the flour. He turned and slapped my mother across the face. Then they attacked my brother—kicking, punching, and slapping him. My father was in prison for a month. After that he was often taken for a day or two of interrogation.

Fatmeh
'Ayn al-Hilweh camp

Activist women like Fatmeh, thirty years old and a mother of four, often recount such stories in discussing their early politicization and eagerness to join the national struggle. For adolescent girls, intimidation, harassment, and the absence of their fathers and brothers constituted early forms of political socialization.

During the period 1948–1969, few women were politically active in pan-Arab political organizations. It was mainly their fathers, brothers, and husbands who were engaged in such activities. One of the consequences was that whole families, like Fatmeh's, were harassed and made occasional targets of violence by *al-maktab al-thani* (Lebanese Military Intelligence Service) and local police in an effort to intimidate activists and arrest them. Women often bore the brunt of such encounters with the Lebanese state. Usually it was women who were home when the police arrived and they were compelled to deal with the intrusion into their homes by unknown and sometimes violent men. This was especially difficult for women unaccustomed to speaking to strange men.

With activist men in flight, hiding, or under periodic arrest, women remained at home to shoulder family responsibilities. For the first time some women had to search for employment to feed their families; they also had to initiate and sustain contact with the larger network of kin, friends, and fellow villagers to obtain financial assistance.

Otherness

I knew that I was not from this country. I didn't speak like they did. I saw it on their faces. I knew that the UNRWA was paying rations for us. My family always spoke of Palestine and how much better off we were there. I felt like an outsider, but I knew I had an alternative—that is, a home in Palestine, a big house, and we owned a shop. But my situation was still better than that of the others. We didn't live in the camps, and I wasn't working as a servant in a Lebanese home. For me the problem was not so much a material one but a psychological one, and it has effected me all my life.

I attended a Lebanese school, and no Palestinians were there except my sisters and me. Until I was fifteen years old we were the only Palestinians there. I was always aware that I was a Palestinian—something different. The Lebanese made jokes about us, especially about our accent. I began to feel more Palestinian than ever.

One day five Palestinian girls from the camp joined our class. They had been in UNRWA schools, and since they were top students they were selected to go on to private Lebanese high school. Soon after they joined the class, I addressed the teacher, and he mimicked my Palestinian accent. Suddenly one of the new girls stood up and began screaming and cursing at him. The Palestinian girls ordered a strike, and all the pupils followed until the teacher was forced to apologize to me. After that I sat with the Palestinian girls.

Layla
Beirut

In her account Layla, a thirty-year-old militant from a lower middle-class family, reveals the sense of being an "Other," present in a group yet not an accepted, integral part of it. The Palestinian accent, slightly different from that of Lebanon, is the most immediate, apparent, and tangible symbol that sets Palestinians apart. Thus it is often the subject of mockery.

The alienation of being a refugee often found expression in nostalgic comparisons to a somewhat fictitious reconstruction of social life in pre-1948 Palestine. Um Muhammad, a widow from Tal al-Zaʿter engaged in subsistence farming in Damur, for example, vehemently insisted that the fruits and vegetables of Palestine were far superior to those of Lebanon. Um Nabil, nearly ninety years old, refers to life in Palestine as the "days of paradise." The unattainable alternative was ever present. Sentiments of solidarity protected against assaults upon cultural heritage and statelessness, and once the Resistance was on the scene such sentiments were accompanied by actions such as Layla's and her Palestinian classmates' that publicly expressed the newfound reality of empowerment.

Class position mediated women's experience of national discrimination. Like Layla, those who lived outside the camps were more exposed on an everyday basis to Lebanese society and thus experienced more hostile encounters. In addition, living in the midst of urban Lebanese society in scattered rather than cohesive settlements, they lacked the group solidarity evident in the camps, where everyone was living under essentially the same set of material conditions.

The mobility of camp women was more circumscribed than that of urban women. The space in which they acted out their daily lives was more bounded. Although they encountered the Lebanese less often, they did consider the world outside the camps an alien one, full of potential dangers but also excitement. After a trip outside the camp, usually for shopping, to see a physician, or to visit friends or relatives, women described in animated detail how people were dressed, how men behaved toward them in public places, and the decor of people's houses and they usually expressed relief to be back in the safety of their homes. The outside world was spoken of as a place where danger lurks, as though people were not bound by the same norms of behavior as in the camps. Despite occasional shelling, there was a sense of security and safety within their boundaries. Doors were rarely, if ever, locked, since theft was rare as was rape. The visible presence of *al-fida'iyyin* gave everyone a feeling of safety. While women encountered verbal harassment in the streets of Beirut, such behavior in the camps was rare. The community was too small and knit together by social ties and shared values for men to attempt such a violation of community norms, though they may well have engaged in such behavior in the anonymity of the urban areas.

Does gender influence one's experience of national discrimination? One difference concerns the degree of exposure, which is contingent on women's degree of mobility. Cultural rules that limit women's mobility insulated them from some aspects of national oppression. Jamileh, from a neighborhood in Shatila camp composed primarily of fellow villagers and close relatives, broached this difference when she said:

> I grew up in a community that was very closed. I rarely left the neighborhood. The camp was such a closed community, and I stayed in UNRWA schools, where everyone was a Palestinian, until I finished junior high school. The only problem I remember with the Lebanese was the lack of privacy. I was small, but I remember that if we wanted to do anything to our house, for example, change the zinc roof, we had to apply for a permit and it was never granted. There were always police searches in the camp and they could enter any home they wished. I remember once my brother participated in a strike at school and the next day the police came and took him away. He was gone for a week, and when he returned he was badly beaten and his head had been shaved.

Circumscribed mobility and near confinement to the neighborhood meant that camp women were relatively less exposed to Lebanese society than middle-class girls. Unlike Haifa's father, Jamileh's father was employed, obviating the need for her to work outside the camp. Thus she seldom interacted with Lebanese and naturally had fewer exploitative or humiliating experiences. For camp women experiences of national discrimination centered on the intrusion of the state apparatus into the once seemingly private domestic realm, the arrest and abuse of their men, and —when they worked outside the camp like Haifa—economic exploitation. In these instances men were unable to protect women or the family from the power and repressiveness of the Lebanese state and economy, exposing the contingent nature and mutability of an ideology of male guardianship over women, as well as reinforcing the sense of powerlessness of the exiled community as a whole. Employment and the necessity of dealing with the state and UNRWA bureaucracy gave men a more frequent and regular basis for acquiring knowledge of the world outside the camps. By and large unemployed and with limited mobility, women did not experience as intimate a relationship between national and class domination.

The rise of the Resistance movement put a swift end to the Lebanese state's presence in the camps. The younger generation, those born since the early 1960s and too young to remember such incidents, have had very different experiences of national discrimination. They have witnessed war and attacks on their communities by the Israeli army and the right-wing Lebanese militias. Yet on an individual basis, during the period 1969–1982 they lived without too many discriminatory incidents from the host population, owing to the power and influence of the Resistance movement in West Beirut and the south of Lebanon, which served to curb individual incidents of hostility.

Refugee status can place women in a vulnerable position vis-à-vis men of the host society. When the Palestinians first arrived in Lebanon, women may have been ridiculed, but physical harm was still virtually unheard of. With the rise of an armed Palestinian population, state and communal (particularly Maronite) ill will toward Palestinians escalated, but rarely were women targets of physical assault. Geophysical distance and the intimidating presence of the well-armed Palestinians inhibited such actions. Even during the 1975–76 civil war in Lebanon, Palestinian and Lebanese women of the various sects enjoyed a measure of immunity from assault. This state of affairs, however, was short-lived. The eight-month siege and August 1976 fall of Tal al-Za'ter camp is the prime example of attacks on women undertaken in an effort to cause population shifts. This was a concerted campaign to assault women in order to ensure a Palestinian (and Muslim) flight from East Beirut, as well as to humiliate and make tangible their increasing vulnerability. Such a policy reached its apogee in the 1982 Sabra-Shatila massacres where women and children were specific targets of rape, atrocities, and murder.[11]

Class Consciousness

Class consciousness, a recognition of shared interests based on a similarity of position in the socioeconomic hierarchy, is not as salient as national consciousness in motivating women to action. The commonality of suffering as Palestinians in exile tends to create sentiments of solidarity and unity that cloak class differences. Such sentiments underlie camp women's popular view of Palestinian history, which glorifies the past, asserting that in pre-1948 Palestine there was little tension between widely unequal social sectors. This conceptualization of history is an idealized reconstruction and presentation of society and culture to outsiders and to the self. Life as refugees was full of misery and insecurities; the past in Palestine, even for those who never experienced it firsthand, assumed glorious proportions. Pronounced differences in income, life-style, occupation, education, and family status do cut across Palestinian society. These differences are frequently denied and glossed over—yet at other times they evoke consternation. Sectarian differences were glossed over even more, which can probably be attributed to the sectarian nature of Lebanese society and Palestinian attempts to rise above such parochialism, as well as the Palestinian political rejection of sectarianism. Those who openly acknowledge class differences are the highly politicized camp or lower middle-class urban women who were full-time militants, usually in leftist parties or the leftist sector of Fateh. However, there is a distinction between an awareness of class position, of which most women are cognizant, and class solidarity and action. An ideology that posits class as a basis for understanding the Zionist success in Palestine and for collective action at this stage of Palestinian political history was fairly limited. The most that can be said is that some women had strong feelings of class domination and exploitation and saw a clear link between national and class struggles. None, however, disputed the primacy of national struggle at this stage.

Camp women perceive economic exploitation more as a function of their position in national structures than of gender. Rarely are class position and exploitation extracted from statelessness. As Haifa recounted in her story about working in the factories, they are exploited because they are Palestinians, not because they are from the working class. If they weren't refugees and powerless, they would not have been so exploited. Economic exploitation is recognized as a consequence of both refugee status and class position, because refugee status, at some point, is contiguous with economic marginality.

Nevertheless, those camp women who have an understanding of the class structure of Palestinian society, the development of colonialism and imperialism in the Arab region, and the varied interests of diverse segments of Palestinian and Arab society, often do perceive themselves as part of an exploited class whose position has been compounded by a refugee status. These women refer to the distant past in Palestine: "If we were still in our country we would have developed according to our own internal momentum and class struggle would have been an inevitable part of it." Clearly, though, national dispossession, which has had adverse effects on large segments of the population (though this is very much a matter of degree), has served to temporarily deflect class consciousness and class-based political action.

The pervasiveness of the Resistance movement in everyday life has had contradictory implications for women's class consciousness. On the one hand, the Resistance and its nationalist stance, as well as a national disaster on a collective level, tend to blur class differences as the motivation or focal point of political mobilization and action. The national crisis has generated sentiments of political and national unity in a culturally and socially heterogeneous society. The commonality of suffering reached a level whereby even women of the poorer classes downplayed class differences. They strove to present their situation as Palestinians as one that transcends class boundaries. Maysun, a young camp woman active in a leftist party, stated quite emphatically that "nobody thinks in terms of class nowadays. We're all suffering the same conditions—we're all refugees."

On the other hand, though the Resistance tended to blur class distinctions on the ideological level, in practice it often perpetuated them. Higher level positions in the staff of a potential state bureaucracy were usually held by middle-class members, lower-ranking positions by camp or poorer Palestinians, indicative of a class-based division of labor. This was especially evident in the social class of fighters. In spite of the rhetoric of equality in struggle expressed in the popular slogan: "Every fighter a politician and every politician a fighter," full-time commandos were nearly always "sons of the camp." In the early 1980s the majority of the leadership of the Women's Union were educated middle-class women; just under one-third of the thirteen-member Executive Committee were from the camps. When someone from the camps attained a leadership position it was a topic of conversation: "So-and-so, who is from the camps, is in the leadership now."

The concept of "women's culture"[12] in gender-segregated societies need not imply either the existence of autonomous domains or a challenge to dominant ideologies of gender.[13] One of the pitfalls of this term is to assign it universality. On the contrary, the term should be used in a culture- and class-specific context. For descriptive purposes, the sharing of physical and psychic space defines the existence of a women's culture and informs a consciousness of the world and of themselves as different from men. Women lead quite disparate lives on the basis of class affiliation. The space they occupy and the work they perform varies considerably from one class context to another, while the cultural norms and rules to which they are held accountable are similar in general content, though their application and severity of sanction for transgressions can vary considerably.

Camp women share a commonality of tasks and sentiments of solidarity in the face of adversity and continuing crisis. The physical layout of the camp and the structure of homes ensure that women are seldom isolated from one another. Houses are built in a patchwork jumble on the sides of very narrow, winding alleyways. The simple fact of crowdedness accounts for a large measure of face-to-face interaction. Cooking and baking bread are often shared among kinswomen and friends, and the bakery itself provides a predominantly female gathering place where visiting and a domestic chore are combined. Homes offer little privacy, as windows and doors give way to public alleys, which facilitates women's calling upon one another while on the way to shop or on trips to the bakery or clinic. When the weather is warm, women sit in their courtyards or in the alleys in front of their homes preparing food, sewing, or minding the children. During the day the alleys are largely the preserve of women, children, and the elderly. In the event of military attacks, women and children sit together in the underground shelters to pass long hours of anxiety-ridden confinement. Upon the loss of their children in battle, mothers are consoled by other women who have had a similar experience and those who are acutely aware of the lack of immunity from such a tragedy. The death of a son in battle is a loss for the whole community, expressed in the common reference to martyrs as "sons of the camp."

Urban women, for the most part, do not share this intimate communality of everyday life. The physical layout of the city is less conducive to shared women's space, and their domestic tasks entail less cooperative labor and movement beyond the home except for shopping. Bread is no longer baked at public ovens, and there is seldom an area in front of their homes, bordering public space, where they can pass the hours preparing food, sewing, or minding the children. For middle- and upper-class women domestic work can be bypassed by hiring a maid. Few lose sons in battle, and thus they do not share a sense of communal loss. The middle-class mother of a martyr wept bitterly, "Why did my son have to die? Couldn't someone else do the fighting? My son was educated!" Such a statement could hardly be uttered in public among camp women—to put oneself above others is to openly defy the prevailing sentiment of shared suffering. It is to risk offending and alienating those women who have lost sons in war and those who will probably lose them in the future. In short, it is to cast oneself as detached from the community and its cultural rules and forms of sentiments.

Class differences clearly illustrate the futility of trying to construe a women's culture; even the kind and degree of national oppression differs by class. The sense of community that occasionally binds urban and camp women is better cast as one of national solidarity derived from national identity and affiliation and support for the Resistance and as subjects of a cultural ideology that at some points disregards class. Thus the term *women's culture* should only be used in class-specific situations.

Women in the camps were pointedly aware of the economic and social differences that distinguished them from middle- and upper-class urbanites. It was patently obvious whether a woman was native to the camps or not by a number of immediately noticeable symbols, such as sartorial style and physical bearing. The peasant custom of wearing colorful dresses over trousers and a white scarf distinguished camp women from outsiders and, of course, from the younger generation, who had taken to donning blue jeans and Western style dresses.

Cadres, visiting or working in the camp, who tended to be middle-class urban women, dress modestly (i.e., no low necklines, bare arms, or short dresses) and simply, but with fashion consciousness. They were quickly identified by their up-to-date fashions and style of interaction with men. They spoke more freely to men, though they themselves were aware of the limits of this openness if they wanted to maintain their reputations and continue working in the camps. Their range of mobility was considerably more extensive than that of camp girls, some of whom had only infrequently left the camps.

But camp women's awareness of the differences separating them from urban women extended beyond these visual signs. They were aware that urban middle-class women were usually more educated and had greater mobility, a higher standard of living, and markedly smaller families. Camp women, whose educational level had steadily increased from illiteracy to stabilize at the intermediate level, expressed inquisitiveness and envy of middle-class women's educational achievements; for many it was a source of pride for the Palestinian community as a whole. Some disdained it as a waste of time and resources. Older women, in particular, considered too much education a liability rather than an asset in finding a husband. Um Nabil, mother of a prominent Palestinian leader, commented on her granddaughter's graduation with an M.S. degree, "Who needs an education to get married and raise children?"

Contact between women inside and outside the camps has been limited by structural and cultural constraints on mobility. Attendance at schools in urban areas and Resistance involvement enhanced contact. Jamileh, for example, was one of the few girls from Shatila to attend a private Lebanese secondary school and later the American University of Beirut. In discussing how she felt about mingling with middle and upper class girls, she said:

> I was always aware that the other girls were rich—the way they dressed, the way they spoke. I always felt different. When I came to the university it was even more obvious. I resolved it between me and myself by avoiding social gatherings or parties. I didn't want to have to face it or any conflicts, and this was my way of adapting.

Over a period of ten years, Maryam, a highly politicized activist from Shatila, had worked her way up the Resistance hierarchy. Her father had been a worker in Haifa, and after 1948 they lived in extreme poverty. Maryam, whose approach to the political situation included a well-developed class perspective, once told me of her feelings toward the bourgeoisie. While we were walking to a wedding party I casually mentioned a mutual acquaintance who would be there. Maryam became quite agitated:

> I hate this woman. Though she knows absolutely nothing about politics, is a bourgeoise and new in the Resistance, she has recently been assigned to be my "responsible."[14] She's only in this position because she is romantically involved with someone holding a prominent military position in the Resistance. She also entertains this fellow and his colleagues in her home, providing fancy meals and alcoholic drinks.

She explained to me why she detests this kind of person:

> Ever since I was young I have had strong feelings about the bourgeoisie. We were very poor and I worked as a servant. This feeling of being so poor made me hate the bourgeoisie. Even now I look at them with hate —even if they are in the Resistance. I always compare the way they work in the Resistance and the way I do. I feel I am from the poor. I feel more with them because I know the meaning of poverty and hunger. They can't really know what it is like. Because of this difference I feel between them and me I joined a leftist party. I believe deeply in the class struggle.

Although political affiliation often puts in contact women from the camp and urban areas, working in the Resistance can also be an isolating experience. Women in the Resistance socialize mainly, although not exclusively, with each other; some seldom enter "Lebanese areas." Dalal had never been to many parts of Beirut and knew little of the city, though she had lived there for years, working with the Resistance. The only time she left the area was to visit wounded comrades in the hospital. She explained:

> Here in Lebanon we—the Resistance movement—are a society in ourselves. Our dealings with the outside are limited. As a movement we face the bourgeoisie, but we are in a position of power. Within the movement we don't feel the class antagonisms. If I weren't in the Resistance I would feel it more, because class differences in Lebanon are acute. I think women in general feel class differences less anyway simply because they move so much less in society; their exposure is more limited than a man's. I feel these differences only when I visit the hospital, for example. There I see all those people from Ras Beirut and from the AUB with their fancy clothes. So I feel these differences only when I mix with the outside world. Our experiences in the movement are very different because we seldom mix with outsiders. Also, we are not an integral part of the labor market here—we are not working and selling our labor. We are a closed society.

Maryam's, Jamileh's, and Dalal's statements represented the parameters and touched the surface of the complexities of camp women's class consciousness. Jamileh lived in two bounded social worlds, the AUB and that of Shatila, keeping to herself in the former to avoid painful encounters; Dalal had no need to interact with people outside her small circle of Resistance friends; Maryam was openly hostile to the bourgeoisie.

Camp women had conflicting attitudes toward middle-class women, Resistance cadres or employees, with whom they were in contact. Much of the reaction depended on the character and comportment of the individual outsider. Nonetheless, some patterns were discernible. Suspicion and doubt were coupled with acceptance and admiration. To camp women, middle-class women had more choices in their lives in terms of education and mobility and enjoyed a measure of immunity from conflict. When the camps were bombed, middle-class women could return to the relative safety of their homes. Yet it was precisely during incidents of external aggression that expressions and actions indicative of national unity were the strongest.

Middle-class women's more "liberated" behavior made them subjects of close scrutiny and at times caution, for fear they might negatively influence girls in the camps. Yet they were also admired and respected for their devotion to the national cause. Older camp women wondered about the intentions and methods of the cadres: "Can they really understand our problems?" "They're so bossy—as if we don't know anything."

These underlying tensions were rarely expressed publicly. A complex and subtle etiquette of public silence glossed over potential conflict, as did the commonality of suffering and struggle. Negative comments were voiced privately. After working in the camps for a number of years, Layla eloquently lamented on the gap in understanding and acceptance:

> I never really knew how the people in the camps felt about me. You know, camp people cheat you. They greet you in a friendly way and invite you to visit, and then you find out they gossip about you. You never know their real feelings. But some of the women supported me and told me about the gossip and who was doing it. Only later did I find out that the women who told me of gossip by other women were usually involved in family conflicts.

Unless they were members of the Resistance, middle- and upper-class women were usually far removed from daily life in the camps with its own banalities, secrets, and constraints. Physical and social distance was expressed in contradictory terms—disdain and admiration. These were the same sorts of attitudes held by camp women toward middle-class women, although the former were looking across a power and privilege gap.

Urban middle-class women had fewer opportunities to develop a sense of neighborhood-based solidarity than did camp women. As discussed previously, the nature of urban middle-class life was not as conducive to a shared sense of work and space. There was less sense of sharing a way of life where women were masters of managing meager resources. Urban Palestinian women were more united by ties of national solidarity, kinship, friendship, and membership in voluntary associations. Their networks lent themselves to mobilization for political work in the form of charitable associations and information organizations.

My fieldwork in the camps was occasionally a topic of surprise among middle-class Palestinians: "How can you go there?" "Aren't you afraid?" "What about disease and the filth [or the constant shelling]?" "Those people are uneducated—you should talk to educated people!" Middle-class Palestinians were rather unnerved by the representative status—of cultural authenticity, of struggle and resistance, of suffering—the camps and their inhabitants had acquired. Madame Haddad, a fifty-four-year-old woman from Jaffa who had lived in the Beirut area since 1948, once asked me where the camps were. Never having seen one, she had no idea of their location in the urban configuration. Yet she admired their inhabitants, who she felt were fighting for all Palestinians, especially those girls who had died in battle for "all the other Palestinians." "If we didn't have the Resistance, Palestinian history would be over," she told me. "As for the rich," she opined, "they should give money to the Resistance because it is working for them, as Palestinians. They [the camp people] send their children to die. The least the rich can do is give money." Madame Haddad exemplified middle-class attitudes toward camp people, but with a twist that some camp women found a bit condescending—camp women were now grudgingly respected by the middle class since they were bearing the brunt of protracted struggle and for their sacrifice: the giving of their sons.

The traditional elites had more disdainful attitudes toward the camps and those involved in the Resistance. Co-optation by the new middle class and, to a lesser extent, by the sons of former peasants of the Palestinian body politic can be held accountable, in part. Leadership positions in the PLO were occupied by the young, educated men of a middle class that was nascent early in the twentieth century and that had become politically and ideologically hegemonic since the 1948 disaster. However, the attitudes of the elite were not monolithic, varying according to past and present nationalist involvement. May, daughter of an upper-class mercantile family of Jerusalem with no past or present history of political involvement, was intensely patriotic and nationalistic. She talked incessantly about the Palestinian disaster and related all upheaval in her personal life to it. It seemed to relieve the bitterness she felt over losing her home in Jerusalem to the Israelis and being denied reentry. To her, the Resistance leadership were a bunch of upstarts who had taken over the political process from those best suited to staff it—the traditional elites. Yet as a Palestinian living in West Beirut, she was begrudgingly aware that the Resistance presence was her prime source of security. She applauded the fighters when they scored a victory and deplored them for their sometimes rough street behavior, and peasant origins. In contrast, Madame Sa‘d, from a politically and financially leading family of Jerusalem, felt closer to the Resistance and those who fight in the name of Palestine. Her sons were in the Resistance, so she frequently played hostess to the colleagues they brought home. She admired them and saw in them "the road home."

Gender Consciousness: Female and Feminist

Um Yasir, whose husband and sons are full-time fighters, used to say, "Women have their rights [huquq] now—they choose their husbands; they go to school, work, and fight in the national struggle." Her ideas were not uncommon, nor was her use of the term *huquq*. That women have their rights now was an idea frequently articulated not just by older women like Um Yasir, but also by a host of young women who believed the national crisis and the Resistance movement had engendered a situation whereby girls had obtained their rights.

If discourse is any indication, younger, politicized, and educated women took a different view of the situation. They spoke of liberation *(taharrur)* and looked to employment and political mobilization as initial steps. Unlike Um Yasir, they argued that women had only just begun to acquire some of their rights. While agreeing that the right to choose a husband or reject one chosen for them was a dramatic breakthrough, they contended that a cultural system that prescribed control over women, vested in the family, circumscribed their personal autonomy and was a major force shaping their daily lives. Initially I attributed this disparity in discourse and attitudes to a generation gap. Upon encountering younger women who held similar ideas I begin to realize the situation was more complex. A more fruitful way to conceptualize what appeared, at first glance, to be a paradox is in terms of female consciousness and feminist consciousness.[15]

Female Consciousness

In pinpointing the distinction between female and feminist consciousness women's lexicon is telling. Those who spoke of women's rights did not seek changes in the allocation of social roles based on gender as much as they sought rights considered legitimately theirs within a division of labor that assigned to them domesticity.

In 1969, one of the first women activists gave a speech to a gathering of camp women. Encouraging them to be active in the national struggle, this middle class, educated activist asked them, "Aren't we equal to men?" She was astounded when they unanimously shouted, "No, of course we're not!" Such experiences made explicit to activists the extent to which cultural ideologies of gender were shared by men and women alike. In extrapolating on the role of politicized women she drew an analogy between women's consciousness and lack of active resistance and that of the working class:

> . . . she sees with the eyes of her husband. She doesn't defend backward ideas, but she cannot see the light of her liberation. It is comparable to the working class; many times, when they aren't organized in parties or unions, they are tools in the hands of the bourgeoisie because they are afraid of losing the few benefits they have. They feel it is their

destiny to be oppressed so they don't struggle. Not because they like their situation, but because they don't have an alternative and are afraid. It is the role of the vanguard to present an alternative.[16]

Equality with men was not their concern or, indeed, their definition of women's rights. Their political actions were rooted in ideas of what they perceived to be their culturally sanctioned rights as women, mothers, and sustainers of life—to carry out their domestic tasks and raise their children in peace and material security and to be protected from assaults. Autonomy in the choice of a husband, the opportunity to attend school, and work before marriage were the foundations of their notion of what actually constituted women's rights.

These ideas and new demands have been occasioned by changing materialities. Daughters and sisters were encouraged to study and work to enable them to sustain their future families during instances of turmoil and material insecurity, an imperative that assumed saliency in a society with a high rate of widowhood. Equally significant was the desire to increase the family's standard of living and finance the higher education of sons. Better-educated young men were seeking more educated women as marriage partners. Rising levels of education designated intermediate schooling a criterion of a suitable wife. Women's education and employment were viewed less as contravening the normative consensus on domesticity and more as augmenting it, as being new criteria of its proper performance. Women worked to provide for their children or to buy things for the house; if unmarried, her earnings went toward preparations for marriage and to assist her family in meeting daily expenses. The economic realities that underlie work are cloaked in two related ideologies and their accompanying discourses. While acknowledging economic realities, a nationalistic discourse confers legitimacy, couching work in terms of "a contribution to the cause" and "working for the people, for our society." The other discourse—intimate and personal—is well rooted in a changing life cycle that now comprises an extended period between completion of school and marriage when women increasingly look to employment for self-fulfillment. However, it is important to note that self-fulfillment—working to "improve myself, to be productive"—is closely coupled with notions of community. Expressions of personal aspirations and actions were embedded in those of community. Working women, mainly employed in Resistance-sponsored institutions, saw themselves as being socially productive and thus achieving personal fulfillment through contributing to the development of the community. Such employment met society's criterion of legitimacy, which increasingly bound women's enhanced opportunities for work to national movement institutions.

Education and work are not expected to displace the primacy of domesticity. Contemporary cultural expectations structure women's lives in a chronological sequence of education, work, marriage, and child raising. As the overlap between employment and domesticity increases, women, young and old alike, are concerned with the management of conflicting demands and loyalties. Um Nabil worried that her granddaughters would be unable to manage domestic work and a job and thus discouraged them from seeking education beyond high school.

The violation of the sanctity of the domestic realm—the searches and arrests of the pre-Revolution period and the bombings, sieges, and massacres in the 1970s and 1980s, the psychological trauma of exile, and the physical hardship of life in the refugee camps—galvanized women into action. Female consciousness was evident, for instance, when mothers organized small but vocal demonstrations and marches to jails to protest the arrest of their sons or husbands, when groups of kin or neighbors baked bread and carried it to fighters during military attacks, and when they drew water from wells under heavy fire and hauled it to the underground shelters to ensure the survival of the camp's children. There were incidents when groups of women mobilized to protest to an embryonic state structure what they considered assaults on the community of women. In the wake of a spate of honor crimes in Tal al-Za'ter, a delegation of women visited Yasir 'Arafat, appealing to him to protect women from such abuses.[17] In early 1982, when a fifteen-year-old married woman in Shatila was raped and murdered, an angry group of women demonstrated in front of the jail where the perpetrator was being held, virulently demanding his execution. It was equally evident when they demanded of the Resistance increased social services and avidly supported the incipient PLO state infrastructure in the camps with its multitude of institutions and services that eased domestic burdens and softened the margins of poverty.

Though eager to participate in the struggle—indeed, they think they have the right—camp women also define the sectors of their participation; most feel that women can best serve the Resistance by teaching, nursing, doing secretarial work, and raising children to be good Palestinians and to fight for liberation. Only a few join the Resistance with the idea that they, or women in general, will become liberated in the process. Um Yasir, whose three daughters teach in Resistance-affiliated kindergartens, told me one evening as we huddled in her one-room home in the camp while it was under heavy bombardment:

If women are not working in the Resistance they are not human beings. It is not shameful for women to work in the Resistance. The Revolution gave women the right to take their role in the battle, in politics. They have a duty to the Resistance—it gave them their freedom. The struggle is a man's battle, and women's role is to help by encouraging him and taking care of him.

The limits in her mind are clear. Yet within those limits women are bound to do their "duty." If they don't, their status as "human beings," as members of a community, is at stake.

The mother of two prominent sons—one a political leader, the other a military figure—Um Nabil spends a lot of time around the fighters, whom she affectionately calls her "sons." She insists on washing and mending the clothes of visiting fighters and asks them, "Wouldn't you like to take a bath?" She prepares food for them and often appears at military bases to cook and clean for them. During the 1936–1939 revolt in Palestine, she and her husband used to hide fighters fleeing from the British and she secreted weapons in the countryside. One evening during Ramadan, the Muslim month of fasting, Dalal, a full-time fighter, and I broke the fast with Um Nabil. We got into a discussion of changes in women's lives since the Resistance had come to power in Lebanon. Um Nabil insists that work and activism should not jeopardize the proper performance of domesticity. Cautioning about the double burden of work and domesticity, she said:

> It's right that women today fight. Men are braver when women are around. By God, it's good that girls are educated these days. But some of these girls don't even know how to care for their homes and children! Who will marry these girls? We worked in the fields in Palestine and took our children with us or left them at home with the family. Now women can leave them at the nurseries, which is okay if the husband agrees. When women work they are helping their husbands. But she should finish her housework before she thinks of going to work. You know what this means? It means women work all day outside the house and then they come home and are faced with all this cleaning, cooking, and washing. Women will be overwhelmed because there is no one at home to help them.

It is difficult to find women who would disagree with the notion that women have a role to play in national politics. But the contours of the relationship between politics and domesticity are contested terrain. Variations in approach to the question are less according to class and generation than they are attributable to extent of politicization and nature of affiliation. The ideas of younger, uneducated, unpoliticized, and unaffiliated girls can closely resemble those of older, uneducated women, while the literacy, politicization, and formal affiliation of other young girls has made a difference in their perceptions of the possibilities open to them. Older women of the *jil filastin* (generation of Palestine) or the *jil al-nekbah* (generation of the disaster), like Um Yasir and Um Nabil, define the contours of the possible differently than do younger, especially though not exclusively, activist women. Political activism should not impinge upon domestic duties and priorities, nor should it constitute a challenge to prevailing norms of domesticity and male authority. They perceive women's current roles in the Resistance to be largely a continuation of their activities in the 1936–1939 conflict and the war of 1948, providing support services—nursing, cooking, fetching water, carrying messages.

While some of the younger, activist women advocate changes in gender structures and relations, older women usually confine themselves to advocating increased education and employment opportunities and a controlled presence in certain female-associated areas of political work. These women may have become more aware of women's subordination, but they did not press for a radical restructuring of gender-based social relations. What they demanded of the Resistance was improved conditions for carrying out domestic tasks. Female consciousness was a powerful force, mobilizing women in defense of the camp and into the social service sector of the Resistance, and was also the basis of their claims on it.

The forms of consciousness that compelled action also defined, to some extent, its parameters. In the case of female consciousness, this was a conservative phenomenon. A radical transformation in consciousness, and thus actions that challenge extant social formations, occur when contradictions surface. For instance, crises such as military assault on the camps blurred distinctions between women's, national, and political concerns. The severity of the national situation was such that any previous semblance of a dichotomy between domestic and public realms was shattered as domestic boundaries were violated and labor mobilized to sustain the community. Yet women were acting within the parameters of cultural convention when they resisted these assaults on the community. Practically speaking, they were acting to sustain and to ensure the performance of the daily routine of domesticity from the disruption and chaos brought about by political turmoil.

The radical dimension to female consciousness has two aspects. First, it dissolves the boundaries between the seemingly distinct domains of public and private, revealing the integrity of social realms. Women's actions dramatically underscored social inequalities, differences in how people experience crises. In a society where ideology postulates women's exclusion from public affairs, lower class women's involvement in defense

93

of their communities makes vividly conspicuous the extent to which the middle and upper classes are removed from the brunt of conflict. This aspect of female consciousness is perhaps more pronounced in instances where women are protesting labor conditions and the state's defense of capitalism. Moreover, when women do participate in the national struggle, the constraints imposed by gender ideology on national mobilization and its impact on the overall potential of a community to resist domination become patently clear. Second, when women seek to act on the basis of what they perceive to be their rights, cultural conventions proscribing women's public participation often come into full play. Some women do protest against a system that prevents them from participating in defense of the community in a way that extends beyond the domestic.

Transformations in Consciousness

If, as is apparent in female consciousness, the parameters of domesticity are being expanded and redefined to encompass tasks imposed by economic crises and political transformation, the crucial questions become: is there a contradiction between domesticity and its expanded tasks, and if so, at what point does it occasion transformations in women's consciousness? Alternatively, does the process of expansion and redefinition itself serve to deflect and dissolve contradictions? Female consciousness can have both conservative and radical implications for transformations in consciousness and actions, depending on the specific sociopolitical circumstances that activate and mobilize it.[18]

Juxtaposing the concepts of female and feminist consciousness need not imply the existence of two opposed forms or that feminist consciousness emerges from female consciousness. Nevertheless, such a transformation can and does occur in some instances. The impetus for transition between forms of consciousness points to the radical potential of female consciousness. Female consciousness was mobilized and activated to such an extent that it transcended its conservative bent to assume a radical character that was an impetus for the emergence of a feminist consciousness among some sectors of camp women and many middle-class activists.

Young women joined the Resistance motivated by concern for the survival of their communities and as nationalists—in other words, out of nationalist and female consciousness. They joined more to ameliorate the conditions of their community and liberate Palestine than they did with the explicit intention of improving the position of women. There was, however vaguely articulated, an idea that women's position itself would improve with participation in national affairs. Yet this ideological commitment to national struggle and actions derived from it ultimately initiated a questioning of the immutability of women's position in the social structure.

The multiplicity and interconnectedness of domination—national, class (for some), and gender—are set into prominent relief as the contradictions between domesticity and activism surface, giving form to a situation where women, empowered with consciousness of domination, are faced with decisions concerning priorities and commitments. In short, they must negotiate the management of conflicting loyalties and demands.

Activism was more instrumental than employment in forcing this process. Women's presence in the wage labor force remained numerically low and did not conflict with domestic demands as much as activism did.[19] To be able to join the Resistance women had to face a struggle with their parents, with the society in general, and within the Resistance itself. When they attempted to assert their national identity and commitment by taking part in Resistance activities, they confronted the full brunt of cultural rules governing women's behavior. At the least, sustained nationalist activity implies a questioning of conventional norms of female conduct. When women acted to preserve their communities by participating in the Resistance, cracks appeared in the ideological constructs that assigned them to the domestic sector. In acting to defend their communities and to safeguard the structures of daily life women defied both their exclusion from public affairs and the ideology that buttressed their subordination, shattering the illusion of a society with clearly defined gendered domains. When they did so the full weight of domination was evident.

At this juncture women became cognizant of the constraining nature of gender structures and ideologies and female consciousness exerted its radical potential. Among these activists, feminist consciousness is informed by several specific experiences: conflict with their families over their commitment to the Resistance or employment, encountering obstacles to mobilizing other women and becoming involved in their family conflicts, and the realization that women are the equals of men. If political activism awakened women to their subordination, it also awakened them to their potential equality with men. Women fought and died just as men did. Over and over women insist that they are able to shoulder the same responsibilities as men and therefore have the right to be equal participants.

Layla had a series of arguments with her family concerning her membership in the Resistance and the proximity to men it entailed. With no end in sight, she left home and didn't see her family for some time. Her organization assigned her a responsible position in women's affairs, a decision to which she was vehemently opposed. She felt women's affairs were not important "political" work and that this assignment was a move against her personally. She complained, "I don't want to work with a bunch of housewives!" In her view, women should be regular members like everybody else, not segregated into their own activities: "Either they are housewives or they are members"! There was no room in her conceptual scheme of activism for ambiguous positions. When she started working with women in the camp to develop their political knowledge and involve them in the Resistance she began to realize the enormity of the task and the problems they faced. Women didn't show up for meetings because of opposition from husbands and fathers or the pressures of child care and housework and because they themselves didn't assign political work a high priority. Her position on the need for a women's section changed as she came to understand the specificity of their problems.

Working with women also awakened cadres to the limits to which the Resistance was prepared to go to ensure equality. While some men supported an active role for women, others continued to insist that women's liberation was not an issue now that they attended school and worked and that any remaining changes could wait until "later" (a reference to a vaguely conceived political entity). Military and political issues (as narrowly defined by the leadership) were zones of prestige and thus were accorded precedence in terms of the allocation of resources. The Resistance also was concerned that an explicit commitment to gender equality would alienate their mass base.

The Feminist Problematic

Fernea aptly captures the problematic of Arab women's movements when she says that they "do not see the existing problems as exclusive to themselves. Over and over again, they say in different ways that the 'feminine condition' cannot be separated from that of men, the family, and the wider society" (1985:2). The current Palestinian women's movement is an integral component of the broader national movement. In 1982, a well-developed and coherent feminist ideology had yet to emerge to accompany the union's mobilization of women.

The movement is similar to other Arab women's movements that have not been separate entities but are firmly grounded, both organizationally and ideologically, in Arab nationalism and the struggle against foreign domination. As we have seen, it is of paramount importance to locate the development of feminist consciousness in the experience of exile and a national movement intent on transforming society and mobilizing the general populace.

The use of the term *feminist* in the Palestinian context can be problematic, as there is not a self-defined Palestinian feminist movement per se. Women's position is conceptualized as inextricably embedded in the larger national question. I use the term *feminist* to describe the ideology of those who perceived that hierarchical gender relations and ideologies that promote the subordination of women at some points transcend class boundaries and, as culturally grounded, preceded national domination. A recognition of the specificity of women's experience of national crises and conflict is also in evidence. Feminists advocate transformations in gender relations and meaning as ways to achieve autonomy and equality rather than simply integrating women into extant structures.

A range of points of view is current among activists. Some consider gender equality to be a future development of the gradual, ongoing process of mobilizing women for national struggle; political participation and employment will integrate women into public life, and through practice eventually cultural notions of gender will be transformed toward equality. Though few demands for radical restructuring of gender relations are voiced, there is a tactical side to women's public pronouncements. Fateh publications and speeches by its leaders pay scant attention to the liberation or equality of women, stressing instead the need to mobilize women for national struggle. In the Palestinian context, a fundamental component of individual liberation means participation in the larger process of national politics.

Highly politicized women, particularly those with long experience working in the camps as mobilizers, opine that gender equality must be an integral component of the current struggle for national liberation, that its achievement will not be an inevitable by-product, but a struggle on its own. The dilemma is to integrate it into a nationalist framework at this "advanced defensive stage."

Locating women's struggle as an intimate part of a national liberation movement in a society where both women and men are seen as victims of the continuing national crisis, Samirah, a Fateh activist, gave succinct expression to a common sentiment among women.

> I think that because women fought side by side with their husbands, their brothers, or with their comrades, after national liberation women's liberation is a natural result. They have the right to say, "I did the same as you; I will take my liberty." We don't say, "Men are our

enemy; we should fight men." This is wrong. The man himself is not liberated. He is disinherited, uprooted; he doesn't have a state; he has no rights. How can we take our rights from a man who has none?

For women like Samirah, gender equality is not an issue to be left until national liberation; it should be an integral part of the national struggle. Yet accompanying such a view is an astute recognition of the limited potential for a major restructuring of gender relations in a society devoid of a territorially based entity with its own polity, economy, and social institutions. Samirah's ruminations also underscore the deep sentiment of community prevalent among Palestinians, the sense of common interests and goals that supersede women's specific concerns, and the comprehensiveness of the process of liberation that cannot be separated along lines of gender. Most women concur that the impetus and legitimacy of the struggle for gender equality accompany the national struggle, but its tangible achievement and legal consolidation can only be realized with the establishment of an independent Palestinian political entity.

Women's political consciousness is more than a consequence of experiences of national, class, and gender domination and subordination. The Resistance movement, as the organizational format for the expression of women's political consciousness, had a positive input in shaping the contours of political consciousness. First, aside from the sense of dignity it accorded Palestinians in exile and the political education programs it offered to its cadres and recruits, it confirmed and reinforced political consciousness by displaying what militant struggle can achieve. The quasi self-sufficient social infrastructure based on mass involvement gave camp Palestinians a heightened sense of participation in the dynamic process of cultural reconstruction.

Second, Resistance ideology ordered and ranked the multiple forms of domination that structure women's lives, their political consciousness and sense of self. Concomitantly, it then circumscribed political consciousness with an exterior quality, marginalizing or even denying the highly internal quality of women's experience of gender domination. In general, the Resistance determined the ranked order of forms of consciousness. It allocated prestige and resources to forms of consciousness and the actions and affiliations occasioned by them. On the one hand, in spite of Resistance ideology, women's participation in its activities often led to an awareness of their equality with men and their subordination in the gender order. On the other hand, participation in defense of the community led to a reaffirmation, though in politicized form, of a female consciousness and form of action.

In the era of the Resistance (1969–1982), young camp women and activists begin to describe themselves and other women with a whole new vocabulary, a repertoire of intensely active, political, and nationalistic terms and categories—activists *(nashitat)*, politicized *(musayyasat)*, fighters *(fida'iyyat)*, workers *('amilat)*, strugglers *(munadilat)*, and martyrs *(shahidat)*. These new concepts of self were squarely located in a sense of national pride and involvement in struggle and, most important, in their sense of empowerment. Yet caution should be exercised in alluding to these terms as reflecting a quantum step in redefining women's position or even in perceptions of their position in the social order. Domesticity remained paramount; few rejected its primacy. As we will see later, political activism was being grafted onto domesticity, politicizing and mobilizing the domestic sector. Near the end of the Resistance presence in Lebanon, after the ripening of the contradiction between activism and domesticity, younger, activist women began to question a gendered division of labor.

Women's political consciousness is not, in and of itself, always sufficient to indicate formal political activism, but it does indicate a constant state of mobilization potential and a readiness to undertake those actions necessary to sustain and defend the community. Political consciousness may not be an absolute prerequisite of mobilization and indeed often emerges and develops during the process of mobilization, but it is essential for sustained political activism. The next chapter examines the processes by which women joined the Resistance and the obstacles they faced.

4

Mobilizing Women

■

The title "Mobilizing Women" is intended to convey an essential aspect of the general process of mobilization. Women mobilize and are mobilized. In short, they are in a constant state of "mobilizing." They have been assigned the task of mobilizing other women and community support in general. And as a category of gendered person, they are the target of these mobilizing efforts. The first part of this chapter examines the multifaceted process of women's political mobilization and the various channels through which they enter the national movement. The second part explores the relationship between crisis and mobilization and the cultural rules called into play when women decide to become active. Channels of mobilization comprise: self-initiative, universities, mass mobilization campaigns, local-level Resistance institutions, kin ties, and crisis situations.

In the pre-1948 period, Palestinian women's organizations did not seek the mass mobilization of women. For rural peasant women, ancestors of today's camp women, political activities were more often spontaneous responses to localized crises. A small minority of urban women were active in charitable or social associations. With the birth of the Resistance movement, mobilizing women into mass organizations and training them as cadres became an explicit goal. A key distinction between these two periods in the class composition of activists and their targets of mobilization. In the pre-1948 period, there was little attempt to directly involve peasant or lower class women in urban, largely elite, organizations in a sustained fashion, nor did they attempt to form formal women's organizations. Though now most activists are middle class, educated, and urban, their goal is to mobilize camp women and integrate them into the national movement in order to build a mass-based women's organization.

The concept of political mobilization has to be fluid enough to encompass a broad range of activities, formal and informal, and accommodate varying and fluctuating levels of commitment. On one hand, the protracted nature of the Palestinian struggle, the absence of a territorial base, and exile in frequently hostile territory have informed the general parameters of the mobilization process. On the other hand, the specificity of the process, the forms it took in everyday life, was intimately rooted in camp social organization and cultural norms of appropriate behavior. Community thinking, as well as that of the Resistance leadership, was that all sectors of the community should be involved in a threefold process of "mass mobilization": to promote national struggle and independence, to defend the exile community, and to develop a network of social institutions as the groundwork of a future Palestinian entity.

The concept of mass mobilization occupies a salient position in Palestinian political ideology, yet the mobilization process itself has an uneven, almost haphazard, quality. At times it is a consciously devised and organized process that aims to harness human potential and energy for social transformation and national liberation via sustained militant action and the training of political cadres; other times it has a diffuse, random quality. Gathering groups of recruits without a clear plan for their placement is one such example.

Under the leadership and auspices of the PLO, camp communities were encouraged to organize to assume control over their daily lives. The establishment of camp municipalities *(lijan al-sha*c*biyyeh)* to manage water resources, electricity, and sewage and maintain order by mediating local disputes is just one example of the assumption of local control. In organizing human resources for social development the Resistance was also attempting to consolidate a national body where the individual's identity and loyalty would gradually be directed more to the (embryonic) state rather than to primordial forms of social organization and affiliation such as kin, regional, or religious entities.[1] Traditional family functions were being augmented by Resistance provisioning of employment opportunities, an array of social services, and protection.

A number of questions can be posed about women's mobilization. Were women a specific target of mobilization? If so, why? Do the mobilization process and policies vary by gender? How did the mobilization process accommodate ideologies of gender? The larger context of the national struggle must not be lost sight of; women's mobilization does not take place in a political or social vacuum. Policies, or the lack of them as the case may be, should be, for analytical purposes, closely articulated with the larger military-political situation of the Resistance movement in Lebanon and its various stages of ideological development. They should also be juxtaposed with the prevailing normative order as it concerns gender.

The period between 1969–1974 was the heyday of the revolutionary tide in the camps. The Resistance had recently arrived from Jordan to link up forces with the fledgling movement in Lebanon. In the absence of an organized and integrated plan for their mobilization, a handful of women, often teachers and former members of the Arab Nationalist Movement, were joining of their own accord. The effect of women's activism during the Jordanian period (1967–1971) cannot be underestimated. Quite a few of the women leaders active in Lebanon at this time had come from Jordan in 1970–71. Experienced in organizing women in the camps in Jordan, they were infused with what they described as "patriotic zeal," which they hoped to translate into a national policy on women's issues. Their example encouraged women in Lebanon to join the movement; their actions challenged the cultural order of gender, and they held positions of responsibility within the national movement. Their years of experience both in the military and in social and political organizing served them well when they entered the Lebanese arena.

The Resistance movement in Lebanon faced a situation of continuous military and political crisis, which, it can be argued, compelled them to adopt a defensive position. Though they were able to acquire and sustain support from certain sectors of the Lebanese population (students, intellectuals, workers, and leftists), the Lebanese right, in conjunction with the state and army, was rapidly mobilized in a campaign to, at the least, cut them down to size or, at its most extreme, force them to leave Lebanon altogether. In 1973, armed clashes broke out between the Lebanese army and the *fida'iyyin,* followed by civil war in 1975–76 and Israeli invasions of Lebanon in 1978 and 1982.

In the course of chronic crises behavioral norms were suspended temporarily, producing a cultural ambiguity that women were anxious to capitalize on to take daring action. It was at such times that they joined the Resistance and undertook more intensive efforts to mobilize others. Conversely crises acted to deflect attention away from the designing and implementation of stringent and well-planned mobilization policies as well as the emergence of a body of theory and strategy for women's integration into the national process. This was particularly the case after the 1975–76 civil war, when a process of bureaucratization ensued. Those women who had so energetically joined in the early 1970s, anticipating that the revolution would offer a theoretical and practical program for the liberation of women, were to be sorely disappointed by the lack of actual advancement. Women who in the early 1970s had been members of cells that focused on politicization found that the war cut short formal sources of further politicization and, for many, work in the Resistance was becoming a salaried job rather than a practical expression of revolutionary commitment. Nevertheless, more women joined the Resistance during the post–civil war period than in the early days. By this time, it was more culturally acceptable, and the employment opportunities it provided were a further inducement.

Fluehr-Lobban pointed out that when militancy, especially armed struggle, characterizes a national movement resisting settler-colonialism "the militance demanded of women is greater" (1980:237). Armed struggle, she points out, requires that a large percentage of the population be mobilized not just to fight, but to staff the ordinary institutions and positions that were normally closed to women. Palestinian women were mobilized less with the intention of informing a new division of labor and more with the intention that they serve in a support capacity to operate the social institutions of the Resistance and as part of a concerted plan to enhance, but not radically alter, the social standards of the Palestinian community. Their participation in formal politics became an indicator of modernization, radicalism, progressiveness, and social development and a sign of the rejection of the "backward past," which Palestinians, intellectuals and ordinary people alike, often assign saliency in facilitating Zionist control over Palestine. The Resistance had yet to develop an integrated and coherent plan to mobilize women, though it was a component part of their vision of the future society they wanted to establish.

The impetus for mobilization came from women themselves, acting first as individuals, then as small collectivities, organized around the Women's Union, and as groups within their political organizations. Their intention, better defined and at some variance from that of the largely male leadership, was to raise the political consciousness of women and gradually involve them in the national struggle. The Women's Union established vocational training projects in order to equip women with the requisite skills for employment, laying a basic material foundation for their liberation. Their eventual equality, which was supposed to result, remained vaguely defined both in terms of substance and the process of achieving it.

In reality, the mobilization of women went far beyond recruiting women for sustained militancy and as a support staff. Mobilization, particularly crisis mobilization, broke through the boundaries of domesticity, but did not alter the sexual division of labor. Women's domestic roles became infused with politics as they were called upon to make available to the national struggle their domestic services (see chapter 6).

Mobilization as Process: "Step by Step"

The process of mobilizing women is at the same time one of raising their political consciousness. The two processes are intimately interconnected. Women are more easily mobilized if they are politically conscious, for the decision to join reflects a desire to assume an active stance vis-à-vis the materialities that influence day-to-day life. But becoming politically conscious is often a process charged by the Resistance and involvement in its daily activities. In pursuing the strategy of mass mobilization and the harnessing of human resources for national advancement, the Resistance fashioned new institutions designed to serve the basic needs of the community as well as expand the process of political education. Participation in these new institutions was meant to and did convey to wide sectors of the population a sense of their place in the historical process of national reconstruction. For example, the clinics established by the leftist organizations to improve health conditions and care in the camps focused on preventive medicine. Largely staffed by camp residents and under the aegis of the Resistance, the clinics' medical philosophy stressed the individuals' and communities' responsibility to maintain hygenic conditions. Health education stressed preventive care rather than reliance on expensive imported medicines and equated raising healthy children with national duty and social responsibility. Unlike the previous passive reliance on the UNRWA's curative services, local-level health facilities and their education programs were intended to instill in residents a spirit of involvement in the process of national construction.

Women's political consciousness is always more than a response to discrimination, for many camp women have such experiences and remain politically unconscious and uncommitted. The Resistance presence in the camps politicized women as a consequence of its mere presence and involvement in so many aspects of daily life, a presence that helped to dissolve feelings of powerlessness and encouraged a sense of autonomy, control, and independence. The mobilization of women is a "step-by-step" process that first involves raising their consciousness and getting them into the work force. Membership in an organization means not merely activism but also a continuously maturing political consciousness. The question that must be posed is: are there transitional points when political consciousness and the politicization process lead into mobilization and sustained militancy? And how does the mobilization process itself further political consciousness? In other words, what are the details of the relationship between ideology, belief, knowledge, and practice?

Following their expulsion from Jordan in 1970–71, the Resistance transferred its headquarters to Beirut. Palestinians speak of the camps as suffused with "an intense revolutionary atmosphere" and a "sense of euphoria" at "being in control of our own communities and future." Zaynah, an activist during the battles in Jordan, reminisced about it: "These were days of fire—we were strong and proud. It was a spontaneous euphoria, but it was based on a deep love of Palestine and the ardent desire of everyone to do something." She went on to say how easy it was to gather women for lectures, demonstrations, and community projects such as digging shelters and sewage canals.

In Lebanon, the Resistance lost no time in taking over the day-to-day running of social institutions in the camps and set up a variety of new ones designed to serve basic needs for education, medical care, security, and municipal services. Young men, eager to join, flocked to enrollment offices. In the euphoria of gaining control over their daily lives and escaping the repressive measures of the Lebanese authorities, the young Resistance men achieved the status of local heroes. Young women also were drawn out of their homes by this revolutionary atmosphere. Their presence was evident in the now frequent demonstrations, martyrs' funerals, and national celebrations that took on ritual qualities, expressive of a militantly assertive national identity and sentiment. Whenever there are demonstrations or funerals of "martyrs," Um Khalid, a thirty-three-year-old teacher in the PLO literacy program and mother of eight, goes around her neighborhood knocking on doors or calling through the windows to her many friends to join in. She was usually quite successful, appearing at these events with a substantial crowd of housewives accompanying her.

A variety of symbols and rituals, old and new, and a synthesis of both gave impulse to mobilization. What symbols and rituals instilled and evoked a sense of national obligation and compelled action? Were there symbols or rituals that appealed specifically to women? The martyr (*al-*

shahid) is an example of a cultural concept imbued with synthetic elements and meaning. Honored for sacrifice, the martyr is remembered in a number of ways. In Palestine, a death in the village or neighborhood was announced from the minaret of the local mosque. If the news needed to be passed to another village or, after 1948, to another camp, messengers would be dispatched to the elders to convey the news. Modern technology has transformed the presentation and communication of death, particularly for martyrs. Mass-produced black-and-white posters with the martyr's picture are plastered on walls around the camps and in Beirut. But they do more than announce death. They inform the viewer that the martyr died for the sake of all Palestinians. Produced by the political organization to which the martyr belonged, the posters end with the statement: "We pledge to the souls of our martyrs that we will continue on the road to liberation." The posters evoke sentiments of affinity among Palestinians. Death in battle for the sake of national community thus carries meaning for everyone, not just the martyr's family. The posters, with their pronouncement of death, and the confluence of martyrdom, sacrifice, and honor inspire feelings of community and militancy and a desire to do patriotic acts.

Contemporary Palestinian rituals of death in martyrdom take their cue from Islam. Mingling the secular and the religious, an *ayah* (verse from the Quran) that claims immortality for the martyr is imprinted on the posters: "You must not think that those who were slain in the cause of Allah are dead. They are alive and well provided for by their Lord" (3:169). Inscribed on the gravestones of those who have died in jihad, they have been incorporated into the mourning rituals for those who died for the national cause. There is a widespread popular belief that the martyr for Palestine ascends to heaven, just as the martyr for Islam is assured of ascending to heaven.

In Islam, the dead are washed and wrapped in a white linen shroud. Martyrs for Islam, however, are neither washed nor wrapped. They are buried as they died; the state of purity effected by washing is achieved by death in martyrdom. The *fida'i* is buried in a similar manner—"he is washed in his own blood."

Martyrs' funerals bring together large segments of the camp community and affirm communal solidarity in the face of wrenching adversity. Attendance gives expression to the bonds that unite people in the camps —shared suffering and loss, vulnerability to death, yet defiance of it as well. These funerals dramatize sentiments at once decidedly celebratory and thus defiant in the face of death and of collective loss. The paradelike procession winds its way through the narrow alleys of the camp and then down the wide city boulevards to the cemetery carrying large poster placards of the martyrs. Women ululate at Palestinian weddings as a sign of joy for the bride and her new status. This celebratory spirit is also evident in the funeral of the martyr, a manifestation of the glory that martyrdom brings. Women's mournful wailing, expressive of community loss and vulnerability, is now accompanied by the defiant salvos of gunfire by guerrillas in full uniform and battle gear. Traditionally the firing of weapons at funerals signified respect for the dead and imparted a sense of honor to the deceased. The firing of the Kalasnikov attests to the honor of the martyr. Celebrating martyrdom for the cause imparts to it a sense of significance that has meaning for all members of the community, not just the grieving family. The glory of sacrifice is displayed in dramatic form. Community expressions of grief engender a sense of sharing in a deeply emotional experience. Eulogies by prominent leaders lend stature to the martyr and formalize the political content of martyrdom. Their presence is also an assurance that his death was not unnoticed and that his family will be taken care of.

The most pronounced symbol in Palestinian cultural life, both of militancy and for mobilization, is the gun. Ubiquitous in everyday life and a pervasive motif in popular forms of culture—poetry, visual arts, plays, dance, and songs—it more than anything else gave symbolic, and yet deathly real, form to the ethos of militancy.

Women find meaning in the same symbols as men, because they do not constitute a separate culture with distinct systems of meaning. Their values and ideals are certainly not at variance with those of the wider society. The same symbols that promote a powerful politicizing and mobilizing effect on men do so for women. Yet there are some symbols that are more meaningful to women. A recurring theme in paintings and posters is a woman in traditional embroidered Palestinian dress clutching both rifle and child. For both men and women the image of a fighting mother poignantly underscores the severity of the Palestinian plight, the pervasiveness of national struggle in daily life, and the involvement of all sectors of the population. For women it equates child raising with militancy—both giving life and losing it. Yet these images hold potent meaning for men as well. On the one hand, it shames them that women must carry the gun and thus gives them greater motivation to fight. On the other hand, it exemplifies the heroic, sacrificial dimensions of motherhood.

Mobilization is a complex process that ranges from recruiting women to join the Resistance, to inducting them into the work force, to organizing ordinary camp women to become involved in community affairs, to general mobilization for military training mandated by the Resistance leadership. Several features characterize the mobilization process of women.

107

It was structurally diffuse, crisis-oriented, and weak in theoretical perspective and practical strategy and was closely related to a woman's stage in the life cycle. Though women perceive themselves as joining out of nationalist sentiment, many also indicated that in doing so they felt they were making a step toward women's emancipation. The mobilization process gradually eased women into resistance organizations without overtly confronting cultural norms of female propriety. Last, it was carried out through a multiplicity of channels, some founded upon women's traditional activities, like visiting, while others were based in the new public space available to them, such as vocational training programs, literacy courses, and the workplace. Still others joined of their own initiative, pressed by the prevailing atmosphere of national struggle as the means of ensuring a future for their communities.

Women are always in a state of potential mobilization or are already mobilized, and then it becomes their duty to mobilize others. The diffuseness of the process was evident from the varied methods and locales where women were targeted—the workplace, home visits, universities, and vocational training and literacy programs. It would be difficult if not futile to try to identify a centralized plan for mobilizing women. Each political organization pursued its own strategies, which precluded higher levels of coordination. Indeed, organizations often vied with each other to recruit women (and men). If the process was diffuse, so were the aims. While the ultimate goal was to form cadres, some segments of the camp population, housewives in particular, were encouraged to take part from their homes and neighborhoods.

Two periods can be distinguished within the revolutionary era (1969–1982) to characterize the mobilization of women as cadres, members, friends, and employees: the pre–civil war period, 1968–69 to 1975–76, and the 1977–1982 period. In the first period, the preliminary foundations were being laid for women's politicization and mobilization into political organizations and the nascent, Resistance-initiated public sector. Yet women's political activities during this period have been described by militants themselves as spontaneous, unorganized, and informal. During emergencies in the camps, such as attacks by the Lebanese army or Israeli air attacks, women rushed to organize relief and social services. Some did join the Resistance during such moments; many, though, returned home once the military threat subsided.

After the 1975–76 civil war, there was a noticeable shift in mobilization policies. Some women leaders suggested there was a collapse of revolutionary ideals; rather than developing according to a consistent and coherent ideological plan, the Resistance was reacting to events around it. Gradually it was coming to resemble a bureaucratic movement. The social infrastructure that arose during and immediately after the civil war was necessitated by the pressing social needs of people in the camps, many of whom were now homeless, unemployed, widows, and orphans. The burgeoning new institutions demanded the recruitment of employees. Some cadres contend that the idea of building a revolutionary movement was giving way in the face of an overwhelming struggle for simple survival and the social burdens imposed by war and dislocation. The incessant attacks by Syria, the Lebanese army and right-wing militias, and Israel had put the Resistance on the defensive. To sustain the camp population, it was imperative to recruit employees to manage the social institutions that provided medical, welfare, and educational services. Other cadres allege that mobilization policies became more stringent, better-organized, and coherent with the spontaneity of the early years giving way to well-planned strategies. Actually, both kinds of processes were occurring at the same time. It is a question of levels of organization and types of affiliation to the movement. The enthusiasm of the early years when Palestinians were recruited with the intention of making everyone a member was transformed into different modes of affiliation. Some people became cadres; others became employees.

Mobilizers adopted a step-by-step approach to reach the mass of camp women. Joining the Resistance took different forms for women and men. Men more readily join voluntarily, whereas women are recruited in a process spread out over time, because of the need to overcome social barriers that obstruct extradomestic activities. Salaried work outside the home is often considered a necessary first step toward emancipation and politicization.

Middle class and mobilized as a university student, Huda was living in Shatila with her husband, a guerrilla. An activist and mobilizer in the camp, she explained that mobilization is not first and foremost a process of inducing women to join organizations:

> I try to mobilize women to work first. Mobilization is not just political mobilization. It is to get women to participate in society. It is to get rid of social obstacles through being involved in production. In this way women build up their self-confidence. Then I try to tie in work with politics.

Huda's approach, that women initially work in order to achieve some initial independence and self-confidence prior to formally joining the revolution, reflects the policies of some mobilizers and their organizations, in particular the Popular Front for the Liberation of Palestine (PFLP).

Women's participation remained limited as a result of forms of social control and values, structurally and ideologically based in the family, the community, religion, and law. This matrix of forms of social control and corresponding legitimizing ideologies that assigned women a subordinate position and status informed their perception of their abilities and the parameters of their social activities. This translated into a lack of self-confidence in political matters and a perception of their role as supporters of kinsmen's activity. At meetings in the camps where men and women were together, women rarely spoke. In women-only meetings, however, there were lively, spirited discussions. The step-by-step approach was intended to gradually overcome these inhibitions and bolster self-confidence in preparation for integrated nationalist activity.

The step-by-step approach was also intended to circumvent overt offense to conservative sectors of society and to avoid the appearance of promoting overly rapid, culturally inappropriate social change. Even more to the point, however, the Resistance hardly had an alternative. Masses of women were certainly not going to rush to leave their homes for the unknown and dangerous world of politics. Mobilizing women became an endeavor of social engineering. Some of the first projects established by the Women's Union and the political organizations addressed women's needs, both financial, to give them a way to earn an income (sewing workshops, typing courses, piecemeal embroidery, etc.), and social, such as literacy courses to prepare them to be active members of society. In planning such services, the goal was to provide women with the means to financially contribute to the household and thus raise their status within the family and, in the process, acquire more authority in household decision making. Economic independence was considered the cornerstone of women's future liberation. Just as significantly, the growing number of widows obliged the Resistance to provide women with the means to support themselves and their children. For example, SAMED, the PLO's industrial sector, initially established workshops and small factories to provide widows of martyrs with salaried employment.

By the end of the 1970s, the mobilization of women was beginning to focus on women as a social category.[2] In effect, the assignment of priority to military and narrowly defined political affairs had limited the extent to which women were able to participate. A dilemma surfaced—how can women effectively participate in the process of national liberation if they continued to be subjected to domination in the same community they sought to liberate?

Huda's approach to mobilizing women combined a focus on the national struggle with problems specific to women. Before I set out with Huda on her round of visits, she explained how she proceeds in imbuing the personal problems of women with a political content:

Through visiting I build a relationship with each woman. Every visit has an aim, which is determined beforehand. My talk during the visit is organized and calculated. I start with social talk, for example, about inflation, about the problems they face daily, and I try to pose alternatives. Then I try to approach the question of women, and of course they have a lot of stories and problems to relate. I use these topics as keys to ask them for alternatives. Then I move to try to talk to them about their own personal problems. The point is to raise their political awareness using their own problems and examples of the problems of others. I attempt to relate their specific problems to the economic situation, for example, divorce and *mahr* [bride-price]. Then I try to discuss politics with them. I start with their economic and social problems and try to link these with political problems, i.e., being expelled from Palestine and living in exile, and link this with joining the Revolution as a solution.

Mobilization is not a one-way process. The phrase *mobilizing women* indicates a multidimensional process where women are not just passive recipients of mobilization campaigns; they also mobilize women. In short, they are enmeshed in a constantly shifting network of women mobilizing women.

Channels of Mobilization

Women are mobilized through multiple channels: in the universities, by self-initiative, mass work and/or mass mobilization campaigns that utilized women's visiting and kin networks, the kinship system, and local institutions such as the workplace. Women were affiliated to the Resistance as full-time members, ordinary members, employees, and friends. Members of an organization are either full-time or ordinary members; the former work in the Resistance to the exclusion of any other employment. The full-time member is a cadre unlike the ordinary or regular member, who receives no salary from the organization and is only obligated to pay dues and attend meetings. Employees are salaried workers in Resistance offices and institutions who may or may not be members. "Friends" is a category of affiliation implying support for an organization and agreement with its political ideology.

Categories of mobilization are not always definite, bounded entities; rather, they are marked by considerable overlap. For example, a member who had decided to join on her own self-initiative may have made this known to other students whose duties as members of an organization included mobilizing other students (a form of mass work). Nevertheless, for the sake of clarity I will attempt to sort out these categories, keeping in mind their nonexclusivity.

Self-Mobilization

Women were often driven by an overwhelming sentiment of national duty and the desire to take an active stance in shaping the present and future of their communities to initiate contacts with *al-mas'ulin* (political and military responsibles) with the intention of joining a political organization,[3] particularly in the early period (1969–1974). Naturally all forms of mobilization involve some initiative on the part of the one being mobilized. By self-mobilization in this particular context I refer to those women who initiated contact with the Resistance on their own, who were not targets of a mobilization campaign. The nationalist and militant spirit that pervaded Palestinian society accounts for much self-mobilization in general. A strong sense of the interconnectedness of the immediacies of one's own life with the Palestinian dilemma in general underpinned with particular acuity self-mobilizing actions. The early era of the Resistance inspired fervor and pride among the exile community, and thousands of young people were ready to commit themselves to its ranks.[4] Self-mobilizers were, for the most part, urban, lower and middle class, and university-educated, and they tended to remain active after marriage. They almost always had some contacts with the Resistance prior to joining. They might be friends of activists or students of nationalist teachers who had encouraged all students to take part in the revolution. One of the few Palestinian social institutions that existed prior to the rise to prominence of the Resistance movement was the General Union of Palestinian Students (GUPS). In 1968 Layla (see chapter 3) was active as a high school student in the GUPS, and she subsequently decided to join the Resistance. The initiative was largely her own. No one actually mobilized her, but once she indicated her eagerness to participate, two GUPS members arranged for her to join an organization.

University Students

Zaynah joined the Resistance in 1973, when she was a university student. She met and fast became friends with another Palestinian student who, unbeknownst to Zaynah, belonged to a political organization. Whenever there were demonstrations they would attend together, Zaynah's friend encouraging her to act on her professed desire to liberate Palestine. When

Zaynah seriously voiced her intention to join the Resistance, her friend confided that she was a member of an organization and would like to introduce Zaynah to the responsibles. Zaynah attributes this longing to be active to the atmosphere in the universities at the time. In the early 1970s, the student movement erupted, both on the right and left, around widely disparate political ideologies.[5] Lebanese workers and students were striking, outrage against the army for failing to protect the south from Israeli incursions was growing, massive numbers of migrants were forming a poverty belt on the outskirts of Beirut, and inflation was rising. Eventually civil war erupted in 1975.

Rihab, a university student at the time, exclaimed, "I was ready to beg people to mobilize me, but no one approached me!" Meanwhile her political consciousness was unfolding as a consequence of involvement in demonstrations and strikes at the university. In a critical vein she offered this comment: "I was very affected by this wave of patriotism and shared the enthusiasm of the students about the Resistance, but I was still very naive politically." After Rihab had spent a year or so wanting to be part of the national movement, a student activist broached the topic with her and found a ready and willing candidate for recruitment. At this point Rihab felt she had matured intellectually from reading political literature and taking part in strikes and demonstrations. Naturally, once she was mobilized her political training was conducted on a more serious level, with a reading and discussion schedule with other recruits and responsibles.

As the cases of Zaynah and Rihab amply demonstrate, the distinction between university students who are self-mobilized and those who are mobilized as students, via their contacts and activities at school, is a fine one. Though they may take the initiative and seek membership in an organization, they must first make contacts with its members on campus whose duty it is to mobilize students.

Interestingly, both self-mobilizers and university students tend to become full-time members and most married full-time militants. By 1973–74, those women still most politically active were urban middle class women mobilized as students or on their own. Only a small number of camp women had gone beyond a supporting role during emergencies to formally enroll in the Resistance.

Self-Critique

In a spirit of self-criticism, women militants began to question an approach that turned to camp women during military emergencies without trying to sustain and develop their revolutionary potential, neglecting to follow them up for sustained mobilization. There was a recognition that camp women could be more successfully mobilized by women from the camps, with whom they were more closely bound by ties of class, neighborhood, and kinship, than by urban women, who as outsiders had little knowledge of camp women's daily lives. This shift in choice of mobilizers also reflected the leadership's apprehensions about creating a movement characterized as middle class when their base was supposed to be the masses, not just for ideological reasons but for strategic and practical ones as well. The camps were the recruiting grounds for fighters as well as a main base of operations and safe ground where the Resistance could exercise authority and control over the exile community.

In the long run, self-initiated mobilization augured ill for women's participation in the national movement. In the absence of a clear-cut policy from above, individual women who joined tended to be urban lower middle- and middle-class, educated women. A mass-based movement that could form the nucleus of a women's organization was hardly on the horizon. Moreover, the embryonic women's movement, embodied in the GUPW, could easily be co-opted, since from inception it was structurally integrated into the PLO and participation was limited. A movement that receives minimal impetus from below faces limitations on its autonomy because of the ability of the larger, formal political structure to intervene in pursuit of national unity and political hegemony by keeping strict tabs on the activities of popular unions and organizations and by appointing their leadership.

Large-scale mobilization can hardly be conducted on an individual basis. It requires a broader structure of organization, personnel, and support. Mobilization policies that come from above have the additional appeal of tending to legitimize women's defiance of the moral consensus. Yet once policies for the mobilization of women became an integral, though loose and uncoordinated, part of the PLO body politic, the PLO leadership had more power as a group and the political structure and means either to facilitate or to block the development of women's issues.

With the advent of the Lebanese civil war (1975–76), the consolidation and strengthening of the Women's Union was under way and within the political organizations the focus of mass mobilization, though still encompassing the spontaneous mobilization of women that crisis demands, shifted to the mobilization and development of cadres. Samirah, a twenty-seven-year-old cadre who worked full time mobilizing camp women, emphasized this shift in approach:

I don't want to gather numerous women around me and not organize them well. This is how we used to work. I prefer to work with a small group of women—say twenty—who with time will become cadres. I want quality, not quantity. I may spend three or four years with this group of girls—it's a kind of investment. I give everything to these girls. After a time, each of these girls can mobilize another twenty girls.

Mass Work

'*Amal jamahiri* (mass work) in the camps and surrounding poor, urban neighborhoods is a task commonly assigned to activist women. The aim is to mobilize the community to support the Resistance, to raise levels of political awareness, and, at the same time, to keep abreast of their needs and provide for them. Motivated by a political ideology based on the cultivation of mass support, it is an expression of the intimate relationship between the people and the revolution. Most important, it fosters genial relations between the Resistance and the masses—to let them know they are part of the national movement and that the latter is responsive to their needs. Maryam, engaged in full-time "mass work" in Shatila camp, explained:

> Mass work is political work—it is social care, health care, and home visits to recognize the problems of poor people and help them. We conduct political education meetings in homes, and we try to deal with women's everyday problems and activities. Mass work also includes mobilizing people into the organizations.

In addition to raising political awareness and forging a link between the camps and the Resistance, mass work is supposed to create supporters and mobilize the community. Yet those women mobilized as a direct consequence of a mobilization strategy carried out via mass work alone are not substantial in number. At the time of this study (early 1980s) it was too early to adequately assess the impact of mass work as a means of recruitment to organizations, since it only assumed its more systematic character in the late 1970s and early 1980s. Nonetheless, it warrants discussion for a number of reasons. It is a prominent form of work for women in the Resistance, and it serves as a vital link between the people and the leadership. Though it overlaps with other channels of mobilization, it is, indeed, a primary strategy in this combination. For example, even when women join the organization to which their fathers or brothers belong and perceive themselves as having been mobilized by their own

115

families, mass work played a role. Women members pay visits to encourage the female kin of male members to join, often taking them to their first meeting or political events. One aspect of the task of mass work is to mobilize these women, with or without the support of their kinsmen.

Through trial and error, mobilizers found a number of channels through which to cultivate and activate camp women's support for the Resistance —family, village, and community networks and the workplace—structures and networks that form part of everyday social life.

In the 1970s and 1980s, women's visiting networks were just beginning to cut across class, sect, and camp-urban boundaries. The pre-1948 urban-rural distinction was probably exacerbated in the first two decades of exile as the distinctions between camp and urban Palestinians were sharpened by widely disparate opportunities for education and employment. When more broadly based nationalist politics began to permeate everyday life, camp women (as well as men) came into contact with middle class, urban Palestinians and the latter became marginally, though on occasion intimately, incorporated into the visiting networks of camp women. Contact was fostered through employment in Resistance institutions, membership in organizations, and activist male kin's friendship and work relationships with men from outside the camp and, by extension, their kinswomen.

Visits are paid back and forth between camp women and to a much lesser extent between camp and urban women, though it is usually the latter who visit the former. Urban women have more mobility than camp women, who are unaccustomed to leaving the camps for extended periods of time. Um Khalid carried out extensive visiting both within the camp and just outside it. Within the camps she visited, at distances far from her immediate neighborhood, women she met in the clinic, wives of her husband's comrades, and her students. She also received frequent visits from cadres and employees in the Resistance, middle class and camp women alike.

In addition to those aspects of social life introduced by the national movement such as political lectures and employment, camp women's everyday social activities like visiting and the *subhiyyeh* (midmorning gatherings of women over coffee) became channels of politicization and mobilization. Mobilizers found these gatherings convenient for talking to groups of women about the political situation and encouraging them to take action. In short, domestic space and the new arenas of public space lent themselves as sites of mobilization. As women paid frequent visits to relatives and friends in the immediate vicinity, their visiting networks were available for recruiting supporters, employees, and members.

Crucial for initiating contact with a wide variety of camp women, networks were established in a variety of ways. For those from the camp who are engaged in mass work the process is fairly easy, as they are already part of a network originating from their own kin group, neighborhood, and friends. Well known to camp families, they easily pay informal visits. When Nuhad, who had herself been mobilized by cadres seeking girls to work in an embroidery workshop, wanted to recruit girls to work in the same workshop, she went around her immediate neighborhood in Shatila, dropping in on fellow villagers (pre-1948), kinswomen, and friends to inform them of the project and the availability of work. In this way she was able to generate substantial interest among her neighbors and several girls then were hired.

For the outsider the situation requires precision and delicacy. Recruited to Fateh as a student, Samirah worked in Shatila camp for nearly ten years and is now well established and respected in the camp. Initially she faced difficulties since, as a single, middle-class activist from outside the camp, her comportment was subject to scrutiny and suspicion. Gradually, however, she built a network of potential recruits. She started by concentrating on the sisters of male members. As an *ukht* (sister), she had easy access to these families, and once she established an ongoing visiting relationship, she expanded her network to include friends and neighbors of these families. The constant informal visiting between women provides a continuously expanding network of women as targets for recruitment:

> Because I'm a girl it's easy for me to enter homes in the camp. Building a relationship with families facilitates the mobilization of their girls. I focus on women who have a brother, father, or husband in the Resistance. This is the easiest way until we become stronger. Then we can expand our work. I tell their fathers and brothers that they should encourage these women to come to demonstrations and celebrations. Another way of approaching such women is by weekly visiting. For example, if I find a girl that would make a good cadre I visit often, but I don't discuss politics much until we are better friends. I go for informal visits and discuss everyday things. These women are not difficult to mobilize because of their family connections with the Resistance.

Huda, a member of the PFLP and new to the camp, relied on the advice of other comrades from Shatila for initial introductions to households and tips about whom to visit. By selecting a household in each neighborhood and establishing and sustaining a visiting relationship that would then draw in women from its visiting network of family, friends, and neighbors, she extended her own network broadly across the camp.

Initial visits can be stiff and formal. The women are only superficially acquainted, and each is well aware of the other's aims: the mobilizer to try to encourage the woman to become active, the woman visited to gauge the situation carefully, especially from the perspective of her family. Women usually show polite interest but are aware that such a decision is not theirs alone to make. Family consensus must first be ascertained.

During visits women are urged to attend upcoming events in the camps such as demonstrations, national celebrations, lectures, films, and funerals of martyrs and learn about Resistance-initiated social services. Women are also asked about any educational, health, or financial problems. Not accustomed to discussing such intimate family matters with outsiders, some find these visits tedious and embarrassing. Others, particularly widows, welcome the opportunity to share their troubles and learn about possible assistance and social services. For younger women, eager to participate in salaried work and the national movement, these visits can pave the way for them to enter public life. If a father or husband is present during a mobilizer's visit, his opposition can be gauged by all present.

Life events such as births, marriages, and deaths are also occasions for visits. Assigned to a particular geographical region of the camps and to the families of members, mass workers pay visits on such occasions, usually accompanying a friend or relative of the family concerned. In this way, they form another relationship to incorporate into their visiting network.

Women's visiting networks have become infused with national political overtones. Mobilizers' visits differ markedly from the traditional visiting patterns, which served to reassert and reinforce social relations, develop new ones, and maintain community harmony. In the past, most visiting was between women neighbors, relatives, and villagers, requiring little mobility beyond the quarter or village. Visiting by mobilizers has quite different aims and crosscuts neighborhood and kinship boundaries. Mobilization visiting is to create and solidify new social relations based on political affiliation to a national body in which women are now being asked to assume a role. Yet similar to the visiting that characterized women's social relations before the period of the Resistance, the end result of the new-style visiting remains similar to that of the past: to maintain and cultivate social relations and enhance community harmony.

The Resistance initially faced difficulties in developing a corps of women cadres from the camps. Even after the civil war and the appearance of more women cadres from the camps, there remained a preponderance of mobilizers from outside the camps. Middle class, educated women, commited to full-time activism, they lived either in the camps or close to them. Initially, their work was difficult and tedious; as outsiders it was incumbent upon them to build a visiting network and acquire community trust in the absence of a kin, regional, or neighborhood foundation. As single women, they had to be careful to avoid gossip. Casual, friendly relations with men and immodest clothing would have aroused doubts about their reputations and thus fitness to visit freely with women. Unable to succeed in sustaining an intimate and trusting relationship with camp families, many drop out of this work, underscoring the need to train camp women cadres.

Kin Ties

Mobilizers often say that the easiest girls to mobilize are those who have active male family members and those who are employed in Resistance offices or institutions. When male family members are politically active, opposition to female political participation tends to be less than in non-affiliated families. The parents are acquainted with Resistance members and feel their daughters have a protected status in the Resistance. Furthermore, they tend to be more politicized and supportive of the Resistance. In addition, girls from these families are already somewhat politicized or at least familiar with political issues. In other words, they are "riper" material for recruitment.

Living in a family where brothers (or sisters) are active may draw women into the Resistance. They are constantly exposed to the political discussions and activities of their brothers and their friends. This exposure, a form of political socialization, can inspire girls to joing the Resistance. Brothers occasionally encourage their sisters to join their political organization, dissuading them from opting for membership in a rival group. Brothers often urge their sisters to help in times of crisis in the bakery or clinic and attend demonstrations and funerals, activities that parents are less reluctant to oppose if a brother is involved or gives his approval.

Kin ties can be endowed with more direct significance. When Rima, a seventeen-year-old student, wanted to attend meetings, her father opposed it on the grounds that politics are not a girl's concern. Her elder, activist brother mediated with their father, convincing him that her attendance would not be harmful and emphasizing his own support for her actions. Eventually her father conceded and she became a member. The elder brother can be a singularly significant influence on whether or not a girl becomes active, and his influence illustrates the nonexclusivity of categories of mobilization. Even seemingly self-mobilized women like Rima required the mediation of a kinsman before joining. Fathers in their

119

old age begin to turn over some of the family responsibility and decision making to sons. As guardians of their sisters' honor they possess veto power over their actions as well as the influence to persuade fathers.

The PFLP clearly recognized the power of the brother's position in the family. In 1981, when more concerted mobilization campaigns were undertaken, its male members were advised, in the form of an internal memo, to pursue more vigorously the recruitment of their sisters. If their sisters did not join, it could be a mark against their political standing in the organization. The implications were clear: male members could rise in rank more rapidly if their female kin were mobilized.

Social Institutions

Women employed in Resistance institutions such as SAMED (the PLO industrial sector), the Red Crescent, PLO offices and departments, and the smaller, private Palestinian social agencies that are closely linked with various political groups are subject to politicization and mobilization campaigns. Mobilizers consider these women some of the easiest to mobilize; relatively minimal family opposition is evident. In working, such women have already achieved a modicum of emancipation and mobility. As a result of their daily interaction with Resistance matters and members, they tend to be more politically aware than unemployed women. Thus the transition to organizational membership is easier.

The workday is often accompanied by political lectures, and supervisors make home visits. Essentially to get acquainted with a woman's family in order to better understand any constraints on her participation, visits also reassure the family, letting them know with whom their daughters or wives are working. Thus these visits can gain parental approval for employment and activism, as they are interpreted as a recognition of and an act of respect for traditional familial authority. By incorporating such displays of respect into mobilization strategies, opposition is somewhat deflected. The visits hold a special meaning for the families concerned; they indicate a genuine concern for the social position and moral values of the employee's family. They are also instrumental in establishing kinlike relations between the employee and the workplace.

Employment in Resistance institutions is an avenue for establishing a support or friendship relation with an organization or, to a lesser extent, for entrance into formal political organizations. The step from employment to affiliation or membership is fairly easy and is widely encouraged by the responsibles in the workplace. In a national movement that is constructing broad-based social institutions, as well as engaged in mass mobilization strategies, a blurring of boundaries occurs between sectors and types of affiliation. In a sense, membership becomes an extension of work. Operating under the aegis of the Resistance movement, these social institutions are categorized as nationalist endeavors. Resistance-affiliated employment makes one part of the revolution; thus it is perceived as a contribution to the national cause and is considered a primary form of struggle for women. But employment can become an end in itself. After the civil war and the consolidation and expansion of these institutions, they needed far more personnel and Palestinians needed jobs. With the collapse of the Lebanese industrial sector and the closure of the port, substantial numbers of working class Palestinians were unemployed. Palestinians faced two choices: join the stream of migrant workers in the oil-producing Gulf states and Saudi Arabia or Germany or find employment in Lebanon. The higher incomes mandated by Lebanon's rampant inflation and the rapidly rising cost of living engendered by the oil boom of the 1970s meant that for many women Resistance employment became a necessity. Although such employment is still considered a nationalistic action, some women decline to become officially affiliated to any organization and considered their work as "simply a job." Such an attitude was not peculiar to women. The disillusionment engendered by some Resistance actions in Lebanon and a failure to achieve quick political results, along with a certain level of open corruption, resulted in complacency about working for the Resistance. It was one of the largest employers in the country, and, as such, not all employees were committed to the Resistance. It was a source of livelihood, a way to make a living, and thus in some cases "simply a job."

Camp women involved in Resistance-sponsored vocational training projects and social programs are another target both for politicization and recruitment. Women activists visit vocational training programs and workshops during work hours for lectures and discussions, providing an arena for political activity removed from the constraints of the home, where parental opposition to a girl's attendance at meetings and lectures is sometimes a source of conflict. An all-female setting, devoid of a gendered power component, is more conducive to animated discussion. The opportunity to talk politics in a female-only setting builds self-confidence. One need only compare these situations to mixed meetings, where women seldom speak.

Demonstrations and funerals of martyrs are occasions for the girls in a class or workshop to attend as a group with the teacher or supervisor leading them, usually an older married woman. Um Khalid used to take her literacy class to funerals of martyrs and national events such as Day of the Land.[6] Parental opposition was assuaged by the chaperoned and thus protected nature of attendance.

In 1982, the PLO launched a literacy campaign in all the camps. In the previous decade, various political organizations had held their own smaller literacy classes geared predominantly to women, who formed the bulk of the illiterate population. The 1982 program was designed to unify all such programs under one centrally coordinated campaign. I often attended class in Shatila with Um Khalid, who taught in one of the initial pilot programs.

Coterminous with the intention to create a literate society through instruction in basic reading, writing, and mathematical skills, the literacy program aimed to politicize women via education in Palestinian history and nationalist politics and as the backdrop to a militant and coherent national consciousness, the eventual goal being to involve large segments of the female population in community development and Resistance activities. The thematic content of the literacy textbook chapters addressed predominantly national issues, for instance, "The Balfour Declaration," the "Popular War of 1936," "Jerusalem, Capital of Palestine," and the "Women's Union." The vocabulary, both in the textbook and in oral discussions and exercises, focused on national and military issues — "weapons," "ambush," "struggle," "organizations," "mobilization," "bullets," "committees," "revolution," "martyrs," etc. The inclusion of material on Palestine and the early history of the national movement imparts a sense of history. As for the direct mobilization efforts of the literacy classes, whenever there were demonstrations, funerals, lectures, or films, the students attended as a group with their teacher. Um Khalid was careful to try to avoid friction with the younger girls' parents. Before taking them to activities outside the classroom, she sent home the younger, unmarried ones to seek permission, telling them, "Go ask your mothers if you have finished all your housework and can attend this event — tell them you're going with me." Several times a week after class she would visit her students' families to inquire after sick family members or ask about a wounded relative or visit the mother of a newly martyred son. This lessened family suspicions as to whom their daughters or wives were seeing every day, and as Um Khalid was the mother of eight children and wife of a prominent responsible in the camp, her visits lent an aura of safety and legitimacy to these activities. Um Khalid's extension of her job as a teacher into the home and the political arena points once again to the obscuring of boundaries between work, political activities, and the home.

A common feature in women's lives was the *nadwat* (seminars) held every two weeks or so in the camps by the Resistance. The *nadwat* cover a wide range of topics—from child and maternal health care to the current political situation. Held in the homes of ordinary women, they are led by cadres. Each week they are in a different neighborhood of the camp, so as to draw in the kin and neighborhood network of the women in whose home they are meeting. When women are asked to attend by the cadres they are encouraged to bring a friend or two. Attendance ranges between forty and fifty women from fifteen to seventy years of age. Groups of girls from the workshops and vocational training centers also attend the *nadwat*. In a *nadwat* I attended, Um Khalid led her class from the literacy course. While walking through the alleys and streets of the camp she drew an expanding crowd as she stopped at the doorways of friends along the way, calling them to join.

These are informal affairs. Women sat with their children on the floor of a large, shaded courtyard drinking tea and eating nuts. Huda, who did mass work in Shatila, presented a short lecture on the current political situation and then opened the floor for discussion. Since it is predominantly women present, they are less inhibited from asking questions and freely enter into animated discussion. The cadres are able to advance women's politicization in a relaxed, informal domestic setting and inquire about their problems and concerns, as well as identify girls for recruitment. Community sentiment on current political realities can also be gauged.

In this informal domestic setting women feel confident to air grievances. They take the opportunity to tell the cadres their problems and concerns, especially their views on the policies of the Resistance in the everyday affairs of camp life. Women complain about the shortage of shelters, the lack of water and electricity, and the need for pest control and demand increased municipal services. They question the cadres about the current political and military situation—"Is attack imminent?" "How should we prepare for it?" Some question the policies of the leadership. One elderly woman asked, "Why do we have so many political factions when we need political unity? We are all Palestinians; we are all suffering the same conditions living in these zinc-roofed huts!" The most lively exchanges were those initiated by middle-aged and elderly women. Still lacking a strong sense of self-confidence in public, even in all-female settings, younger women and teenagers are more reticent. At the *nadwat* I attended, the most vocal women were Um Khalid and her star pupil, a widow with two young children who was determined "to overcome my ignorance and better understand the conditions of my people."

In sum, women are mobilized in a process that also attempts to integrate them into national public life through a multiplicity of overlapping channels and categories; some of these channels, such as visiting networks and the *nadwat,* are integral parts of everyday life, yet their form and purpose have been infused with political content and meaning. Other channels arise from new arenas of activity opened to women by the Resistance such as literacy courses, employment, and national events.

Mobilization and Crisis

During my period of fieldwork, September 1980 to May 1982, there were no crises comparable to the 1975–76 civil war or the 1978 Israeli invasion of South Lebanon or that of the summer of 1982, all of which I experienced but during which I did not carry out sustained research. While I was doing research, crises that sparked a state of emergency or alert among Resistance forces were sporadic and short in duration—the Israeli attacks on Rashidiyyah camp in the summer of 1981, the spate of car bombings and the Israeli air raids in Beirut in July 1981, and a series of PLO-Lebanese clashes throughout this two-year period. It was the civil war and its aftermath that loomed so large when I did my fieldwork. It has caused untold numbers of deaths and left in its wake a multitude of displaced people.

Given the pervasiveness of crisis in everyday life, it fast became a salient channel of mobilization. In Damur, a community in severe crisis, substantial numbers of women were developing a relationship with the Resistance. Crises can rapidly mobilize large numbers of women to participate in the civil defense of their communities. Subsequently some become formally affiliated while others become friends and supporters. The two cases presented below illustrate how crisis mobilized one woman as a full-time member and another as a friend.

When I first met Randa, she and her five-year-old daughter were living in the remains of a bombed-out school in Damur. Several other families from Tal al-Za'ter had settled there, each setting up housekeeping in what was once a classroom. Despite the absence of electricity, windows, and running water, her sparsely furnished room was impeccably tidy. Water was hauled from a common tap outside the school building in large, colorful plastic containers. A common bathroom was shared among the inhabitants of the school, which included Randa's widowed sister and her two children.

Randa joined the Resistance when she was twenty-five years old, by then a widow and mother of two children. She had lived most of her life in Tal al-Za'ter camp in East Beirut, which fell to the Phalangists in August 1976 after nine months of siege and heavy bombardment. Her husband, along with hundreds of other men between the ages of fourteen and sixty, was lined up against a wall and shot the day the Phalangists entered the camp. The remaining residents fled to West Beirut. She had never been active or had an interest in politics, nor had she worked outside the home after marriage. A strained financial situation led her to broach the subject of employment, but her husband forbade it. Unlike many women in Tal al-Za'ter, Randa did not participate in defending the camp during the siege. Seven months pregnant just before the fall of the camp, she went into premature labor and delivered a stillborn child in the underground shelters. Her eldest child, six-year-old Muhammad, contacted polio during the siege and now lives in a special children's home in Europe paid for by the PLO.

When Randa and her widowed sister, Jamal, and the latter's two children left Tal al-Za'ter, they initially lived with their parents in Rashidiyyah camp in South Lebanon. Accustomed to living on their own, they were unable to tolerate reverting to a daily existence controlled by their parents and Randa's in-laws. The two sisters stayed with the family only a few weeks and then moved to Damur, a small coastal town about ten kilometers from Beirut, whose Christian Lebanese inhabitants had fled or been expelled during the 1976 civil war. The PLO opened Damur as a refuge for the thousands of Tal al-Za'ter widows and their children, repairing (minimally) war-damaged houses, setting up schools, kindergartens, and clinics, and opening small factories to provide employment and vocational training.

When Randa first arrived in Damur she lived on a widow's monthly indemnity of 250 L.L. (then about $60.00) from the PLO's Office of Social Affairs. In need of more money, she began to work in the social affairs section of a political organization. Her first task was to visit families to determine who needed food, blankets, stoves, and medical care. At the same time she started to embroider for the organization's workshop and was subsequently elected to be the responsible. She says she wanted to work for two reasons: "I needed the money and wanted to do something, to get out of the house and be productive. Our society almost imposes political activity on us. If I live here I must be involved— there is no escaping it." While she was in the workshop, the responsibles of the organization would drop in, asking her to read their newspapers and magazines, pressing her to join as a full-time member, which she eventually did. Though her in-laws strenuously opposed her new political activities and employment—"What do women know about politics?"— she ignored their entreaties and persisted. Living far from them, financially independent, and in custody of her children, she was able to ignore their opposition and that of her own parents.

After the fall of Tal al-Zaʿter, Haifa (see chapter 3) settled in Damur with her widowed mother and two sisters. Now politically inactive, she had initially joined an organization during the 1973 fighting between the Lebanese army and the Resistance that centered on the refugee camps. Sitting in her small two-room house bordering the fields in Damur she related what transpired in May 1973:

> I was at home trying to paint the house. There was a lot of shelling that day, and a shortage of nurses in the clinics was becoming apparent. A *rafiq* [comrade] came to ask my younger sister to help out in the infirmary because they were expecting more heavy shelling during the night. So I went along with my sister and the comrade. I told myself, *I can do something to help*. Well, I spent fifteen days in the infirmary. I wasn't in the organization, but since I had now acquired a little knowledge of nursing I started to work in the infirmary off and on, as I still had to work full-time in the factory. A few weeks later the responsible asked me if I would like to join the organization and I agreed.

After the fighting subsided Haifa remained a member of the organization but in a support capacity, since she still had to work full-time in the factory. She explained:

> I worked with the Resistance but not on a full-time basis—I took no salary. Whenever anything happened in the camp I didn't go to work, but stayed to help. There were many girls like this—some of us would go to the infirmary, others would bake bread, and others would prepare food and take it to the fighters during the battles. Now, here in Damur, though I'm not working in an organization, whenever there is an air raid I go to the infirmary or to where the bombs have fallen to see if there are any wounded and to prepare to evacuate them. During the siege of Tal al-Zaʿter, the factory was closed, of course—everything was closed—so all of us girls, whether "organized" or not, used to go to the infirmary to help the wounded. Those girls who had been through military training fought alongside the men. Generally speaking, the rest of us helped with nursing and preparing food. I used to work days in the infirmary—giving injections, changing bandages, etc. During the night I took food to the fighters. When there were wounded people we girls would rush from the clinic under shelling to carry them to the clinics.

Haifa is not currently a member of an organization, yet she is quickly mobilized in the event of a crisis. She spends her days in agricultural labor in the nearby fields, selling vegetables and fruits on the streets or to traders to resell in Beirut; the rest she keeps for the household. Her sister remains a full-time activist, and between the two of them they manage to support their aged mother and younger sister.

Randa and Haifa's stories illustrate how crisis affects women's mobilization potential and how it draws them into political organizations for a variety of motives and reasons—the desire to be an active and contributing member of the community, to help defend their communities against attack, and to attain financial security. Haifa most accurately depicts the cyclical response of women to crisis. Unlike Randa, her mobilization was not sustained and transformed into full-time militancy.

Haifa and Randa represent two distinct responses to the same sort of crises. Both were from Tal al-Za'ter and had survived the 1976 siege and expulsion to provisionally settle in Damur. Yet Randa, who had never been involved in politics, became a full-time member of an organization, while Haifa, who had responded to crises in the past, was now inactive and had never become a full-time militant. Aside from individual differences in character, their experiences of the fall of the camp and the family structure that remained in each case shed light on why one was permanently mobilized and the other was not.

Now a widow and the sole support of her daughter, Randa had also taken on responsibility for her unemployed, widowed, and illiterate sister. Vividly aware that she had to support herself and a number of dependents, she quickly found work, which eventually led to her mobilization through the persistence of several women cadres who encouraged her to join. The material and emotional security of being politically affiliated in a situation where the larger Resistance movement controls nearly all resources for employment and social services in the community cannot be underestimated. Randa was alone, with no men to support and protect her, and the Resistance provided a sense of belonging and identity, a source of protection, and facilitated access to scarce resources.

Haifa, on the other hand, was still living with her family (mother and sisters) and she had a brother who occasionally stayed with them. The family had not broken down to the same extent as Randa's, whose relations with both her own family and that of her dead husband were strained. Nor was Haifa's financial situation as dire as Randa's. She was accustomed to working and supporting herself and contributing to the household budget. Her previous political involvement and her sister's membership gave her family an edge in obtaining much needed social services.

Randa was mobilized as well as politicized by extreme crisis—she witnessed her husband's execution and experienced the birth of a stillborn. Uprooted and traumatized by the siege of the camp and the expulsion and massacre of its inhabitants, she faced a domestic life essentially in ruins. In sum, she was completely alone to fend for herself and her daughter. Randa was faced with few options. Clearly her political consciousness unfolded and matured after her move to Damur, reflected by her willingness to work for her community in the immediate days of chaos following resettlement. Randa commented:

> Our situation imposes on you that you should be politically active. Before this disaster I never thought about politics or joining the Resistance, but now my situation is so different. I now know more clearly who are my enemies. For all these women here in Damur it was the loss of their husbands and sons that pushed them into political activities.

In short, the inability to live according to the cultural norms of domesticity and uphold conventionally sanctioned female behavior figures prominently in prompting entry into the national movement during crisis. The absence of familial authority removed barriers that might otherwise have stood in the way.

Damur was in no uncertain terms a community in crisis. The overwhelming majority of families were, like Randa's, female-headed households. Many of these women were traumatized by the loss of husbands and sons. In the absence of men their economic future was bleak. The Resistance organized community institutions and was the only sure source of economic security providing widows with indemnities and employment. In such a situation, where women had few alternative options, those who worked did so in Resistance enterprises. As discussed above, such employment is often the first step in the process of mobilization.

The protractedness of the Palestinian national struggle and yet its cyclical character—periods of prolonged, extreme tension as in the civil war and periods of relative quiet interspersed by occasional flare-ups as in the years between 1977 and 1982—have contradictory implications for the mobilization of women. Crises draw women into community and political activity in a support capacity. Yet most drop out once the crises have subsided. For some, activism is cut short by onerous domestic duties; others perceive their role in the national struggle as supporters in times of crises. Haifa exemplifies those who would willingly work with the Resistance when their camp was under siege but did not make the transition to full-time militancy.

Although crises and the protractedness of the struggle can have positive consequences for the mobilization of women, they also deflect attention from the stringent planning of mobilization campaigns and from explicitly women's or social issues, emphasizing narrowly defined political and military ones instead. Yet the civil war was to provide the real impetus for the development of Palestinian social institutions. The Red Crescent, for example, rapidly expanded in response to the growing need for medical care during this period. Samed expanded, providing more work opportunities for the numerous widows. Thus some social institutions thrive during crisis, but not necessarily the Women's Union nor the prominence and prestige accorded women's issues.

Much criticism of the GUPW by militants and union members has focused on this issue. Over and over it was the same story: the union is quick to mobilize women during an emergency but fails in follow-up recruitment. Samyah, a Fateh member who had once worked in the union, called their way of working "charity work," as did many critics of both the union and the mobilization policies of the Resistance. In the Palestinian context, "charity work" is a particularly strong appellation that subsumes a series of negative political meanings. It signifies the "old way of working before the Revolution," the "bourgeois way" of dealing with the Palestinian problem as well as that of the international community exemplified in UNRWA policies. It implies a relationship of inequality, an uneven balance of power, and a tactic to deflect attention from the root causes of the Palestine problem.

Another consequence of crisis mobilization is a politically ambiguous status for women. It keeps women in a support capacity category distinct from sustained militancy. Although Haifa called herself a member of an organization, she means that she is affiliated through ties of kinship (her sister and brother are members, and their cousin is a prominent martyr) and allegiance to a particular organization. She serves in a support capacity in times of *istinfar* (alert or emergency) and then returns to her home or salaried job once the emergency diminishes.

While Damur represents an extreme case of crisis, continuous, smaller crises punctuate everyday life. Over the years, the camps in the south faced many such incidents as a result of geographical proximity to the Israeli border. The camps in Beirut also shared the burden of periodic attack, clashes, and sustained war, as in the 1975–76 battle with the Phalangists and the Syrians.

The spring and summer of 1981 were marked by continuous political tension and an escalation of attacks against PLO offices and the camps in the form of anonymous car bombs and Israeli air raids. The 1981 crises brought a new form of terror somewhat different from the usual quick-strike air raids. Car bombs, random and without warning, killed hundreds of people and devastated whole city blocks, terrifying Beirut's residents, who now hesitated to move around in the streets. In neighborhoods populated predominantly by Palestinians and sites of the PLO offices, residents were packing up and dispersing around the city. A general alert *(istinfar)* was proclaimed, and all the fighting forces were readied to engage in battle.

During the air attacks on the camps, activist women visited families in underground shelters, reassuring and explaining the situation to them and assessing their immediate needs in the way of food, water, and medical care. "Ordinary" camp women baked bread and prepared food for the fighters. The union stepped up its first-aid training courses in the camps and those neighborhoods likely to be attacked and organized groups of women to visit the wounded in the hospitals.

Although crisis mobilizes women, for the most part temporarily, it conversely immobilizes many of their ongoing social projects directed at camp women and their political plans. In June 1981, when the al-Fakhani district was bombed by the Israelis, Layla, for instance, who had left the Resistance following the civil war and had been visited several times over the past few years by cadres to convince her to return, willingly went to work at one of the emergency day-care centers and nurseries set up by the Resistance to operate twenty-four hours a day to look after the children of cadres. With schools closed, the older children had nowhere to go while their mothers were working. Yet once the intensity of the emergency had diminished she went back home and refused to rejoin her party, even though this temporary return to activism encouraged her former comrades to again try to convince her to return on a full-time basis.

In June 1981, I was accompanying Huda on her daily round of visits in Shatila camp, part of her task of doing mass work. A series of Israeli air raids began over the city. Most of the offices emptied as cadres spread around the city and the environs of the camps to avoid large congregations in likely targets. With the air raid sirens blaring, Huda, Faten, a responsible in the camp, and I sat in an office listening to the newscasts on the radio and drinking tea. It was a hot, dusty day, and the usually noisy and bustling camp was completely silent except for the sounds of bombs dropped from low flying airplanes, the sirens, and artillery that was all but useless against the planes. Most families had taken refuge in the shelters or left the camp for safer neighborhoods where they had friends or relatives to put them up. The only people visible were the fighters, cadres visiting the shelters, and those still scurrying around searching for safe shelter. The nursery where Huda normally left her three-month-old daughter was closed. It had one of the largest and safest shelters in the camp, but most mothers preferred to keep their children at home during air raids, fearing separation or the family's sudden move outside the camps. Huda was forced to take along her daughter, since the nursery was closed. Such closures during emergencies oblige mothers to stay home with their children rather than participate in defense of the camp. Huda debated whether she should continue with her plans to make visits in her immediate neighborhood. On the one hand, she felt it a burden to have to take the baby along with her and she was well aware that other women would have their children at home, making conversation difficult, but on the other hand, crises were opportune times to engage in political dialogue with women and explain what is happening. In the end, we stayed in the office for the rest of the morning. As the shelling intensified, both of us were too afraid to leave the safety, although largely illusionary, of the office.

By the afternoon the shelling had diminished enough for people to start returning home. I spent the rest of the day with Um Khalid. She had decided to hold class, since the situation has calmed somewhat. But just as we were leaving the house, shelling resumed. Naturally she hesitated to leave. Within minutes neighbors were coming in and out of her house to see if she knew what was happening: "Where is the shelling coming from?" "Who is doing it this time?" "Should we take the children to the shelter?"

Um Khalid sent her son downstairs to the office to get news of what was happening. She was still debating whether or not to go to class when Um ʿAli, her neighbor, asked, "What are you going to do? Are you going to class?"

Um Khalid grabbed her infant son, held him tightly to her, and said, "How can I go? Would you leave your children when there's shelling ?"

Class was canceled and we stayed at home waiting for the shelling to die down.

In sum, crisis draws women into politics, but at the same time it deflects attention away from issues of concern to them. Most women respond to crises in a cyclical fashion: temporary mobilization and then rapid demobilization as the crisis subsides; for others it is the beginning of their political activism. The response to crisis depends on its extent and severity and its impact on family structure. The cyclical character of women's mobilization was a problem for the cadres as well as the national movement as a whole. It made it difficult to build up a corps of members and skilled and experienced organizers. For the leadership of the movement, it was compatible with a limited vision of women's role in the struggle.

Ambiguous Status and the Life Cycle

Mobilization potential and strategies corresponded closely with specific stages in a woman's biosocial life cycle. Before the advent of education for girls and a later age of marriage there was little time lapse between puberty and marriage. In Arab Muslim societies, marriage is the official, legitimate means of regulating female sexuality and reproductive potential. The time lapse is now considerable, nearly ten years; thirteen is an average age for the onset of puberty, and twenty-two or twenty-three is the average age of marriage for young Palestinian women.

The "dangerous years," beginning with puberty and indicating sexual maturity and marriage or control over potentially dangerous sexuality, have expanded in time as women's education has been extended and a later age of marriage has gained acceptance. Singleness is certainly not an obstacle to activism, for it is precisely during these years of ambiguous status, when women are subjected to the greatest restrictions, that they are now working outside the home, engaging in militant politics, and are most receptive to mobilization campaigns. School, the workplace, and politics constitute a new public arena in which women now move during these dangerous years. As a result, the consensus on what constitutes women's proper space is being assaulted. It is precisely the fact that they are undertaking employment and political activism during the years of dangerous/ambiguous status that enhances activism's potential to pose a challenge to conventional notions of gender.

Before exile and the formation of mass political organizations and the growing trend toward neolocal residence, position in the life cycle was less influential in determining the extent of women's political activism. The most active members of the Arab Women's Executive Committee were married. In this period, elite married women had time to involve themselves in national affairs. The availability of servants alleviated domestic responsibilities (though not management responsibilities), freeing them for a variety of extradomestic endeavors. Peasant women's participation in defense of their communities required little sustained pattern of activism. They were not organized into associations or political groups that required a prolonged commitment of time and energy as are women today. Their actions were more spontaneous, in reaction to attacks on their villages or to assist their male kinsmen or fellow villagers in battle.

The "dangerous years" just before marriage (eighteen to twenty-three) are when women are more likely to engage in extradomestic activities and be most responsive to mobilization appeals. The majority of women leave the Resistance upon marriage, though this has begun to change in the past few years. Indeed, the leadership of the women's movement, both the union and the heads of women's sections in the political organizations, are mostly married women of middle-class origin. What has changed significantly is the target of recruitment—younger single women.

Women's conceptions of femininity and self are salient aspects of mobilization potential. They color mobilization potential on both sides of the spectrum. Few married women consider it possible to make a sustained commitment to engage in politics after marriage, and mobilizers hesitate to give much attention to married women or women over thirty-five to forty years of age. Marriage, the most momentous event in the life of a young woman, signifies a fundamental transformation in status, self-perception, and extradomestic roles. Marriage usually assumes primacy both of identity and loyalties over others such as employment and national activities. Once they have undergone the marital rite of passage, formal political activity and employment drastically decline as women uphold the cultural consensus on female propriety. Women militants acerbically comment of those who leave work and politics upon marriage, "She has graduated."

Few married women over the age of thirty-five to forty are targeted for mobilization. They may be asked to assist the fighters or help in the clinic in times of crisis, but they are not considered mobilization material, as being able to give a sustained amount of time and energy to the Resistance. When Samirah went on her visits around Shatila she always targeted young unmarried women of around eighteen to twenty years of age. When I pointed this out, she remarked, "I don't bother with married women, as it takes too much time to convince them to do anything and they rarely join an organization." She thought her time would be more productively spent with unmarried women, who were more likely to join organizations. When setting up a literacy project in Shatila in the spring of 1982, the organizer found the most enthusiastic women were between the ages of twenty and thirty-five. Few women over forty signed up or showed any interest. She commented, "Women over forty feel they have no life left in front of them and little to give the Revolution." The cadres see middle-aged or older married women with children as "prepolitical."

With the onset of menopause, women in the Arab world acquire increased power and prestige, taking a more publicly vocal role in domestic and community decision making. The desexualization that is assumed to accompany menopause accords women greater mobility. Older women (over forty-five to fifty), particularly poor widows with children to support, are the cooks and cleaners of the offices and military bases. Older housewives, especially those whose sons and husbands are guerrillas, are fairly easily mobilized during military crises to staff kitchens and clinics.

They feel themselves an intimate part of the Revolution and their duties toward it as an extension of their domestic roles, referring to the young fighters as "my sons," obscuring boundaries between domains.

The younger activists make a distinction between sustained militancy and the temporary militancy of these older women. Temporary militancy is lauded as a manifestation of steadfastness in face of communal adversity and as an expression of patriotism. But it is also deemed as lacking in a political consciousness that can be transformed into a long-term commitment.

Middle and upper class urban Palestinian women over thirty-five to forty years of age are also less likely to be mobilized as full-time militants. Like their counterparts in the camps, they are mobilized for support services, in this case charitable work or fund-raising, in which their contacts among the bourgeoisie can be crucial for access to funds.

The predominance of unmarried girls in the Resistance attests to the shift in the significance of the life cycle for extradomestic commitments between the pre-1948 period and the era of the Revolution. Formerly, elite women were usually married to political leaders. Those who remain active after marriage in the contemporary period are also often wives of leaders and belong to the middle class. Whereas the bulk of activist women are young and single, the leadership is slightly older and usually married. Marriage may be necessary for organizational advancement. There is the possibility that upon marriage an activist's commitment will be diminished. Singleness is equated with a certain social immaturity— marriage confers adult status while also implying control over women. With marriage, particularly to a leader, an activist gains a following— the wives of her husband's coworkers and subordinates—that may facilitate her political advancement. Her activism complements her husband's, for it is assumed that they hold similar political ideologies and belong to the same factions. Therefore, in the event of a power struggle or schism, she can deliver more members—that is, her followers—to her husband's faction.

Obstacles to Mobilization

Obstacles to mobilization are multifaceted. Aside from the PLO's own lukewarm commitment to the sustained mobilization of women, cultural conventions and family restrictions present formidable impediments. Yet obstacles to mobilization and sustained militancy can also be located in the double burden of housework and activism and perceptions of propriety. Not all women are propelled to activism in the face of violations of domesticity.

The consequences of challenging the consensus on gender relations and structures may be more easily dealt with by women than the consequences of challenging family opposition, for if the family supports a woman's activism society's disapprobation is more easily faced and overcome. Furthermore, the more numerous and visible politically active women become, the less frequent and malicious the gossip. People tend to gossip less about others when their own kinswomen are militants. During the general mobilization campaign of 1981–82, coordinated between all PLO organizations, high school girls were required to take military training courses after school and during the weekends. This generated remarkably little opposition from camp families. The father of a fourteen-year-old girl succinctly expressed community sentiment: "Everyone's girls have to go, so it is a shame for no one." If his daughter had been the only one of his family or neighbors to suddenly undertake military training it is likely he would have reacted differently.

The Family

The family has a double-edged role in mobilizing women; it is crucial both in facilitating and obstructing it. The family is the primary social institution entrusted with the task of enforcing society's normative order on women. In societies where the state is weak or its power and authority are contested by other agencies, the family remains the single most effective locus of control over women. Accordingly, seldom do women join the Resistance without arousing family opposition. Few families readily confer approval on a kinswoman's decision to engage in political activism. In many cases they are effectively able to hinder women's actions; in other cases women engage in protracted and occasionally volatile conflicts with their parents for their permission to participate. By examining several cases that illustrate the variety of problems and the kinds of tensions women face with their families over the question of militant activism some patterns can be discerned.

Amal was a nineteen-year-old university student in Beirut when she joined the Resistance in the late 1970s. Her father, opposed to women's involvement in politics, had no idea that she had done so. She did, however, tell her mother, who was apprehensive, fearing Amal would be in dangerous situations. To ease her mother's worry Amal told her she was only involved in social, not military, work. So her mother reluctantly accepted the idea and devised schemes to cover for her with her father.

135

When it was Amal's turn to do housework her mother would tell her, "I'll do your work for you. You go and do the tasks required of you." When her husband approached the house she would alert Amal to his impending arrival, rushing to tell her, "Put your things away; he's coming!" She would also warn Amal when she knew he would be home earlier than usual, advising her, "Manage your time before he comes home."

Siham was the responsible in a sewing workshop in Damur. Initially her father opposed her going out to work, but after numerous discussions and with the mediation of her younger brother, Abid, he relented. Now she is the sole financial support for a family of six: her mother, father, and two younger sisters. Siham was encouraged to join the organization sponsoring the workshop, which entailed evening meetings. Her father, however, refused to let her leave the house after dark. He still tries to prevent her from attending, but prior to each meeting she sends word to her brother, Abid, who is her organization's responsible in Damur, to intercede with her father. Abid, ten years younger than Siham, manages to convince their father to allow her to attend. The same process is repeated nearly every time she wants to go out at night.

I first met Nawal during the civil war when she was fifteen years old. Her father was a full-time member of an organization that was trying to recruit her to work in their kindergarten. At the time, she was typing at home on a piecemeal basis to earn money. Hers was a large—twelve children—and poor family. Several of her brothers were in the same organization as their father. When her father was out of the house, women cadres visited and urged her to work. If he returned, the visit took on ordinary social overtones. He was staunchly opposed to her involvement in the Resistance. She was not allowed out of the house except to go to school, and she dared not try to secretly join an organization. Appeals from women cadres to allow her to work were to no avail.

The next time I saw Nawal was in the winter of 1981, when I happened to meet her in an office in Shatila camp, where she was sitting with a group of about nine or ten men warming their hands around a small fire. Now twenty years old, she seemed at ease and self-confident. She accompanied me to the home of some mutual friends, where she related what had transpired with her father over the past few years. Using the argument of patriotic duty, she finally convinced him to let her work in the kindergarten. From there it was only a small step to joining the organization. Subsequently she became engaged to a man from the West Bank, though in her family such an exogamous marriage is rare. She emphasized this last point to illustrate the extent to which her father had changed due to the influence of his children's compelling nationalistic arguments and their political activities.

ʿAblah, a middle-class university student, secretly joined the Resistance during the late 1960s when it was just becoming more openly active in Lebanon and when the dangers of arrest, imprisonment, and torture by the Lebanese authorities were still possible. Parents were quite skeptical of their children joining such a new movement, having little idea where it would lead. Her parents supported the idea of building a Palestinian movement, but they were upset and worried when they discovered ʿAblah had joined. They said, "Why should you join?" "Let the others go!" "Why only you?" "We are with the *fidaʾiyyin,* but others should be fighters, not our daughter." They were apprehensive that the neighbors would find out and start gossiping about the late hours she was keeping.

Wafa, recently married and mother of a one-year-old son, spent most of her day at home alone in Shatila. Her husband was a full-time fighter. Fadiyah, a cadre, tried to mobilize her to work on a health survey project that would have required her to conduct interviews with women in her immediate neighborhood. She would have been able to bring along her child. Wafa was very eager but anticipated opposition from her husband. Unable to obtain his permission, she was reluctant to commit herself. Under pressure from cadres who were visiting her daily, she finally agreed to do so without his permission, though she remained anxious about his eventual reaction. When he finally came home on leave he was very angry that she had acted without his permission. He called the women with whom she was working "loose" and said that if she associated with them she would be called similar things. He was particularly galled that it was Fadiyah who had initiated her involvement. She had a bad reputation among the fighters and people in the camps. Insisting that Wafa should devote her energies to her son and the house, he forbade her to continue with the survey project. The cadres continued to visit her, but it was in vain. She remained at home, rarely leaving its confines.

From these five brief stories—two middle-class university students and three camp women, two single girls and one married woman—it is apparent that women, regardless of class, face similar kinds of familial control and interference. Opposition is constant, though variable in form and content. Both fathers and brothers occupy critical positions. Opposition is located in vertical kinship relations; families are divided in their approach to women's activism along generational lines. More opposition comes from fathers than from brothers. Mothers, like Amal's, occasionally play a supportive role, interceding with their husbands to try to win more autonomy for their daughters. Many sympathize with their daughters but do not voice their opinion, conceding authority to their husbands. The family divides along a generational rather than a gender axis, with sons and daughters questioning the authority of the father. The mother often will join this group in solidarity with her daughter. I knew of only one case where a mother openly and avidly opposed her daughter's activism, fearing a scandal that would upset her kin, whereas the girl's father displayed little sustained opposition.

Siham's case illustrates the supporting and mediating role of brothers who are themselves involved in the Resistance. These brothers possess a distinct form of influence in the family. Their level of political education equips them to argue cogently with their elders, and in the camps the power of the younger members of the Resistance has substantially co-opted the functions of the traditional elders. As cadres or employees, brothers are often the economic mainstay of the household, which enhances their voice in family affairs. Equally significant, brothers are vested with the task of protecting their sisters' honor and as such are conferred much control over their actions. Nevertheless, brothers can play a negative role. Two instances of opposition come to mind, one from the middle class, the other in the camps. In the latter case the brother was not active in the Resistance and was opposed to his sister's involvement in what he considered "leftist politics." He used physical coercion to prevent her association with the cadres. In the former, the elder brother feared his sister's involvement would endanger his business investments in East Beirut (an area under the control of the Phalangists). He took little concrete actions to stop his sister, instead expressing his opposition in persistent exhortations to "think of the danger you're putting us in."

Nawal's case is perhaps representative of the typical situation. The family battle is a process that drags out across time, with no clear-cut results. It appears to be a no-win, no-lose situation that can go forward or backward at any time. In Nawal's case she was finally able, after years of negotiating with her father, to become formally active, though he never did completely lift his opposition. Nawal persevered and thus the battle was carried on over the years. Marriage offers a way out of such situations.

In the 1970s it is probable that the economic situation weakened family opposition. Given the high rate of inflation and increasing consumerism in Lebanon, the extra income that women brought home was sorely needed. In Siham's case, she was the sole support of her family.

Wafa's situation showed some of what motivates male opposition. Her husband was adamant that involvement would jeopardize her performance of domestic duties and expose her to criticism damaging to her reputation and his honor. It is worth noting that neither Wafa nor her husband had any relatives in Shatila camp. Her husband bore full responsibility for ensuring her proper behavior.

In the case of ʿAblah, parental opposition focused on danger and transgression of social norms. Like most parents, ʿAblah's were wary of gossip that would damage her reputation and that of the family. Her parents openly voiced the sentiment that the Revolution should be served by "others." Middle-class parents could voice such concerns more openly, whereas camp families were more hesitant to publicly state such opinions. It would contravene the norms of loyalty to the Resistance and the ethos of equality of suffering.

Domesticity and Self-Perceptions

The easiest women to mobilize are the unmarried; most active women, aside from some of the leaders, are single. Upon marriage the drop-out rate from both employment and political work increases drastically. In addition to the actual rigors of domesticity and child care, women's perceptions of them as primary present obstacles to mobilization and activism. Identification with domesticity is considerably pronounced after marriage, as is the striving to perform well in order to fulfill norms of femininity.

There has been little serious questioning of the implications of domesticity either among the Resistance leadership, the Women's Union, or ordinary women themselves. The moral consensus is firmly entrenched and retains its legitimacy. Politics and employment are now part of "girlhood," and the transition to the marital state, or "womanhood," usually indicates a nearly total immersion in domesticity at the expense of extradomestic involvements. For those who do continue to work after marriage domestic commitments do not diminish in intensity. As we will see later, nurturing and caretaking tasks have themselves been imbued with a political content and meaning.

Women couch the choice of domesticity over politics by endowing child raising with patriotic meaning. Jamilah, a young mother of two children in Shatila camp whose husband did not mind if she were to work as a nurse in the Palestinian Red Crescent, explained why she opted to stay at home: "If a woman raises children she is contributing to the Revolution one way or another." Motherhood is both an excuse and a justification—"raising children takes all my time"—and yet child rearing has incorporated a political meaning.

The Resistance leadership is well aware of the drop-out problem and the high cost to its social institutions. Vocational training for women only for them to drop out a few years later is a costly and wasteful expenditure of scarce resources. The Resistance has tried to remedy the situation through the provisioning of day-care centers and after-school activities for children. The aim is not to alter the gender-based division of labor but to ease women's load in order to facilitate their entry into the national arena. The proximity of family and women's exchange of domestic labor also provides women with another source of day care. Full-time activists with children often avail themselves of a mother, mother-in-law, aunt, sister, or elder daughter to look after their children when they are away. In spite of the availability of day care, many women still drop out upon marriage. Mobilizers' decision to direct recruiting campaigns to unmarried women made sense given their greater availability for scheduled activity, their generally higher levels of education, and the absence of a domestic commitment aside from helping their mothers at home.

Some married women were mobilized after marriage and child rearing. Um Khalid, mother of eight children, enrolled in a teacher's training course and subsequently taught twelve hours a week in the literacy program in Shatila camp. Her eldest daughter, fourteen-year-old Muna, looked after the children. Um Muhammad, a widow with two young children whose husband died in Tal al-Za'ter and who could be called a self-mobilizer, is determined to become a cadre and to this end is avidly pursuing her studies in the literacy course. She states with vehemence, "I want to improve myself and become a full-time cadre, but in order to do so I must learn how to read and write." Her mother lives with her and takes care of the children while she studies and attends political meetings. Um Muhammad's reaction to women who leave the Resistance pleading "too much housework" is to tartly reply: "I, on the contrary, have lots of time. If one is really enthusiastic and commited, one finds time. Housework is boring and can be cut down and done quickly, and visiting can be reduced." Fatmeh decided after her fourth and last child was born that she wanted to work and join the Resistance. Aside from belonging to an organization, she works full-time as the headmistress of one of its kindergartens. She explained, "My life was empty and my husband encouraged me to join the Resistance and work." Her husband helps out at home, and her mother-in-law lives next door and looks after the children when she is out. Thus the actual demands of domestic labor don't necessarily impede mobilization; just as crucial is how women manage the dual tasks of domesticity and activism and how they consign priorities.

The Resistance did not attempt to mobilize women around explicitly women's issues such as day care, improved community services, legal reform in women's status, and equality for women. If they had done so would results have been very different? Arguably, they could have been worse. Men might have exerted more opposition to something so radical and threatening to their own position of power in the gender hierarchy. Furthermore, it is precisely because their participation is in a nationalist struggle that it is accorded a modicum of legitimacy. The national threat is perceived as so dire that there is a readiness to realign some aspects of the normative consensus on women's assignment in the gender structure and concede them a limited freedom to engage in political activities. And in the process of constructing sociopolitical institutions and new forms of social relations to confront their political status gender structures begin to undergo a process of reformulation, incorporating new cultural elements, recasting existing features, and rejecting others outright. The effect of this process of cultural reformulation on gender structures, relations, and meaning was to readjust positions in and elements of the gender hierarchy.

The demarcation line between politicization and mobilization is a complex one. Intimately interconnected, the relationship between ideas and actions at times appears distant, as if they are two distinct forms in social life. In reality, they are seamless. Politicization is an intended outcome of the mobilization process and yet a necessary precondition. Mobilization is unlikely without political consciousness, and political consciousness remains an individual, unactivated quality unless it is mobilized for action.

5

Action, Ideology, and Gender in the National Movement

■

What is it that women actually do in the Resistance—what positions do they occupy, and what tasks do they perform? In a more theoretical vein, Palestinian national policy, and that of the GUPW, recognizes a multiplicity of forms of subordination. However, this official discourse on politics and struggle designates them as primary and secondary, ignoring the complex ways in which forms of power are interrelated and yet may also have an existence independent of one another. This hierarchically ordered and ranked conception of power and subordination points to a hierarchically ordered and ranked conception of forms of resistance and struggle and their political appropriateness and acceptability. Such a twofold inquiry suggests the contours of the relationship between ideology and practice in this particular instance.

Affiliation: Members and Friends

Women are affiliated with the Resistance in a number of ways: as friends, members, or cadres (full-time members). The key to being affiliated is action, however loosely defined, on behalf of the national cause.

There is a very clear distinction between friends and the category of members. When I first went into Shatila camp, I sat with small groups of women in their homes and offices and asked what kinds of tasks were entailed by their participation in the Resistance. Invariably, they began by identifying who was "organized" *(munazzamah)* and who was a "friend." Those who are organized—that is, formally affiliated to an organization—are the activists: members or cadres. The distinctions become more refined as equal care is taken to distinguish between cadres and regular members *('anasir)*. The latter are formally affiliated with an organization, have an organizational rank within it, are subject to the authority of a political responsible, and are expected to attend meetings and carry out assignments; these women may be students, housewives, or employees in Resistance institutions or in the private sector.

Cadres or full-time members *(mutafarrigh)* usually work in the political and administrative sectors of their organizations. They are a select group targeted for future leadership positions. They undergo special training, both military and political, in programs abroad or at local cadre schools *(madrasat al-kawadir)*. On salary, in some organizations, they are forbidden to engage in other paid employment. The single most significant distinction between full-time members and members, however, is the former's status as cadres. Fluehr-Lobban defines cadres as ". . . militants attached to a political party." Militancy does not necessarily indicate involvement with armed struggle but rather is a ". . . type of political involvement where women cadres are linked to political parties, even taking on leadership roles within that party" (1980:242). The term *cadres* indicates the potential for political advancement; as one continues to evolve politically, acquiring more proficiency in the organization's political theory and displaying leadership abilities, she will advance up the hierarchical ladder.

On average, full-time members or cadres are in their late twenties or early thirties and have attained a high school or university education. They are about equally divided between those from the camps and those who reside in urban areas. Full-time activitists from the camps usually have a high school education; a very small number have university degrees. Obviously education, or literacy at least, is imperative for full-time activism. Most full-time activists from urban areas were university educated.

Members are more varied than the category of cadres, with its stringent requirements. About half of members are married. They are invariably married to full-time cadres. They are rather evenly divided between camp and urban origins, and their educational level varies widely—about half are university educated; the remainder either are high school graduates or have an elementary school education.

It is a rather common supposition that women leave the Resistance and employment with marriage. Young single women are trained in a skill or mobilized after months of intensive effort and political education only to work one or two years and then quit to marry. Officials with Palestinian social institutions such as the Red Crescent and Samed, the PLO industrial wing, consider this a grave problem, since the turnover rate results in a substantial loss of human resources. Full-time activists run the gamut in marital status—a substantial number are married, slightly fewer are single, and a few are widowed or divorced. Regardless of the fact that many full-time members are married, substantial numbers of women do drop out upon marriage, before they have attained full membership. Becoming a full-time member requires a number of years of commitment and study; thus those women who advance to this stage may well be married by then, usually to militants in the same organization. Those who drop out with marriage are usually still in the process of becoming members or are friends or employees—that is, "ripe for mobilization." Thus marriage has uneven consequences for women's activism. For some it signifies rapid demobilization and an embracement of domesticity; for others, however, it can actually consolidate their political positions. Being married, a woman acquires a certain status—she is respectable and serious, having made the transition to social adulthood. Marriage to a full-time militant can improve her political position. Her followers can be substantially augmented by those of her husband's and their wives. Male militants are not as likely as non-Resistance men to encourage their wives to drop political work.

The average age of members and full-time members suggests that both groups were part of the radicalization process that occurred in the camps during the late 1960s and 1970s when women began to join the Resistance on their own initiative. It also suggests that once they attain the level of member their political commitment is rather stable and they are less likely to waver with marriage.

It is difficult to delineate fixed, categorical boundaries between forms of affiliation. Ordinary camp women quite naturally draw a distinction between formal political affiliation—being "organized"—and their own fluid form of community based involvement. Political leaders and ordinary camp residents alike often repeat with an easy assurance that nearly every camp household is affiliated, in one way or another, with the Resistance. If a father or brother is a member of an organization, his immediate family is usually considered by others and by themselves to be its supporters. Women are no exception to this sort of self-identification. Um ʿAli, a neighbor of Um Khalid's in Shatila camp and mother of seven children, was not herself formally affiliated to any organization, and she rarely attended national events in the camp. But if one asked her if she belonged to an organization she responded, "We belong to Fateh." Her husband was a full-time fighter with Fateh; it was the family's sole source of income, social services, and security. Because of the nature of membership—the tangible services that accrue to members and the sacrifice required of their families—and the continued embeddedness of individual identity in the family, the meaning of affiliation extends beyond the individual to encompass the family. Material recognition is given to "family membership" in the Resistance. Salaries include a stipend for wives and each child of its members. PFLP salaries also include a stipend for husbands of female members and their children.

The category of friend connotes clearly delineated patterns of action and thus affiliation. To be a friend *(sadiqah)*, the most common category of affiliation for camp women, means that one identifies with and supports the policies of a certain group, assists them during crises, and can be counted on to attend their political and national events in the camps. Friends become affiliated through a family connection or on their own initiative.

With an average age of forty, friends tend to be older than members. They are rather evenly divided between married and single women and widows. What does characterize them fairly uniformly is their educational status; the majority are illiterate and the rest have some elementary education. Thus, unlike members, they tend to be poorly educated, a reflection of their chronological age, since in pre-1948 Palestine education for girls in rural areas hardly existed.

Friends are actually involved in and/or are employed by a particular group. Cadres refer to their activities as belonging to the realm of the "prepolitical." Underlying such an appellation is the assumption that political involvement is a unilineal process. Yet popular movements are linked to their mass base in a complexity of ways. "Prepolitical" indicates that cadres' perceptions involve a dichotomization of behavior into the categories of political and prepolitical, imposing a distinction that recognizes the significance of informal political action but relegates it to a secondary position.

145

Twenty-year-old Khadijeh, a self-described friend of the PFLP, was employed in its sewing workshop in ʿAyn al-Hilweh camp. She distributed its literature on the streets of Saida and in the camp, and her closest friends were members or friends. A small, intimate group of four or five girls who worked together gathered in the mornings before work to drink coffee at Fatmeh's home. Two were members; the others were in the category of friends. Fatmeh is the wife of one of the organization's responsibles in the camp and is herself a member. One of her tasks was to oversee the process of transition from the "prepolitical," friendship stage to that of member. Indeed, the morning coffees fit into a pattern of mobilization conducted through everyday activities that invested them with a new intent and meaning.

The overwhelming majority of friends were women from the camps. And, by and large, their husbands were members of the Resistance. Upper middle- and middle-class urban women were also to be found among the ranks of friends of the Resistance. Their activities contrast with those of friends from the camps. Whereas the latter are spurred to action by attacks on their communities and act to sustain it, the urban friends are active in fund-raising, establishing charitable institutions, and collecting and distributing materials for people in the camps. Yet it must not be lost sight of that they are also spurred to action by crisis. Like the activities of their counterparts in the early women's movement, many of their charitable works are in response to social upheavals and disasters in the camps such as those imposed by the civil war.

Women's political affiliation is not a unilineal process in which a transition is made from one hierarchical category to another. Of course this does occur in some cases and the national movement may aspire to such a state of affairs, but in reality friends do not always go on to achieve full membership. Instead there is a pattern of movement back and forth between categories of affiliation. Members may become friends if their level of activism lapses, as often happens during periods of calm. The birth of a child may also serve to remove women from the political arena for a few years, during which time they may act as friends or supporters of the movement.

All categories of affiliation specify practice. There is no affiliation without action. However the popular, "unofficial" meaning of affiliation has been stretched to encompass women like Um Ali, who define themselves as activists because of a life-style imposed on families as a whole by activist members.

Activism

Women are active participants in all sectors of the Resistance—military, political, and social. They do, however, have a more concentrated presence in the social fields—(mass work, education, information, and health) and/or in the lower echelons of the administration, serving as secretaries, clerks, telephone receptionists, etc. They appear least in higher level political positions and the military. Their participation in the contemporary national movement dates from the origins of the movement in the 1960s. Popular lore claims the first woman activist was Um Jihad, wife of Fateh military commander Abu Jihad.[1] A Gazan, she participated in the embryonic post-1948 underground Palestinian movement based in Gaza and Egypt and currently heads the PLO's massive Social Affairs Department. In spite of a few highly visible and powerful women, the vast majority remain distant from the centers of power and decision making. In 1981, thirty women were elected to the Palestine National Council, a parliamentary body, nearly tripling their representation (from 11–12 to 30) in the 301-member body. Women leaders were quite adamant that they had no wish for quotas to ensure their presence in national bodies, preferring instead to go through the long process of developing capable cadres and attain political power on their own merit and hard effort.

Organizational and Administrative Work

As a full-time activist Samyah was involved in building up her organization via mass work in Shatila camp. She spent her days visiting young women to try to involve them in the Resistance and arranging political meetings and activities. A few hours prior to national events such as demonstrations and funerals, she would go door to door rallying girls to attend. During the civil war she joined the Student Brigades (the military branch of Fateh's student organization), temporarily halting mass work.

In short, organizational work builds the organization, its mass base, and social institutions and extends its political theory and practice. Full-time cadres, like Samyah, do the bulk of organizational work; this is only logical, since it requires the full-time commitment characteristic of cadres. For women, concentrated in the less powerful and prestigous positions of building the mass base and institutions, organizational work often resembles an extension of their traditional domestic tasks. The aim of mass work, where women are concentrated (described in detail in chapter 4),

147

is to mobilize community support for the Resistance and to cultivate the relationship between the masses and the revolution.

Administrative work, which can be done by cadres, members, or non-member employees, implies proficiency in a skill rather than organizational rank or affiliation. As a regular member, Fatmeh attended her organization's political meetings and was employed full-time in its affiliated nursery. She was trained in preschool education, and her employment was considered an administrative assignment separate from her organizational duties and rank. A cadre, Sa'dah's linguistic skills were put to service in the information section, where she translated foreign news bulletins into Arabic and wrote the newscast for the radio and daily press reports.

Those engaged in administrative work are often members, but there are quite a few employees (men and women) in administrative offices who are not. In spite of their nonmember status, employees consider their work a contribution to the national struggle, building its social institutions and developing the self-sufficiency of the exile community. Employees in the sewing workshop in Shatila saw themselves as active nationalists because they sewed uniforms for the fighters and linen goods for the co-op to enhance the economic self-sufficiency of the camp.

Extensive overlap between these categories is evident. They are not bounded entities that exclude activism in others. Indeed, many activists carry on with several tasks at once. Dalal, for example, was a full-time member of an organization. When Shatila or Resistance-controlled areas of the city were under bombardment she was quickly mobilized to fight. She fought full time during the 1982 Israeli siege of Beirut. Ordinarily her organizational duties encompassed serving as her organization's liason with some of its foreign supporters, handling arrangements for delegations, and serving as an escort for visitors. In addition, when she was not overseeing visitors, she worked in the information section writing, translating, and editing articles for publication in her organization's journal.

Concentrated in social work and in forging and maintaining Resistance relations with the masses, women are rarely in formal positions of power. In a sense they serve as links between the Resistance and the camps. Friends and supporters of the Resistance will be discussed in chapter 6, since they are not a formal component of the political hierarchy, though they represent the kind of relation most women have with the Resistance.

Military Service

I met Bassimah at the home of mutual friends in Beirut in the summer of 1981 while she was on a few days' leave from her guerrilla unit in South Lebanon. She was one of hundreds of women university students undergoing military training during the 1981 general mobilization campaign. But as a potential cadre she was also being groomed politically. She had passed a rigorous political education course in her organization's cadre school and was now enrolled in an extensive military training program. Upon completion of her military service, she began working in the political offices of the Resistance. Bassimah was not militarily demobilized; when an alert was sounded she donned her fatigues and joined the fighters. She was one of the women (and men) who exemplified the popular slogan: "Every fighter a politician and every politician a fighter."

Illiterate and unskilled Rula, a full-time fighter since the civil war, felt the military was the only work for which she was suited. *Al-fida'iyyin* in her unit were trying to teach her to read and write, but it was an unstructured effort and her slow progress was a measure of her ambivalence. Her father and sisters and brothers had been killed during the siege of Tal al-Za'ter; only her widowed mother, whom she now supported, was left. In 1976, she decided to fight in defense of the camp. Following a few introductory lessons on the handling of weapons and basic guerrilla tactics, she fought for several months, only to be captured by the Phalangists when she and several other fighters tried to escape to the mountains when the camp fell on August 12. I probably wouldn't have known of her experience had it not been that one day when we were taking showers I noticed that her stomach and chest were heavily crisscrossed with deep scars. I asked what had happened, and she explained that in hand-to-hand combat a Phalangist militiaman had repeatedly slashed her. Unable to fend off his attack, she was taken prisoner. She was blindfolded and bound for fifteen days, and her untreated wounds became badly infected. An exchange of prisoners two weeks later led to her release. Just before the 1982 war, Rula left her guerrilla unit in South Lebanon and went to the Arabian Gulf, where she had found a position as a nanny.

Like other illiterate or uneducated fighters, Rula was not a member of an organization. Regular members undergo military training, but not as extensively as cadres. Several of the university-educated women had served in the military in a sustained fashion during the 1975–76 civil war in the well-known and respected Student Brigade.

The examples given above of Rula and Bassimah explored some of the different reasons for sustained military involvement and what it means for women of different classes. National commitment is a given in both instances. For Bassimah, who aspired to rise politically in the ranks of the Resistance, it was part of a more general political grooming for full-time militancy. She was a cadre in whom the organization was willing to invest time and resources. For Rula, military work was a way to survive when few other options were available. With little formal education, to become a member or cadre was a near impossibility for which, in any event, she had neither the inclination nor the qualifications.

It was not unusual for new recruits to demand military training and service. Indeed, several women, particularly those who were self-mobilized, explained that they had insisted on it when they first joined the movement. New members were usually anxious to enroll in a training session at the bases in the south. Layla, for example, recalled that when she joined the movement in the late 1960s she strongly resisted efforts to persuade her to channel her energies into mobilizing women. She didn't consider this "real political work," insisting instead on undergoing military training; she subsequently became commander of a base.

Insistence on military service was a way to prove themselves as capable as men in serving the national cause. It was also a test of one's commitment; not everyone can go through the rigors of training and sustained military duty. The military experience was an essential component of grooming for sustained militancy and leadership positions. Crisis roused others to fight despite an apparent unwillingness and/or inability to become a member or cadre.

The military experience gave an abrupt jolt to cultural conventions of gender. Needless to say, the terrain was male-defined. Women, determined to be equal to men, had to confront the content of the female gender. Shedding gender stereotypes, casting off the culturally defined female traits of passivity and weakness, was akin to a rite of passage.[2] Palestinian women describe a "startling and euphoric" transformation of self and consciousness during military training. They confronted an internalized sense of domination through a set of actions that were radical departures from conventions of female behavior. Within a limited temporal and spatial framework, women and men related to one another as near equals. Camaraderie between men and women was a consequence of facing the same dangers and trusting one another's military abilities.

Women acquired a sense of empowerment, however ephemeral, from being armed and trained to use those arms. Training in guerrilla tactics and self-defense and the strenuous routine of daily exercise sessions spawned a self-confidence in their abilities to be equal participants in the national struggle. Women spoke of an "euphoria," "a new sense of who I am and my strengths," and "carrying the same load as men." Thus women's heightened consciousness of their abilities unfolded through action, an action motivated by national consciousness and the conviction that women have a right to participate. Most important, the military experience awakened women to their potential equality to men. The belief in women's unsuitability, both physical and emotional, for training and combat was contested as they proved themselves as committed and able as men. Their strengths were made apparent to themselves and others.

Subsequently, some women discovered that military participation was less of a feat than was mobilizing and working with women, a task requiring infinite persistence and patience and a test of one's commitment. Yet such tasks are less endowed with the prestige and glamour of carrying the gun—the public display of power.

During the 1975–76 civil war, women members of organizations, employees in Resistance institutions, and members of mass organizations such as the GUPW were given military training in sessions ranging from a couple of weekends to two to three weeks. In the winter and spring of 1982, an Israeli invasion was widely discussed and anticipated in Palestinian and Lebanese political circles. Thus a general mobilization campaign immediately preceeded the 1982 Israeli invasion of Lebanon,[3] during which high school girls in the camps were trained on weekends and after school. In any case, few women were called to fight during the 1982 Israeli invasion and siege of Beirut.

If the PLO did not encourage women's military participation, why then were they trained? No unequivocal or coherent policy was ever articulated by the PLO on the issue of women and military training. The existence of training programs can be attributed to the demands put forth by the GUPW to the PLO leadership and by women members of the PLO's constituent organizations. One must keep in mind, however, the absence of a unified training program. Each political organization had its own military structure and training programs. The GUPW also offered women training programs under Fateh sponsorship. The intent underlying training programs varied in time and according to sponsor.

The intent underlying these programs is difficult to pinpoint, since no distinct policy guided their operation. When the PLO initiated the 1981–82 general mobilization campaign the intent was less to engage women in full-time military work than to impress upon the Palestinian community the seriousness of the situation and prepare a population to defend itself in the event of a worst-case scenario. Since the 1960s, the PLO has sponsored paramilitary youth clubs for boys *(ashbal)* "tiger cubs" and girls *(zahrat)* "flower's."[4] In these Fateh mass organizations, along with the youth clubs of other political organizations, young girls were ostensibly trained to form a militia as a second line of defense in case of all-out war.

The ambiguous stance toward women's military participation was also partly a consequence of a surplus of young men willing to fight. During military crises, for example, when women turned up at PLO offices to enlist to fight, they were often politely told they weren't needed, as were highly educated men. Concern with alienating a conservative mass base also served to circumscribe women's military mobilization. Women's military contribution is reflective of the gendered division of labor that permeates the Resistance.

Training and arming women were prominent and persuasive symbolic gestures. Women toting the weapons of war signified the extent to which even the most protected members of society embodied the suffering of the community, how this suffering and resistance to it had transformed even the most conservative aspects of society, and the extent to which the community supported the Resistance.

Militancy, Femininity, and Status

In a society where men gain prestige and status from sustained militancy, what kind of status accrues to women who express national sentiments in militant fashion? Has female militancy informed permutations in the elements that give definition to femininity?

Women's activism has not always been accompanied by a concomitant positive transformation in status. Indeed, in some instances women may have acquired a new negative status. Often called "loose" and "immoral," individual women in the military only seem to gain in status if they go beyond what is expected and achieve martyrdom, are wounded, carry out incredibly heroic acts, or abide by high moral standards. But the collectivity of women has gained in status. Palestinians now see women as capable, active nationalists. Material deprivation and the repeated emotional and physical traumas endured by women in the camps have acted to ensure that few men view women as weak or politically compromising. But it is as individuals that women endure an ambiguous status. National crisis may have legitimized women's new activities, yet tensions and ambiguity as to femininity do ensue from this rather sudden appearance in public politics. A small snippet of conversation between two cadres is indicative.

Abu Samir said sardonically, "Our women aren't women anymore;

they have become men. Now I know they have to be this way because of our society, but even when they go home they are no longer women."

Abu Munir, commiserating with his friend, said in lamentation, "My wife complains about housework and cooking, but if she does these same activities outside the home for the Resistance she feels differently about them."

Clearly activism impinges on private lives. The private domain is not immune, and indeed its privacy is thus questionable. If this conversation is any indication, men want separate spheres of action and relations. When women blur the lines, when they become "no longer women" due to their exposure to other men and Resistance activities, their status as feminine is questioned. Women's domestic work, when done in the context of the Resistance, is accepted by Abu Munir's wife, but she complains about the performance of these same tasks in the private realm. Activism leads to women's consciousness of and questioning of domesticity as it is performed privately.

Aspects of femininity have been suffused with new meanings derived from activism and the demands of a community in constant turmoil. Women who stubbornly and defiantly remained in the camps during attacks, a potent manifestation of *sumud,* steadfastness in the face of adversity, sent a message that the community of Palestinians would not be forced out, that they were prepared psychologically to withstand attack. Women took the concept of *sumud* and carved a niche for themselves within its bounds of meaning. In Lebanon the term *sumud* as used by Palestinians acquired a specificity of meaning. Attacks on Palestinian camp communities were designed to expel them. Palestinian steadfastness was a powerful, and yet also poignant, symbol of the failure of enemies' attempts to dislodge an already uprooted people. In short, *sumud* had potent political implications and meaning. The qualities that comprise *sumud* are also those that are characteristic of femininity—silent endurance and sacrifice for others (family and community). When in fear of imminent expulsion, nonaction, the act of not acting, of staying put, became an act of political will and commitment; it was a recognized and lauded act of resistance. The prominent place accorded *sumud* in popular Palestinian political discourse paved the way for many ordinary women to see, and for others to see, their actions as politically significant.

The political and military division in the Resistance is reflected in women's position in both and attitudes toward them. The military is the preserve of the "sons of the camp"—the poor and the uneducated, in other words, those with few opportunities. University students and cadres undergo military training and may have fought for extended periods of time, but it is the poor who remain fighters. Each displays markedly

153

different attitudes toward female activism.[5] Women in the military are more respected and accepted as equals by their male counterparts than women in the offices. In part, it could hardly be otherwise. To fight together requires the utmost in trust among colleagues. Female fighters were able to inspire this sense of trust in their male comrades. Women in the military are considered by their male counterparts as capable as men; if anything they are thought to have more endurance. Husayn, a well-known longtime guerrilla, once commented firmly and with conviction:

> If you can't trust a *fida'iyyah* then you can't trust a *fida'i!* They are better for longer missions, for there is no patience and stamina like that of a woman. You see, women work in the house and bear children—this requires tremendous strength and resolve. There is little difference between men and women fighters.

The physical and psychological qualities that make women equal to men in the military arena, the quintessentially masculine domain, are women's potential (because women fighters are nearly always single) reproductive attributes and the demands of domesticity. Husayn's words weren't empty. In selecting fighters to form teams for patrols and battles he usually chose one woman in particular, whose fighting skills were greatly admired.

Standards of femininity are class bound. Women's strength is not as valued by middle class men accustomed to mothers and sisters who do relatively minimal heavy labor, enjoying the assistance of household help. Idleness and seclusion have long been hallmarks of prestige for the middle and upper class. A double standard is more prevalent among middle class men who profess to support women's involvement in general, but when it comes to their sisters, wives, or daughters it is for other men's women.

While in the military, women occupy a gender neutral, or desexed, position. Displaying some behavioral traits associated with the feminine (beautification techniques, passivity, demureness, and shyness) does not qualify one for consideration as a fighter. But, ironically, to be considered a good fighter one must display, in exemplary fashion, some feminine qualities. Though women fighters are single, the qualities that render them respect and consideration as the "sister of men" are those of married women and mothers—morally correct behavior and stoicism in the face of adversity. While morally above reproach, an essential attribute of femininity, women fighters are not passive, another female attribute.

On the base where Rula was stationed there was another woman, Majidah. They were the only two women on the base. Rula was not very well respected as a fighter or as a woman; her suggestions on policy on the base and comments about politics were rarely listened to. The men didn't like her much, and she frequently argued with them. Rula didn't engage in sexual relations with anyone or in flirtatious behavior, although she did have a boyfriend on a neighboring base who occasionally visited her. However, her clothing (tight T-shirt with tight khaki trousers) and makeup put her in the category of woman first, militant second. Majidah, on the other hand, university-educated, intellectual, and straitlaced, was highly respected; the men called her "the best fighter in the south." She was frequently sent on important missions and was often in command. Rula, on the other hand, was complaining to her responsible that she was losing her fighting skills as a result of being on guard duty during military alerts rather than in the guerrilla units sent out to fight.

Majidah maintained a serious, almost stern demeanor, rarely joking or laughing, and kept her exchanges with men on the level of politics and military affairs. Her clothing was strictly military—even in the heat and humidity of summer she would wear full military dress with the heavy khaki shirt buttoned up around the throat and the sleeves buttoned around the wrist. Majidah was known as the "sister of men," an apparent reference to the establishment of a fictitious kinship relation between her and the fighters. Her behavior and sartorial style, and her designation as a "sister of men," desexed social interaction, negating the potential for sexual relations in a physically desegregated setting fairly new to Arab society, where men and women can still be awkward in socializing together, let alone sleeping in the same room for weeks on end.

Majidah, unlike Rula, was an "honorary man"—tough and brave but not really a woman in the sense of sex. She had joined the ranks of men, and rather than bringing with her any particular female traits, she was assigned a gender neutral role, akin to a sister with whom sexual relations are forbidden. The construction of a gender neutral space *for women* in the military (not for men), where women assume the desexed position of "honorary men," may be related to the concept of *fitna* in Arab culture. *Fitna* is the state of chaos that would reign if men and women were to interact without the legal-religious regulations set forth in the Quran and by the rules of Arab society that govern male-female interaction.

The performance of heroic acts exempts women from being held accountable to accepted standards of female comportment. Dalal Mughrabi,[6] for example, did not have the best reputation until she died leading a commando raid. Now she is held up as a role model by younger girls and her martyrdom has placed her in the ranks of the national heroes. A word of caution should be interjected at this point. The presentation of Dalal Mughrabi as a hero and role model is more prevalent for foreigners than among families in the camps, for whom her premartyrdom behavior is a subject of gossip. Amneh, prisoner for ten years in Israeli jails, whose torture, including sexual violation, has been made public, is widely respected, and no one would dare to *openly* criticize her behavior. To do so would verge on treachery. The fighters call her "a true struggler" in reference not just to the torture she endured, but to her unwavering revolutionary commitment, unshaken after ten years of imprisonment. Majidah and Amneh are objects of veneration, but they are not defined in female terms. They are symbols that are above judgment by the normal standards of female conduct.

In a society where armed struggle was seen as a salvation from exile, militancy was highly valued as the ultimate expression of political commitment. Women's militancy, as we have seen, dilutes expectations of them to conform to some of the normative prescriptions of femininity—those associated with passivity in particular. The task of mobilizing the community and gaining its support for the Revolution compels women to adopt a mode of behavior that goes beyond what is expected of women in public—modesty, determination, and sacrifice. As militants they carry the moral load of representing the Resistance to the community, and thus their behavior must be exemplary to avoid offending and alienating their constituency.

Thus militancy has had an uneven impact on women's status—some women acquire unparalleled status through heroism and exemption from family-imposed control. Those unfortunate not to have had the opportunity or inclination for heroism may be labeled "loose women." Cadres who do mass work are held in fondness by women in the camps, since they link them to available resources and services. But they are often the butt of jokes by men many of whom feel that women who work with the national movement must have something wrong with them, since they are not married.

Mechanisms of Control

With the decline of traditional social mechanisms of control, expressed in physical means of segregation like the veil, separate quarters and educational facilities, violence by male relatives for transgressions of the modesty code, and single-sex socializing, new forms have emerged to maintain and reproduce domination. Activist women are subject to various kinds of social control. The form, content, and location have been altered, but the effect is remarkably similar. Social control vested in the family is being augmented by that operating within the Resistance, bolstered by its moral authority and legitimacy. Militancy of a sustained nature, especially that accompanied by heroic acts, diminishes family control over women but not necessarily that of society in general. Women militants transcend family belonging to become revered daughters of the community. In a sense they become a public concern. Authority is transferred out of a family context to that of their political groups and leaders. New forms of control maintain asymmetrical power structures and relations and serve to obstruct women voicing their concerns and interests. In short, structures of domination contain within them the means to hinder and slow down but certainly not halt, in the long term, their transformation.

Verbally expressed mechanisms of control encompass ridicule, sexual innuendo, and political discrediting. The fear of ridicule was evident when the mother of a two-year-old boy had difficulties arranging day care to match her work hours in the Resistance. She hesitated to raise the subject in her weekly meetings. As she said, "They will just snicker at me and won't take the whole thing seriously." She never did broach the subject openly with her comrades and continued to complain privately and miss meetings and work.

There is abundant use of sexual innuendo. Women activists are sometimes called loose by ordinary men and those in the Resistance. The slightest transgression can give justification for such gossip. Talking intimately with men or laughing freely in their presence can bring about disparagement and sexual labeling. Men who recognized the absurdity and danger of bandying about such epithets were often too intimidated to protest, for then it would be assumed they were intimately involved with the woman in question.

Such sexual labels can have deleterious consequences for a woman's political credibility. Two cadres had been trying for several weeks to mobilize Munifah. She was considered intelligent and politically knowledgeable and therefore ripe for recruitment. After several weeks of casual visiting and discussions, their interest in her waned abruptly. When I asked why, they replied, "She sleeps around and has a bad reputation. How can we take her seriously politically when she behaves in this way?"

One of the most powerful terms used against women, both by men and women, is *bourgeoise*. Interestingly, it is rarely applied to men, having acquired an almost female connotation referring to a way of life determined by women's material tastes and desires. Yet it has ambiguous connotations in that it is applied to a number of situations. Political disagreements or deviation from accepted policy may be termed bourgeois, as may be interest in women's rights. *Bourgeois* seems to imply that a concern with anything other than the immediate political and military situation is deviationism and potentially dangerous. It can be more efficacious in producing conforming behavior than sexual slurs because of its inherently negative political implications.

157

The National Movement on Gender

This section examines the position on the gender question of the organizations in the Palestinian national movement and the GUPW, as well as the ideas of liberation and the conception of relations between the political and the social spheres of society that underlies them. In addition, tensions between the dominant ideology and emergent, competing ones will be discussed. A theme that weaves its way through this section is the relationship between ideas of liberation and social change and action toward those ends.

In spite of social arrangements instituted by the national movement that have benefited women and advanced their social standing, there has been no serious attempt to articulate a specific vision, ideology, or platform on the question of gender. At this juncture it is imperative to pose the question: what was the intent of the Resistance? The PLO was certainly not a coherent or powerful enough political entity, nor did it aim, to engineer a radical social transformation. Nor did the Resistance intend to undermine the power component in gender structures.

Rather than pronouncing an officially sanctioned ideology on women or gender relations, the national movement found itself compelled, by force of circumstance, to take action on a number of social issues that ultimately brought in their wake unforeseen social consequences. Initially employment in Resistance institutions was envisioned as a means of easing the responsibility of men for household finances. Women were to assume a role in financial responsibility for their families during male absences or in the event of widowhood. But unmarried women's access to income gave them a greater voice in family affairs, challenging male authority. This was an unanticipated consequence of employment that by the 1970s and 1980s was recognized as essential for raising women's political consciousness and mobilization potential.

Gender equality was not construed as a moral issue by the PLO. If the intent was not to restructure gender relations but was to promote social development with women's participation, the dilemma increasingly recognized by women was how women can participate if they are not emancipated.

The Palestinian national movement, comprising nationalists, Marxist-Leninists, Communists, independents, and Islamically inspired members, is organizationally fragmented and correspondingly lacks ideological clarity and unity on social issues or objectives. With the Palestinian people scattered across a wide range of states and a national movement in continuous flux and adaptation to constantly shifting objective realities, long-term social policies and their implementation are difficult on a scale other than an immediate one. The Resistance has yet to define the kind of state, or society, they aspire to create in an independent political entity. This is attributable, in part, to ideological disunity in the Resistance and the absence of a pressing need for such formulations. The Resistance leadership finds it divisive of national unity to expound upon the nature, structure, and ideology of a future state. Similarily, the leadership, both men and women, consider it divisive to support an independent women's movement and avoid clearly articulating the role of women in a future state. The leadership consciously avoids detailing the social and ideological parameters of a future state in order to retain the support and goodwill of the Arab states and to retain the support of their own mass base, perceived as traditional and conservative on social issues. This ambiguity may also be explained by reference to Palestinian intellectual history. Women's position had not been identified and equated with the state of society as among nineteenth-century Egyptian reformers (Qasim Amin and Muhammad 'Abduh) and the twentieth-century Turkish reformer Ataturk.

I asked everyone I interviewed to explain their organization's theoretical stance and policies on women. Not surprisingly, the overwhelming majority had very little knowledge of what these policies were. This only made sense as I gradually became aware that such policies were, in fact, of very limited development and quite ambiguous. Nevertheless, the absence of a formal commitment to women's liberation should be weighed against the complex of social institutions promoted by the Resistance, such as kindergartens and nurseries that allowed women to pursue activities outside the domestic realm, clinics that eased the burdens of medical care in the family, and vocational training and salaried employment.

The point could be strongly made that the PLO has been reactive to changes in women's position rather than affective.[7] It has posed less as a mechanism of social engineering than in reaction to processes unfolding in its midst. New norms and values have been fostered by women's experience of exile and participation in the Revolution, and it is to these new norms that the PLO has been responsive, rather than explicitly informing their emergence. For example, most Palestinians now strongly support women's right to choose their own husbands. The Resistance has taken no formal stand, yet on occasion it will intercede to prevent a forced marriage, just as it sometimes does to prevent incidents of domestic violence directed against women. Interference in domestic matters must be examined in a specific sociopolitical context. Is this a policy to protect women and ensure their newly formulated rights based on an ideological commitment to gender equality, or is it an attempt by the PLO to assert and maintain control over their well-armed mass base?

The Political Organizations

In discussing theories on women I will only distinguish between the largely nationalist Fateh and the self-styled Marxist-Leninist Popular Front for the Liberation of Palestine (PFLP). As the largest political and military groups within the PLO, each represents the two main approaches to the question of how to organize and struggle to regain the homeland. Fateh has what has been dubbed a "maximizing strategy" distinct from the PFLP's "minimalist strategy." The former signifies ideological ambiguity as the cost of Fateh's strategy of becoming the largest and most representative group. The latter stressed the Marxist-Leninist concept of the party and quality of cadres and ideological unity at the expense of size (Amos 1980:43–44).

Irrespective of their differing organizational strategies and political ideologies, on the question of women little of substance distinguishes their theoretical expositions. On the level of practice there is even less distinction. In discussions with leaders of the women's movement, cadres, and women in general, no one was able to distinguish between the practices of one group and another and nothing I observed led me to notice any such distinction. There are, however, some formal, theoretical distinctions predicated on the class-based position of the PFLP and the national unity position of Fateh that could give rise to a different practice. Neither organization has detailed the parameters of a future state, nor have they propounded a vision of social change or the sort of social order they would wish to emerge either now, in the stage of national struggle, or in a postrevolutionary phase of state construction.

When discussing the question of women or, for that matter, probably any other issue in the Resistance it is useful to distinguish official voices from those of individual members. This is especially so given the intellectual climate among the Palestinian community in Beirut, where social and ideological experimentation with a multiplicity of ideas on society and social relations was being discussed, debated, and lived. Fateh's official policy on women is, in some respects, at variance with what individual women leaders and cadres proclaim. Fateh's official position on women can be garnered from political texts (the PLO Charter, the political programs of the Palestine National Council meetings, the *PLO Bulletin* [a monthly magazine]), the statements of leaders, the pamphlets and brochures published by the Information Department of the PLO and the Women's Union, and interviews with members and political cadres.

Fateh holds that women's participation in national struggle establishes the foundation for their eventual "liberation," without however, defining the term. It was assumed that the social implications of female activism would lay the foundations for ideological and social changes. Cultural constructs defining a restricted social life for women were seen as an impediment to their freedom to engage in national struggle. Participation in national struggle, initially by a "vanguard" few, would alter their social position, and new attitudes toward women would emerge, which would then enhance the ability of increasingly larger numbers of women to act. In short, action will give rise to new ideologies of women's capabilities, which will then inspire and permit greater levels and kinds of action. Given such an approach, strategies for bringing women into the public domain included raising their national political awareness and equipping them with wage-earning skills. It was recognized that extensive progress could only be consolidated in a liberated territory where national institution building could proceed free from outside interference and accompanied by judicial reforms under the protective umbrella of state legitimacy.

In spite of the existence of a variety of angles on the question of gender, some common denominators do produce a basic ideological unity. One sector of Fateh policy has consistently held that struggles other than the national one, such as that of women, are of a secondary nature and must wait for the opportune time, in this case after national liberation and the establishment of a state. This fragmented vision denies an intimate relationship between polity and society. In his acerbic article "Propositions on the Struggle of Women," published in 1977 in an intellectual organ of the Resistance, the monthly journal *Shu'un filastinniyyah,* Fateh member Munir Shafiq contends that men and women have identical political interests and outlooks. Women, not subject to a specific form of oppression, should not be mobilized any differently than the rest of the Palestinian people, nor do they have concerns apart from that facing all Palestinians—the national crisis. Any reforms or changes in their position must wait until after national liberation. He delivers a scathing, misogynist critique of militant women. In essence, he accuses them of trying to be like men and in the process alienating the mass of women. Discounting economic independence as an issue of concern to women, he declares that mobilization should not jeopardize the proper performance of domestic duties, nor should men be called upon to share the burden of household labor. Activism should not endanger women's association with domesticity. In other words, redefining gender should not be an issue for Palestinian women. Indeed, women should strive for complementarity between activism and domesticity.

Within Fatah much of the discussion on gender issues has been by left-wing women who are also leaders in the Women's Union. In 1974, May Sayigh, Executive Committee member of the GUPW, well-known early Fateh militant, and poet, was part of a minority group within Fateh that opposed the idea of a "national authority" *(sultah wataniyyah)* on areas of Palestine (rather than all of Palestine) liberated from Israeli occupation. In a booklet published by the GUPW, she rejects both "bourgeois feminism" and the Islamic conception of women's liberation. She called for a materialist analysis that relates women's liberation to economic and political transformation but also recognizes the crucial need for ideological struggle. Women can only attain equality through an organized struggle that is an integral part of a larger movement to end all forms of oppression and discrimination. While noting the specificity of gender domination, Sayigh points to its embeddedness in the national equation. Specificity arises from restrictive cultural values so deep-rooted that to make headway against them requires a special place in the struggle for national liberation. She does not, however, define the specificity of women's struggle. The closest she comes to identifying the specificity of women's struggle is when she states that women have no need of an independent organization, unaffiliated to the Resistance. Rather, they need a "kind of semiindependence but belonging to the Revolution" because women have a "specific reality" of family duties and an underdeveloped consciousness.

Women's participation in the Resistance, Sayigh maintains, should not be confined to self-mobilized individuals or heroic activities but should be on a mass level. Responsibility for improving women's conditions and ensuring their mobilization falls upon the leadership of the Revolution and women in prominent positions. She blames the "reactionary ideology" of the male leadership for the low rate of women in command and organizational leadership positions.

Sayigh is critical of the Resistance for its low level of interest in the woman question, reflected in the lack of policies on women and the neglect of cadres' education on the issue. Contending that the Revolution should encompass political and social transformation, she accuses the Resistance of a general disinterest in social questions and a tendency to see the Palestinian people only in a political context.

On a more optimistic note, she proposes that changes in morals and values occur during revolutions, particularly during crises, and need not necessarily be preceded by economic transformations. As for the Resistance's fear of alienating its mass base, Sayigh makes a very valid point when she says people willing to die for the Revolution will accept ". . . the moral values produced by the revolution" (n.d.:51).

Jihan Helou, executive committee member of the Women's Union and a left-wing Fateh militant, was also concerned about the relationship between women's struggle for equality and the national movement. She maintains that the two struggles are intimately linked in that the national struggle will not succeed with only half the population and, conversely, that women cannot effectively participate unless they are freed of the restrictive practices and ideologies governing their lives. She said, "The fact that we have a Women's Union means that we should have a separate program of struggle, which is mainly a social program." The social programs to which she refers are aimed at equipping women for a more productive role in national development and enhancing their status within the family and society in general.

To Helou priorities have been determined by the objective conditions in which the Revolution finds itself since the civil war in Lebanon. She describes this as an "advanced defensive stage," where the Resistance is concentrating on defending its existence. In the absence of a state, or even a secure territory, and given the geographic dispersal of the Palestinian people, it is unable to formulate reforms in women's legal status. For instance, laws mandating a minimum age of marriage or equality in divorce would be impossible to introduce. (Palestinians resident in host Arab countries are legally bound to observe their laws.)

Helou does consider extensive ideological change possible in this advanced defensive stage. She sketched a portrait of a self-consciously dynamic society in the throes of redefining elements of culture when she said:

Dropping backward values usually takes place during an uprising. Sometimes when it is quiet things go backward. But as a revolutionary organization we have to make use of these uprisings, make use of changes in mentality, and deepen these changes and make them part of our culture and tradition.

Military and political defeat, as occurred in Jordan and which resulted in the PLO's expulsion, deprives the Palestinian community of those institutions that advance women's position—such as kindergartens, vocational training projects, literacy courses, etc. But defeat, Helou emphasized, cannot deprive Palestinians of the political and social consciousness garnered during a particular stage of the Revolution. Changes in ideas and "mentality" will remain to inform new kinds of action. They will

163

restructure social relations and in doing so will imbue culture with new elements.

In 1979, the PFLP, the second largest group in the PLO, published an article in its English language monthly, *PFLP Bulletin,* that marked a departure from past nebulousness on gender. The PFLP attempted to expand its class analysis of national oppression to touch on the unique situation of women. Fundamental to its analysis is that the main contradiction governing the lives of women is the same as that of men— national and class oppression. Contradictions specific to women are expressed in a cultural complex of institutions, mechanisms of control, and ideologies devaluing women and depriving them of autonomy. Women's liberation, though, remains an integral part of class struggle, since the origins of their oppression are intimately connected to the emergence of private property and class differentiation.

The PFLP also contends that new values emerge during the period of revolutionary social transformation, but national victory does not mean an end of the struggle for women's liberation, which must be the subject of a long and continuous struggle. Therefore the PFLP claims to emphasize consciousness raising of both men and women, since improving the economic situation of women in and of itself solves very little.

Most noteworthy in this article, and in a speech made by Secretary-General Habash of the PFLP on the occasion of International Women's Day in March 1982, is the contention that women's liberation is a moral issue. Habash states that it is a question of both moral and principle and the PFLP's "... position on women and their right to equality and liberation comes as the result of moral values ... a people who exploits another is not free." [8]

In the genre of a self-critique, the 1979 article identifies two problem areas. First, the Resistance has failed to develop a policy on women, for which the PFLP itself takes some blame. As the self-proclaimed left wing of the Resistance, they had failed to set a strong example and put forth a coherent policy. Second, the PFLP criticizes the Resistance's reliance on traditional forms of social organization and ideology as a basis for recruitment into and the operation of the Resistance movement, noting their obstruction of women's full participation.

The PFLP and Fateh seem to display theoretical differences on the question of women—the PFLP appearing to have developed a more coherent analysis recognizing the moral dimension of the issue and the need for consciousness raising. Both, however, insist on the complete integration of the women's movement into the national struggle. Neither accords room for women to define their own priorities and organize and struggle for them in an autonomous organization.

The Women's Union (GUPW) [9]

A Woman's Union exists, one of its leaders told me, because there is a women's cause and struggle. The union set for itself several tasks: national liberation, to involve women in the struggle by raising consciousness or level of awareness of the national situation and their role in it, and to initiate socioeconomic programs to enhance the position of women. The aim of the latter is to prepare women for national struggle. Augmenting their ability to be independent wage earners would result in a shift in the balance of family authority, thus rendering more possible women's presence in extradomestic domains. A high level of literacy among women would also elevate their chances to participate more fully in national life and consequently develop their confidence in their abilities.

In terms of consciousness, the union's aim, and this applies to women's sections in the various political organizations, was not to uncover and root out a sense of internalized domination through organized sessions in consciousness raising. Palestinian women were confronting domination through action, through participating in the Resistance. Lack of self-confidence was recognized as a manifestation of the internalization of domination. The Resistance and women's groups, while recognizing the public aspects of women's domination, were hesitant to bring to the fore as an issue the seemingly private dimensions of domination—the realm of male-female relations and sexuality. Once again a dichotomy was imposed on social life and gender, on private and public. Yet in their approach to the question of women—national participation will lead to women's liberation—they forced women to confront seemingly private forms of domination. These structural and cultural forces of domination intruded upon, actually imposed themselves upon, attempts to participate in the revolution as male, family, and societal opposition asserted itself. Participation, it was assumed, would raise consciousness of one's role in ending national subordination and accord women a sense of their capabilities. It was not supposed to awaken them to their own subordination. In short, the Resistance strove to awaken women to national domination and their role in struggle, not gender domination. But in activating national consciousness and a spirit of revolution, the manifestations of internalized domination obstructed women's activism and thus revealed the nature and extent of gender subordination and its effect on activism. Some women surmounted imposed fragmentation of forms of consciousness. As they developed an awareness of subordination at home and in relations with men, the self-confidence and sense of empowerment they acquired as a consequence of activism began to suffuse these social relations. These unspoken, if unintended, consequences of national action suggest that a dichotomous conception of domination, consciousness, and struggle begins to give way under the force of women's actions.

The union bases a substantial part of its approach to the question of gender equality on the perceived impossibility of radical structural change in the absence of an independent Palestinian state. It is perceived as a process whose foundations are being laid during the stage of national struggle. The movement will continue after national liberation, when it will have the potential for realization under the authority and legitimacy of an independent state that can confront traditional cultural and religious forces. A GUPW Executive Committee member avowed, "Our long-term aim is to totally liberate women, but we don't necessarily say it now." The new, unwritten norms stemming from social transformations set in motion by exile and revolution are changing perceptions of gender and women's position, which will form the foundations for the later struggle. Vividly cognizant of the consequences of the absence of state structures in which to institutionalize their gains, women operate on a tactical level trying to initiate and sustain the bases for their advancement —education, employment, and an awareness of their ability to play an active role in the national struggle.

Tension between the national and gender issues is evident in women's awareness of the extent to which crisis obstructs their movement and glorifies violent militancy in which men are in the forefront. On the eve of the Palestine National Council meeting in Damascus in 1981, for instance, for which the union had drawn up proposals for increased funding for projects and was toying with the idea of proposing discussion, on the legal level, on the issues of marriage, polygamy, and divorce for members of the Resistance, Lebanese-Palestinian clashes with serious political implications broke out in West Beirut. I was sitting in the offices of the union when the shells started falling in the next street. One woman said in exasperation, "We can't go before this group of men and ask for anything for women. We will be laughed out of the room. All attention will be directed to the military situation."

Factional politics is a germane frame of reference for examining union policies. In the thirteen-member executive committee, Fateh domination is apparent—half the seats plus one. The rest are divided between six other groups, each of which has one member on the committee. Within the union, women are perceived and relate to one another more as members of different, competing political organizations than as union members with varying theoretical or practical approaches to gender issues. There is also, on occasion, tension and competion between the left-wing, younger generation of Fateh women and the slightly older, more moderate Fateh women. These are divisions of affiliation that reflect minimal differences of opinion. Executive committee members are described by others: "They are all attached to a man and his political line." And indeed, some committee members are wives of politically prominent men. But it is important to point out that they are not in these positions solely because of their husbands' positions. These are the early, self-mobilized militants who would likely be in these positions anyway simply as a result of their own political status and years of committed work. Yet their husbands' status does lend a certain air of importance to their positions and gives their voice substantially more weight.

During their second conference in 1974, the Fateh-dominated GUPW took an intrepid and autonomous stand when it voiced public, formal opposition to the idea of establishing a Palestinian national entity (or *sultah wataniyyah*) on any liberated territory,[10] a policy supported by Chairman 'Arafat and most of Fateh. This was part of the political program adapted by the PLO during the Twelfth Palestine National Council,[11] from which eventually emerged the Rejection Front, which, as its name implies, rejected a political strategy based on negotiations, international conferences, and the idea of a mini-state in any liberated territory.[12] The Fateh women in the union incurred the anger of the Fateh leadership for this show of independent thinking, and some were suspended from membership in Fateh for six months by Yasir 'Arafat.[13] The conflict within the union over the political direction of the PLO, which signaled the union's second transition, divided women along factional organizational lines and within Fateh itself. Some stood against a negotiated settlement with Israel while others choose to support PLO diplomatic approaches.

It is not uncommon to hear criticism of the union by former and current members. The nature of the criticism can be reduced to a couple of essential qualities: factionalism and the charitable, short-term, and crisis-oriented nature of their work. Stories circulate about the tension between women members of various political organizations. Naturally the complaints come from those in the minority, non-Fateh groups, who feel they are merely tolerated while being made to feel unwanted and excluded from decision making and important events. Maryam, a PFLP member and responsible for a section of the union in Beirut, always felt that she was unduly criticized for the quality of her work simply because she was not a Fateh member. She was virulently opposed to suggestions by Fateh members that other organizations shut down their programs and facilities geared to women, such as literacy courses, day-care centers, and vocational training projects, and consolidate them all under the Women's Union. Maryam and women from the other non-Fateh organizations saw this as an attempt by Fateh to dominate the social service sector of the Resistance.

Another frequently voiced criticism is that individual members, when mobilizing women to join the union, are really more interested in recruiting for their own organizations. Samyah commented:

> In meetings most of these women spend their time quarreling with one another, not over women's issues but as one political party against the other. They aren't working for women; each one is working for her organization. When we work in the camps, women from the union are less interested in mobilizing women for struggle in general than they are in recruiting for their organizations and taking credit for it. This is why I don't participate in the union anymore.

Such perceptions aren't confined to dissatisfied members. Camp women often hold parallel views. The union is seen as less concerned with women's problems; individual members' own organizational loyalties are considered as primary. Membership and work in the union do not unify women around gender affiliation; a sense of affinity and loyalty that can crosscut political or organizational boundaries is hard to discern.

Maryam, Khalil, a male cadre from the same organization, and I were sitting around Maryam's house in Shatila one afternoon when a heated discussion began about the union's projects. Khalil casually asked if women were eager to take part in a newly initiated sewing course in the camp. Maryam maintained that the problem with the union is the kind of relationship they encourage with the masses and then launched into a long lecture-discussion on the faults of the union:

> Women are enrolling and are displaying an eagerness to learn. The problem is the way we, as a union, are teaching them. For what purpose does the union establish these courses? Are we offering courses solely so that a woman can learn a skill and work, or do we want to raise her consciousness of her abilities, of her potential, and teach her about the Revolution? What we are doing is teaching traditional jobs. And what happens afterward? What is just as important as teaching women a skill is the kind of relationship we sustain with them once the course is finished. For me this is the most important issue—I don't want these women to finish their relationship with the Resistance once the course is over. I want them to come back to us. A woman can go to any bourgeois sewing center, pay a fee, and learn more skills than we can give her. What I want is to give her something besides a skill. If we don't move women to act, if we don't change things in our society, the union is nothing. I think we should stop all our activities and do a

research project to find out what exactly women need and how we can help them. It will only take six months—what is six months? We're not going back to Palestine for another sixty years!

Underscoring structural dissonance in the Resistance, Maryam also expressed doubt about the practice of training women in skills for which the Resistance was still unable to provide employment. A newly graduated class of seamstresses, for example, was unable to find jobs because the construction of workshops had not kept pace with the number of graduates. She argued that the Resistance gained very little if these women worked in the private sector. From her point of view, little in the lives of these women would change, since they would not be exposed to the politicization prevalent in a Resistance work setting and their domestic lives would continue in much the same vein. She stressed the need to build a more comprehensive and inclusive infrastructure to ensure women's concrete realization of their achievements.

Samyah, who had been active for about seven years in the union and then dropped out, described their style of work:

> They give things as gifts without any plans or strategies for work. They don't understand that if they give people things they should be getting something back for the Resistance. For example, during the war they distributed flour to many people in the camps. They gave it freely, but they didn't establish friendships with the people. They didn't visit them or try to bring them into the Resistance. Their style of work is charitable. If you have a social plan and establish a rapport with people, when you give them something they won't just disappear—they will give back something. This doesn't mean you force people to join the Resistance—just to let them know about the Resistance, about politics.

A related common perception of the union is that it is active only during crises—organizing first aid and relief, with little ability or initiative to follow up its projects.

Why does an organization ostensibly devoted to women avoid directly examining gender structures and relations with an eye to transforming them? Was it a paralysis of theoretical development and an undeveloped feminist consciousness? How much of the blame can be attributed to the union's lack of autonomy in decision making and political stances and the fear of ridicule and censorship that often accompanies discussions of women's problems and demands? To some extent the lack of feminist development is a matter of political expediency, the "don't rock the boat" syndrome, but it also suggests an awareness that the acuteness of the national crises deflects attention from social matters when issues of survival, the actual physical survival and cultural existence, of the community are in jeopardy.

A member of the Executive Committee said the main obstacles to the union's work and progress are the crisislike atmosphere in which the national movement always finds itself, which doesn't give women a chance to work on social issues. The other reason is the leadership's concentration on political issues. In seeking to understand union policy, I would expand upon her comment to once again refer to a narrow conception of the political in Palestinian discourse and the imposition of a dichotomy on social life and struggle. Then I will examine concepts of women's liberation or feminism, another equally important facet of this problem.

The predominant conception of relations between the national movement and the women's movement is one where the latter is assigned a secondary, appendage like position. The Resistance has tried to maintain the appearance of a distinction between the private life of women and men (the world of personal relations, emotions, and sexuality) and public matters, reserving the designation and legitimacy of the "political" for the latter. Such distinctions assume powerful meaning in a society imbued with ideals of resistance and political struggle. By ascribing primary and secondary ranks to the national and women's struggle, respectively, in effect, the appearance of distinction begins to take on a reality. Those aspects of struggle deemed secondary are allotted fewer resources, and by the struggle being labeled secondary their adherents remain low in number. Like Layla, many women "don't want to work with a bunch of housewives"; they want to do "political work." In short, secondary struggles do not possess the prestige or power of the primary struggle— they command neither significant resources nor support. They assume their assigned status.

When Palestinians speak of "women's liberation" *(tahrir al-mar'a)* and "women's rights" *(huquq al'mar'a)* they are referring to the rights of gender as women, not the rights of men. Indeed, since Palestinian men are considered as deprived of rights such a designation takes on an added importance. The concept of women's liberation is undergirded by the notion of a future egalitarian society comprised of men and women— different primarily as regards reproductive potential and its impact on social roles—organized around a gendered, though nonhierarchical, division of labor. This is what Offen has referred to as the "relational" mode of discourse, that along with the "individualist" mode constitutes "two distinct modes of historical argumentation or discourse" on feminism in nineteenth and twentieth-century Europe and the United States (1988:34). In the relational mode, women's reproductive contribution to society gives them the basis to make "claims on the commonwealth" (ibid.:136). The individualist mode of discourse, in its origins distinctly American and British, stresses individual autonomy and rights. From this distinction it is abundantly apparent that a "relational" perspective is a more appropriate frame of reference for understanding Palestinian feminism. Relational feminism recognizes diversity and complementarity between the sexes and calls for state support of women's duties as mothers and for the performance of housework. But in addition, Offen argues, this feminist discourse advocated equal rights for women in education, employment, and civil law (ibid.:139). Palestinian feminism, predicated on their unique experiences and historical and cultural traditions, certainly combines these two elements of feminist discourse.

The family remains the basic unit of Palestinian society, ensuring survival in face of turmoil. Structurally speaking, those aspects of social life that give rise to women's demands for individual rights and personal autonomy are increasing and expanding throughout society. Although women—working, studying, active in the national movement—are asking for their rights, they are doing so in a manner consistent with the structural and emotional centrality of the family. Their vision of their rights as individuals is solidly rooted in the family and the notion of general societal development. They ask for the right to work in the same jobs and for the same pay as men, for equal opportunities to pursue an education, for the right to choose a husband, and for the right to participate in the national cause. These demands obviously imply greater freedom of mobility. Personal autonomy in the sense of mobility, decision-making powers over life choices, and sexual freedom is still a highly contested issue cutting to the core of male familial control over women. As a whole, Palestinian society has not developed in the direction of individualized wage earners residing in nuclear units. Living away from their families is nearly inconceivable, and few women express a strong desire to do so. For most it is financially out of reach and it still carries significantly negative cultural associations. Being alone and enjoying it is considered almost deviant in a society that places a high value on emotional closeness and cooperation within the family.

But most significantly in terms of the debate on feminism and its definitions,[14] Palestinian women are not zeroing in on the division of labor by sex as a terribly crucial issue. Demands for political participation and equal rights have not been accompanied by a demand for restructuring of the asymmetrical gender-based division of labor. Maryam was very clear about this, and about the need for women to assist one another in order to pursue activism, when she said:

the problem of women is first and foremost a problem for women. We have to demand our liberation. If we don't ask for it nobody is going to hand it to us. If we don't ask I can't blame the leadership and the Revolution. If we have problems within the Resistance, for instance, a woman wants to go to a meeting, but she doesn't have a place to leave her child, we won't ask the father. We don't want to make a fight at home for her. We'll ask another woman comrade to watch the baby. We have to do this if we want woman to be involved. We as women have to organize if we want equality. We can't achieve anything by shouting about how awful men are. This accomplishes nothing. We can meet and rant and rave for hours, but we all have to go home and sleep with our husbands and play the game of women. So if we really want to change we have to do it ourselves by organizing and helping one another.

Maryam calls for women to empower themselves through solidarity and organizing as a preliminary move before efforts to persuade the leadership to adopt more radical stances on gender, rather than pursuing changes in the sexual division of labor, which at this stage may risk alienating men.

Feminism is imbued with a number of negative associations, a consequence of Western colonialism and cultural imperialism in the Arab world, which manipulated notions of women's emancipation in an attempt to disrupt family structure in colonial society; the prime example is Algeria under the French. Feminism is also associated with the pursuit of sexual freedoms in a society where women are still fighting to freely choose a husband and for access to higher education. In a society that values social consensus and collective action based on primary forms of solidarity, which are now being supplanted by national loyalties, what is seen as "individual" concerns or expressions of discontent is perceived as disloyal and disruptive of family and community solidarity and sentiment. Feminism evokes negative responses, by and large, because of a misunderstanding of its multidimensionality. For Palestinians, feminism is usually equated with the Western "individualist" mode of discourse rather the "relational," which is closer in essence to their experience and culture.

The issue of sexual freedom, which would directly challenge family control and continuity, remains problematic at best. Palestinian feminism, which combines elements of relational and individualist discourses, has not directly addressed the question of sexual and reproductive autonomy (see chapter 6). Yet this usually unarticulated question pervades popular discussions and strongly nuances formal debates and arguments. To begin to openly discuss it is perhaps too dangerous, cutting to the heart of the matter—the control of women in the utmost of personal, yet political, ways.[15] Muteness on sex points to a confusion among women, activists and ordinary alike, about the position to be accorded sexuality in mapping the terrain of gender equality. Activists usually dismiss questions of sexual relations as "irrelevant" or "not related to the cause." Although the official discourse on sexuality is one of denial of its existence as a problem and its assignment to the personal, bounded world of the interior, distant from the realm of the political, in the sphere of practice an unspoken shift is discernible. In spite of an official silence about the issue of sex, in practice the sanctions for trespassing on the code of morality have eased.

Activists in the early period (1969–1975) displayed a public behavior that was exemplary of the cultural norms of female conduct. They expected of themselves and were expected by their comrades to be above reproach. If the masses were to support the Resistance, its representatives in the community had to display the utmost sensitivity to community norms. They were to suppress individual desires and exert self-control. To do otherwise would indicate that one only wanted to enjoy oneself, using the Resistance as a cover. The political mission and sincerity of the Resistance to assert itself as the representative of the exile community would have been in serious jeopardy if behavior by women militants that flaunted cultural dictates had been tolerated. The self-assigned task of the national movement was not to transform social structure and relations and overturn established normative codes of morality as such, but to transform authority structures and relations insofar as would facilitate national liberation. But the social implications of such transformations were unforeseen.

In reality, sexual relations among the unmarried were increasingly evident. Knowledge of these relations is usually confined to a very small group of intimates. When they do become public knowledge the wheels of disapprobation and censorship are set in motion. Gossip is a pervasive and powerful form of control that achieves much of its potency from its location in seemingly ordinary everyday life and discourse. The simple fact of being *public* knowledge serves as a warning of the dangers on the horizon. However, such relations have gained some legitimacy and acceptance among younger activists who question the constraints of tradition. Certainly the repercussions of such relations have been restrained by the Resistance, which acted, on occasion, to prevent physical abuse of women by their families in such cases, and shifting cultural conceptions of male-female relations that allowed for sexual relations. These new cultural conceptions were a result of men and women working together for the national cause. In daily working contact, men and women were associating as individuals with a similar interest in and commitment to the national cause. As such their relationship was uncontrolled by their families and was governed by a set of cultural concepts of gender that increasingly diverged from that of their parents' generation.

Behavior that was above reproach was mandated for activists' interaction with the "masses." But among small, intimate groups within the Resistance, usually university-educated middle-class women, a different set of norms was established and applied, which included a more open and tolerant attitude toward premarital sexual relations. This experimentation with social norms among middle class intellectual sectors of the Resistance was another barrier between ordinary camp Palestinians and the "vanguard" of the national movement. Women behaved, dressed, and talked differently in the camps than they did with their comrades in the offices or at home.

In sum, there are a number of common denominators between the views of Fateh, the PFLP, and the GUPW. A paralysis of theory is a common characteristic in that none has enunciated a clear, concise theory of gender domination and the process of social transition, nor do they have a coherent and systematic set of policies designed to alter gender structures. The specificity of gender subordination is obscured by submersion in a framework of national or class oppression that gives scant recognition to specificity. Submersion, though, enforces not just an appendage like status to issues of gender but a rank as well. Vis-à-vis other forms of power and subordination, that of gender is secondary and subordinate. This is a further and very telling index of the power of a dominant gendered discourse to define the "correct" kinds of subordination and the parameters and legitimacy of resistance. The union and the PFLP have gone farther in identifying the specificity of gender subordination. Nevertheless, neither the women's movement nor the Resistance in general has called for a transformation in gender structures, relations, or meaning; the basic common denominator among all Palestinian organizations and the Women's Union has been the call for greater participation by women in the national struggle. Given this configuration of participation in national struggle and an uncontested gendered organization of social life and power, how women manage the double burden of domesticity and political activism is explored in the next chapter.

6

Activism and Domesticity

■

How do women manage the competing demands of domesticity and political activism? In other words, what has domesticity meant for female political action and what has women's activism meant for their affiliation with domesticity? Women have fashioned a space for themselves within the political realm that is compatible with domesticity to some extent, and alternatively, others engage in forms of political action that are based in domesticity. In politicizing domesticity they have exposed the seamlessness between public and private. On the ideological level, central components of the cultural system have been reinterpreted in such a way as to give meaning and legitimacy to women's political action.

The Organization of Reproduction

In the Arab world the family is still the most vital and basic social institution in which men and women derive emotional sustenance and material security. In return, loyalty to the family is expected of all its members. Political instability and war strain family resources, yet they also leave the family as the only viable institution for individual security. Sayigh cautions that Arab "familialism" is not just a cultural remnant, but an ". . . ancient adaptive response to insecurity; group cohesion is as important for survival under state oppression as it is for survival in the absence of the state" (1981:267).

In juxtaposing the family and the Resistance it is prudent to keep in mind Rapp's observation that family boundaries are continuously ". . . decomposing and recomposing in continuous interaction with larger domains" (1979:175). Family organization, relations, and sentiments adjust to new conditions in the social fabric and yet also temper, and indeed shape, their impact. For women, the family offers a form of both solidarity and oppression. Families are the primary sites of the control exercised over women, and yet it is in their families that women find the support of other women, relations that cushion and help them manage, or resist subordination. And it is in families that intimate bonds with men are formed, bonds that unite men and women to face life's often harsh vicissitudes.

In spite of multiple stresses, the Palestinian family retained its essential structure and relations and remained a viable and cohesive social unit. It is not female-centered, as is often the response to poverty and unemployment, nor are Palestinian men marginal to its functioning and viability.[1] They may be absent for long periods of time because of migration to the Gulf for employment or for military purposes, but they do not abandon their families, nor does their absence necessarily make life easier for women. On the contrary, they regularly send remittances and make annual visits. Female-headed households are neither a permanent way of life nor do they constitute an adaptive strategy; they are temporary formations. Prolonged male absence may thrust upon women increased decision-making responsibilities, but ultimate household authority is usually shifted to male kin such as a brother or father.[2]

Structurally, the Palestinian exile family forms fluid, expansive networks of agnatic and affinal kin that contract or expand to circulate resources and assistance. Although the neolocal residence has become more commonplace, extended kin obligations have not extensively diminished, giving rise to what has been termed the "functionally extended family" (Farsoun 1970:257). As families accommodate new material and political realities, their elasticity and ability to expand both structural and ideological boundaries is evident.[3] During limited crises, such as bombing of the camps, families seek out extended kin in other areas, remaining with them for a few days or weeks until the violence subsides. Money is often borrowed from a network of extended kin to finance a young man's education abroad and later paid back, often in kind, after he is earning an income.

Instances of extreme crises, intermittently experienced by the exile community as in Tal al-Za'ter in 1976, push to the limits family structure, obligations, and sentiments. In Damur the number of widows with custody of their children living far from their kin was striking.[4] In response to my questioning about why they were living in Damur when they had kin in other camps, stories were told of women who had initially sought refuge with their families or their husbands'. Husbands' families did not always receive them hospitably and were usually in no position to assist them financially. Most of these families showed no interest in taking custody of their dead sons' children from his widow.

Family sentiments were clearly taxed by extreme crisis. Women in Damur preferred living close to others from Tal al-Za'ter who had passed through the same experience rather than trying to reactivate extended kin ties. At an informal women's gathering in Damur at the home of Um Iyyad, a cadre in charge of the social affairs section of her political organization, I asked her how all these women were related. "They are all friends," she said. "None are related by blood. All people from Tal al-Za'ter are relatives because they suffered the same experience." She added, "When you face death and starvation together you are relatives. It doesn't matter if you are from different villages or political organizations. We are one as Palestinians." Another woman in the group, Um Ibrahim, an elderly widow who cooks for the fighters to support her five children, pointed to each woman, naming her village in Palestine, and stated eloquently, "We are all one people; we are the people of Tal al-Za'ter." Selwa, a young schoolteacher, and her family initially lived with relatives in Rashidiyyah camp. In spite of Damur's harsh conditions—no running water or electricity and empty window frames—they moved there because they felt more comfortable with Tal al-Za'ter people. In short, conceptions of kinship, and indeed sentiments, are transformed in response to the severity of the crisis.

Rapp notes that ". . . all states promulgate, enforce, and depend on a family policy." The judicial realm has both defined legitimate family forms and relied on the notion of family to reproduce state authority" (1979:179). In the early 1980s, PLO family policy could be vaguely discerned in their behavior on questions of marriage and reproduction—those actions they tolerated and encouraged. Although policy remained vague and undefined, the Resistance had assumed some of the protective and defensive functions of the family while simultaneously acting to limit family control over the means of violence.[5] For example, rumor quickly spread through Shatila that a father intended to kill his daughter for a breach of family honor. She was involved in an intimate relationship with a young man that had become public knowledge. The Resistance-composed police force warned the father several times that an act of violence would not be tolerated and that if he harmed his daughter he would be arrested, tried, and sentenced. Reaction to honor killings did seem to follow a fairly uniform pattern, with the Resistance trying and jailing those caught harming their sisters or daughters.

In some instances, the Resistance confronted Islamic laws of personal status that were legally out of their jurisdiction, normally being handled by the religious courts of Lebanon. The following short case provides a succinct example of this process of co-optation and direct circumvention. Kamal, a member of the Resistance, had been beating his wife, Lubna, and had inflicted permanent kidney damage. Both Lubna and her family were asking for a divorce, but Kamal adamantly refused. In desperation, Lubna's activist sister finally went to the leadership, explained the situation in detail, and appealed for their assistance. Several responsibles then called for Kamal, Lubna, and her family to meet. They brought along already drawn up divorce papers that they forced Kamal to sign and also made him sign over permanent custody of the children to Lubna's parents.

Increasingly, the Resistance was being called upon to intervene in domestic affairs. With the influx of fighters from Gaza and the West Bank, marriages between camp girls and "strangers" were on the rise. These young men were at a disadvantage in marriage arrangements in that they were not known and thus had few avenues for opening negotiations with a prospective bride's family. Girls who wanted to marry such men often encountered considerable opposition from their families. In the absence of their own families, Resistance leaders took an active role in representing young men in marriage negotiations. They visited the reluctant girls' fathers to try to convince them of the men's respectability and good intentions. They also help to negotiate the bride-price (*mahr*), and full-time members are given a lump sum of money by their organizations upon marriage to be used as *mahr* or to furnish their new homes. In the early 1980s an internal rule in one of the leftist organizations specified that members who force their daughters to marry against their will are subject to expulsion. Such rules can only be applied to members over whom the Resistance has legitimate rights of control and the power to impose sanctions.

Whether or not the Resistance has attempted to reorganize reproductive relations is highly debatable. Policy on birth control is rather ambiguous. Resistance doctors did not feel it was yet an issue, since women were not avidly asking for birth control and the Resistance was neither discouraging it nor promoting it. While they didn't deny access to birth control, they certainly didn't readily disseminate information about it. The topic was publicly broached, however, during health lectures in the camps where nurses and cadres from the union would encourage women to space their children to ensure the health of mothers and children in order to improve the quality of Palestinian society and preserve their own health. Women who ask for IUDs at PLO clinics are given referrals to private gynecologists; for birth control pills they are given a prescription that can be filled at any pharmacy.

Regardless of outwardly pronatalist attitudes, families of over four children are becoming rare among young couples. Finances simply don't allow it, and while the tasks associated with motherhood have expanded, the extended family has declined. Women in the union, for example, encourage smaller families and the spacing of children. Some Red Crescent doctors like Nadya say, "We are against any kind of birth control, even for spacing." If a woman comes to her and she finds that for health reasons birth control is mandated or if a patient really insists she refers her to Planned Parenthood. Interestingly, Dr. Nadya says she does not want children. Other doctors are more forthcoming and will assist women to learn more about and use birth control and will arrange abortions. What accounts for so much leeway in individual physicians' behavior is the absence of a policy from above. Birth control has not been an issue for this largely male leadership because until now the birthrate has remained rather high and women have shown little inclination to reduce family size in a way that would inform a discernable demographic shift in the Palestinian population. The smaller families of the present are not cause for lamentation but are considered the results of a wise decision to maximize one's resources in an uncertain world.

"Girls Are Liberated Now"

In a society where arranged, endogamous marriages[6] were the "official definition of reality" (Bourdieu 1977:37), both education and the Resistance have left a durable imprint on marital strategies and arrangements among camp families. Freedom to choose a husband, which had gained widespread acceptance, is considered a welcome and radical departure from the cultural rules of marriage by nearly all Palestinian women— young and old alike. Older women frequently comment with approval and scarcely concealed envy, "Girls are liberated now—they choose their own husbands." What does choice mean in this context? It certainly does not mean that women are marrying on the basis of independent, individual strategies of action. Marriages remain enmeshed in larger kin structures and strategies. In contemporary Palestinian society, choice means the right to have one's refusal of a suitor's request for marriage honored, even when the family supports the marriage. It also indicates the permissibility of love as the basis of marriage. Women are now choosing their spouses, but they must go through the appropriate steps of gaining family approval. This points to the dilution of direct family control over a woman's marriage, although the retention of control is evident in the continued parental power of veto. To bypass the procedures to gain parental approval would be to stretch the ideology of women's subordination to family control in pursuit of its interest to the limits in a public way that in essence would proclaim its impotency. A few intrepid women marry against the wishes of their families after carefully weighing their strengths, both financial and emotional, and their ability to risk future insecurity. In the event of a failed marriage, it can be difficult to return home if one's parents had opposed the marriage. Change in attitudes toward marriage are also evident among the older generation, who now accept, though reluctantly, their dwindling power over choice of spouses for their children. Thus key concepts of gender ideology have been diluted but not redefined. Within these expanded, but not transformed, ideological boundaries, women are aggressively pursuing strategies to maximize their own desires and interests. They act not just in the interest of the family,[7] but for their own interests, which may indeed conflict with those of the family.

The reordering of the sexual geography of space and women's access to education made available to them an arena in which to form social relations outside the confines of home and family. Jamilah, the young nurse from Shatila, was in the UNRWA office applying for a scholarship when she met a young man there for the same purpose. They proceeded to see each other secretly at the university for a few months and eventually decided to marry. They went through the steps necessary to gain parental approval. He visited her father, pretending he and Jamilah had never met and that he had seen her at the university and wished to marry her. Permission to marry Jamilah was given after a check of his background, and they married soon afterward. Samyah met her husband, Nabil, at the Resistance office where they both worked. Theirs was a mixed marriage—she was Muslim and he was Christian. Intersectarian marriages were no longer infrequent among Palestinians in the Resistance. Nabil began visiting her family and eventually asked permission to marry her. Her parents did not oppose the marriage. But such is not usually the case. When Rihab decided to marry Adib, whom she met while working in the Resistance, her parents reacted violently, forbidding her to see him or to leave the house. He was a Muslim active in the national movement while she was a Christian. In a bold move, bolstered by their belonging to the Resistance, which provided employment, housing, and a real sense of protection from vengeful parents, they eloped. It was only two years later, after the birth of a son, that Rihab's mother broke the ice and started to visit her. To even find her in Beirut took some gumption on the part of her mother, who simply walked around the camps and Resistance areas of Beirut for several days looking for her daughter and asking people if they knew anyone fitting her description. Rihab's father did not speak to her until the war of 1982, when she went to stay at their house.

Working for the same political cause offered young people an arena in which to meet and arrange their own marriages. Women members and cadres are expected to marry from within the organization, and few establish romantic relations with men outside the Resistance. The family-like atmosphere that is fostered among cadres has expanded to encompass subtle forms of matchmaking and an endogamy based on political affiliation. For example, during a speech and celebration marking the anniversary of the Resistance, Maysun, a PFLP cadre, was busily trying to seat those occupying the front rows of the room according to who she thought might make prospective couples and was quite explicit about her motives when asked what she was doing. Endogamy within political organizations can crosscut sectarian and class boundaries. Intersectarian marriage highlights the strengths of Resistance-inspired secular ideologies and their practice. Sectarian boundaries, however, remain firmly entrenched; it is still rare for a Muslim woman to marry a Christian. Such marriages are grounds for more opposition than that roused by a Christian woman marrying a Muslim man. In any event, intersectarian marriages underscore the extent to which women felt empowered by secular ideologies, their backing by the Resistance, and their own abilities to pursue independent courses of action.

The family as an arena for marital arrangements was being bypassed, as was corresponding family control over marriages. New spatial arenas open to women and alternative sources of authority empowered women enough to pursue marital strategies initially independent of the family. Although with changes in the function and meaning of corporate agnatic groups, women's once crucial position as alliance builders between groups has lessened, a girl's marriage continues to be a critical issue to her immediate family. Marriage does remain significant for the formation and consolidation of certain kinds of alliances. Whereas previously land-ownership, political alliances, and status were critical factors in arranging marriages, concerns about security have superceded concerns about land, while political alliances and status have assumed new forms. As late as 1967 some marriages were still arranged on the basis of land ownership. Um 'Adnan recalls that in one week two men asked her father for permission to marry her. The one she preferred to marry was educated but poor; the other was uneducated, and she disliked him enough to comment, "He had eyes like olives and didn't know his head from his foot." Yet her father insisted she marry him. Her mother feared to intervene and counseled her to accept to avoid being beaten by her father. Her father found this man preferable as a son-in-law because his family had had large landholdings in Palestine and he figured when they were able to return home his daughter would be rich.

While concerns about a prospective spouse's land assets have declined, economic and security considerations are in the forefront of marital arrangements and are salient factors in parental opposition to a daugh-ter's choice of a spouse. Parents dread and usually oppose a daughter's marriage to a fighter or full-time cadre, aware of the high chances of her becoming a widow and their low salaries. The preferred husband works in the Gulf, sending sizable remittances to his family.

Marriage can be an alliance creating access to influential members of society and valued resources. Families expand their network of political supporters through the marriages of their children. When Kamli, a cadre, wanted to marry Ahmad, a guerrilla from her organization, her upper middle class family was upset and for months tried to talk her out of it. They feared he would be killed, leaving her a widow, and that if news of this impending marriage were made public her brother's business interests in Lebanon and the Arab world would be harmed. Although her family never did warmly and unconditionally accept the engagement, they resigned themselves to it and made the best of it. In fact, they turned it to their advantage. During and after the civil war, security in West Beirut was provided by the PLO and to have kin connections with a prominent guerrilla had its advantages. Protection of their property and business was guaranteed.

Although the Resistance could not formulate a code of civil law to protect women's marital choices, they did support them both by mediat-ing in cases of arranged marriages opposed by women and in cases where parental opposition to a love marriage was an obstacle. Abu Khalid, a member of Shatila's Popular Committee *(al-lijneh al-sha'biyyeh)*, was negotiating for a young fighter from the West Bank who wanted to marry a Shatila girl. Her parents opposed the marriage, but Abu Khalid was mediating to try to convince them of the young man's worthiness and to keep to a reasonable *mahr* in the likely event their professed opposition was a form of pressure for a higher bride-price. There is a fairly broad consensus against a marriage taking place where the girl has expressed her opposition. Popular sentiment is clearly on the side of Resistance interference in these cases.

Domesticity and Activism

The management of the demands of family life and the exigencies of the national struggle is best cast in terms of a complex interaction between family structures and ideology and the nature of activism. Women have assumed a dynamic stance in shaping the contours of their participation and mediating its impact on domesticity. Women have invested reproduction and domesticity with political meaning and given a domestic content to activism. This section explores the uneven impact of the Resistance on women and the various strategies they utilize to manage and ease the tension between conflicting loyalties and demands.

Reinterpreting Domesticity

Women's domestic labor is in the process of being politicized and put into national public service—that is, appropriated by extradomestic level social categories and given new meaning. The national struggle has mobilized domestic duties and politicized their meaning. Changes in the meaning of domesticity are most apparent in women's lexicon. For women who describe their daily chores as a form of "struggle" *(nidal)* and themselves as "strugglers" *(munadilin),* just to survive and maintain the family in the face of attacks that penetrate domestic space is perceived as a form of participation in the national struggle. Women's discourse is pervaded by terms like *nidal* and *sumud* (steadfastness), particularly during attack, when to remain in the camps was to publicly, and defiantly, display steadfastness and therefore was an action that furthered the national cause. To stay put in the face of assault has a particularly potent significance in Palestinian culture, where the act of flight is equated with surrender and the loss of Palestine in 1948. Both as a collectivity and as individuals, staying put is a defiant, positive action that proclaims history will be not allowed to repeat itself.

In the event of shelling or air raids, children as well as old people must quickly be fetched and a decision made whether to stay put or go to the underground shelters scattered throughout the camps. During prolonged stays in often hot and overcrowded shelters, provision must be made to secure food, milk, and water for the children. Repressing their own anxieties, women stoically attend to their children's needs and try to calm their fears. The whereabouts and fate of the men of the family bring worry and frustration. The daily routine of cooking, cleaning, shopping, work, and school attendance is disrupted. Attacks bring the loss of loved ones, providers, and homes and the prospects of being widowed or losing a child. Homes must be repaired continually or new ones found.

Reproductive capabilities have acquired a new value as a national act. The Palestinian birthrate in Lebanon was declining as a result of a higher standard of living, higher female literacy and employment rates, later age of marriage, and a desire for smaller families. With extended education, the cost of raising children has risen dramatically, contributing markedly to a lowered birthrate. It is fairly common knowledge that large numbers of children hinder women's political participation, tax their health, and are increasingly difficult to maintain in the face of rising inflation, unemployment, and the necessity for higher education. Nevertheless, it is not uncommon for women to state that it is their national duty to bear many children to replenish the human losses incurred during wars. Women do not actually bear children for the nation, but by conceiving of and talking about fertility and reproduction in these terms they gain a sense of contribution to the national struggle. Childbearing is very tightly interwoven with notions of femininity and the achievement of position and status within the household or family.[8] Women's traditionally high fertility has assumed a political urgency. Several times I was asked how many children I wanted. When my response was "only two" most were shocked. One woman poignantly summed up what they meant when she exclaimed, in all sincerity, "But what if they die? Then you'll have none!"

In the 1970s, as the camps increasingly came under military attacks that shattered any illusions of domestic insularity, women begin to speak of giving birth and motherhood in terms of a national act and duty. This is particularly so among older uneducated women who are friends of the Resistance. They express support for the idea that women should contribute to the national cause, but without upsetting gender structures and relations. Their views on what constitutes contribution differ substantially from those of the organizationally affiliated, educated younger generation. The latter are more critical of motherhood as the primary and most fulfilling role and have fewer children, advocating smaller families to free women for a wider role in society.

Um Muhammad, a survivor of Tal al-Za'ter, mother of several martyrs, and friend of the Resistance, said, "We Palestinian women, we have a *batin 'askari.* [literally: military womb; figuratively: we give birth to fighters)." One woman, who lost her husband and four sons in Tal al-Za'ter, explained with a hint of resignation, "We Palestinian women, we give birth to them, we bring them up, and we bury them for the Revolution." A middle-aged woman, complaining about the rationing of cooking gas in Shatila and how all women were contributing to the national struggle, stood up defiantly at a *nadwi* and declared, I'm giving the Israelis a hit, too—my four sons and my husband are guerrillas!" All these women have had their homes violated and lives disrupted by war and perceive themselves as involved in the national struggle. The suffusion of their discourse with political terms points to more than a superficial militancy; it gives voice to sentiments of solidarity and support for the Resistance and underscores the communal burden of exile and struggle. There is an implicit sense of sharing intimately and painfully in the struggle, though perhaps more by force of circumstances than choice.

Although the "mother of the martyr" may never have been politically active in the sense of belonging to an organization, her maternal sacrifice is extolled as a supreme political act. Women, givers and sustainers of life, whose status in the household traditionally rested on the number of sons they bore, are not expected to willingly sacrifice their children. It was out of respect for her sacrifice that the mother of the martyr was always visited by mass workers and leaders on religious and national commemoration days. In addition, mothers of martyrs were invited to attend Resistance celebrations with the leadership. A newly acquired stature in the community and easy access to the Resistance leadership imply a transformation in status. Outpourings of sympathy and acts of respect serve to cushion the loss. After losing a son, some women become quite visible and do play an active political role in camp life as intermediaries between the leadership and ordinary women, transmitting requests or appeals. It is said of them: "They have the ear of the Resistance." The stature accorded the mother of the martyr epitomizes the process by which the meanings of reproductive and domestic roles have become enmeshed in the political matrix.

Women act fiercely to protect their children, risking death, as in the 1976 siege of Tal al-Za'ter, when numerous women were killed carrying water to their children. Maternal sacrifice has become a potent symbol of the extent of the national calamity and suffering. Over time, several rituals and practices, such as annual visits by cadres, mass workers, and the leadership, evolved to console and express solidarity with a grieving mother, including this chorus sung at funerals:

> O Mother of the martyr, rejoice,
> For all youth are your children.

Reproductive roles are embedded in a new social context as women find new meaning in their childbearing capabilities, a clearly political meaning. The martyr's mother is an indigenous form of Palestinian women's struggle.

"Land Before Honor"

Honor and shame are dominant idioms governing the behavior of Palestinian women and men. The honor, social standing, and prestige of the family are contingent upon their female (and male) members' publicly acknowledged comportment, particularly in matters of sex and love. Families and men secure honor and lose face through the public actions of women kin. Shame is brought on not solely by the actions of women but by their becoming public knowledge.[9] But shame is not only a sexual matter or a matter of individual behavior. Communities can loss honor through collective shame.

Among the exiled community, the concept of honor was in flux and of contradictory meaning. Initially, honor was lost because the community was unable to defend itself, lost autonomy, and ended up dependent on international charity and, as refugees in a foreign country, women were exposed to strangers. Yet some women now worked outside the home to help support the family. Men often sent women, or preferably children, for the humiliating task of collecting UNRWA rations. With the breaking down of village insularity and the new proximity to strangers, some women were faced with new restrictions on their mobility.

When Palestinians encountered Zionism they were patently unable to respond to it in such a manner as to prevent their own ultimate dispossession. Refugees from 1948 recount fleeing Palestine to ensure their women's honor in face of potential Israeli violations.[10] A crisis of such magnitude exposed the utter incongruity, if not indeed failure, of traditional cultural forms and key concepts such as honor in confrontation with powerful external forces and ideologies intent on establishing hegemony in Palestine. Notions of honor, which in another context might have compelled action to protect the community, in this case contributed to its demise. A self-conscious critique of culture in an atmosphere of cultural creativity and reflection fostered by the Resistance in Beirut in the 1970s and early 1980s took up the issue of honor. Rejecting a key cultural component, honor—as vested in women's behavior—was attacked as an impediment to struggle, independence, and national sentiment.

The Resistance promoted new symbols of a culture of resistance, such as the gun, the flag, militancy, and steadfastness, while others were invested with new meaning that emphasized national rather than kin and village loyalties. The concept of *ʿard* (honor) was linked with *ard* (land), in a play on words and meanings. Rhetorical devices such as *"al-ard qabl al-ʿard"* (land before honor) point to a more inclusive national rather than narrowly based family honor. Another, in slogan form, posted at the entrance to a military base, read: "Those who enter here drop all backward ideas of *ʿard.*" Such a pointed slogan demarcates clearly distinct modes and standards of behavior corresponding to one's position in space (in the base or outside its perimeters) and to affiliations (those admitted to the base, thus members of the Resistance and expected to adopt its behavioral norms). Such slogans represent self-conscious changes in behavior and relations.

Although family opposition to women's participation in public life is still common, these assaults on traditional notions of honor, whether real or symbolic, cast activism and new forms of social relations in a national light and in doing so imbue them with legitimacy. Moreover, they impart the stature and value of national standing to cultural and gender issues.

Domesticity and Activism

How women's national consciousness and activism articulate with their role in family organization, maintenance, and ideology is problematic, as is evident from the surfacing of tensions centered around conflicting demands and loyalties.

The most apparent structural change in the family, gaining increasing momentum, is the transition from extended family residence to neolocal residence and the ideological concomitants of such a shift—more emphasis on the conjugal unit and love marriages.[11] Like reproductive capabilities, domestic labor has acquired new functions and meaning. As in capitalist society, where women's unpaid domestic labor underwrites the reproduction and maintenance of labor, camp women's domestic labor subsidizes nationalist activity by men.

Unmarried activists face less conflict, since they have less responsibility for the maintenance of a household and children. Married activists negotiate between family and political activities in a situation beset by conflicting loyalties and demands. How they manage the double burden or, as one activist gibed, "the triple burden" of domestic labor, salaried employment, and political work depends to a great extent on the proximity of kin, level of political consciousness, domestic participation by the husband, and presence/absence of female children. The daily lives of three women illustrate how women negotiate between the demands of domesticity, political activism, and employment.

Um Khalid: Politicized Housewife   A thirty-three-year-old mother of eight, Um Khalid was born in a village in Upper Galilee. Raised in ʿAyn al-Hilweh camp in South Lebanon, she had lived in Shatila since the early 1970s, though neither she nor her husband, a full-time member of the Resistance, had any relatives there. She says blithely of her arranged marriage to her paternal cousin, "That's the way it was done in those days." Her family still resides in ʿAyn al-Hilweh, his in the north of Lebanon. In spite of this widely scattered family—some members live in camps in Syria—on occasion Um Khalid travels with her two youngest children to visit her family or her husband's, especially in the event of a birth, illness, death, or marriage.

By camp standards, Um Khalid's apartment is large. In the middle of the camp, it is in a four-story cement building whose ground floor is occupied by Resistance offices and a sewing workshop; the other floors house three families each. Her home has four large rooms, a kitchen, and a bathroom. The salon, with rather newly upholstered Western-style furniture, was reserved for visitors. Two other rooms served as bedrooms, and the third was the common room for eating, watching TV, and receiving informal visitors.

Unlike many camp women her age, Um Khalid finished intermediate school. As she explains, she came from a small family: a father who died when she was young, two sisters, and a schoolteacher brother who encouraged her to study.

When newly married, she went to live with her husband's family. Although her in-laws were also her aunt and uncle, she says they treated her badly: "I couldn't go out when I pleased or visit whom I wanted, and if I was able to go out my mother-in-law would come with me!" She is unflinching in her conviction that married couples and their children live alone: "If a woman lives with her mother-in-law there is no freedom." She prefers living in Shatila with her husband and children, where, as she remarked, "I have the freedom to come and go as I please."

In 1981, a diploma from a teachers' training course gave her the skills to teach in the PLO literacy program. The pay is small, but short work hours, from 3:00 to 5:00 p.m. daily, suit her heavy domestic work load and the fact that two of her children are not yet of school age. Um Khalid had wanted to work for some time.

> We need the money. I wanted to work in the PLO's Social Affairs Department, but the hours are from eight to three. I still have two small children at home, so it's impossible. My job is good—it's only two hours in the afternoon. Once all the children are in school I'll look for full-time work and do my housework at night.

Um Khalid's day begins around 6:00 a.m. After rousing the children and helping the youngest to dress, she prepares them a quick breakfast of bread, cheese, olives, *za'ter* (dried thyme), and tea. The two younger boys (three and one years old) stay at home with her. Abu Khalid leaves home only to return for lunch and dinner, leaving Um Khalid alone to manage the housework and child care. She is lucky to have five daughters to help her, especially the eldest, fourteen-year-old Muna.

Um Khalid's mornings are spent looking after the younger children, cleaning, shopping, and preparing the day's meal. On alternating days she bakes bread or washes clothes. Baking her own bread, a main dietary staple, is much less expensive than buying it from the bakery. She spends about three hours preparing the dough, which she then carries to the bakery piled high on a large, flat, round tray, gracefully maneuvering through the narrow, winding alleys of the camp. The local bakery, where young girls and women gather to bake bread and cook the afternoon meal, provides a unique site for women to meet and exchange news of their children and families and discuss the latest military and political events.

By the time she finishes baking bread or washing clothes, some of the children are beginning to arrive home from school. The girls are quickly put to work washing dishes, sweeping, minding the younger children, preparing and serving tea for visitors, and fixing lunch. Running small errands to the nearby grocery shops is a task often done by her eldest son. Like his father, though, thirteen-year-old Khalid doesn't do house-work. Her daughters rarely leave the house except to go to and from school, whereas her son is frequently in and out of the house during his free time after school.

In the course of the day, friends and neighbors drop in to chat and drink tea or coffee, sometimes helping in housework and cooking. After lunch the girls tidy up and Um Khalid, if she has time, visits friends before her 3:00 p.m. class. Her visiting network is voluminous, extending all over the camp and into surrounding Lebanese neighborhoods. Visits that carry her out of her immediate neighborhood are to women she made friends with through her husband's political work, usually wives of his co-workers or women members of the Resistance she meets at the clinic, during national events, or in her own work as a teacher.

She frequently plays the role of broker, relaying messages and requests to her husband. Since she is literate, she is sometimes asked to read magazines and newspapers to groups of women. They are interested in general news, but are most intensely concerned with the news of wounded or dead fighters. Um Khalid also tries during her visits to mobilize young men into the Resistance, offering her husband's help if their situation requires special attention. Abu Khalid is a member of Shatila's Popular Committee *(lijneh sha'biyyeh),* and thus people often come to Um Khalid for help in solving problems, such as access to electricity and water, that are handled by the committee. It is assumed that she will intercede with Abu Khalid to assist their case. Moreover, as her house was hooked up to a main water supply, women often came by with their large plastic containers to fill water at her taps when it was low in their houses.

Hurrying off to work, confident that her eldest daughter is able to care for the younger children, Um Khalid arrives relaxed and eager to instruct twenty or so young women in basic reading, writing, and math. After class she often visits her students' homes or they may gather at her house. Dropping in at her students' homes establishes cordial relations and reassures families that their daughters or wives are with someone known and trusted. Friendly relations with the teacher can make it more difficult for men to try to compel women to drop out. When there are social or political events in the camp such as *nadwat* (seminars), lectures, demonstrations, or funerals that coincide with class hours, she takes the class, first sending home younger girls to obtain parental permission.

Returning home in the early evening, she relaxes as her daughters do the housework. Students occasionally drop in for help with their lessons. She is rarely idle; even when talking to visitors she keeps busy knitting, sewing, or breast-feeding her baby son. On holidays and feast days she bakes quantities of cakes for the fighters or for friends and neighbors.

Um Khalid coordinates the schedules of her six school-aged children and helps them with their homework every evening, making sure each child has completed his/her assignments. To further complicate matters, UNRWA schools have instituted split shifts because of overcrowding. Since her children span nearly all grade levels, their schedules differ; some attend school in the morning session, others in the afternoon. She is responsible for all their medical problems, taking them to the clinic when they injure themselves and to the doctor for checkups.

Although not a member of the Resistance, Um Khalid calls herself a "struggler" by virtue of her community activities (attendance at funerals, demonstrations, *nadwat,* and national events) and her teaching job. She is fairly representative of the category of friends of the Resistance. She would prefer to be more active but says, "How can I join the Resistance? I have too many children and too much housework!" She is a keen participant in political discussions at the *nadwat* and with her pupils and is usually at the forefront of demonstrations and funerals, having gone door to door to gather a good-sized crowd of friends and neighbors. A nationalist, she is very proud that Palestinian women are participating in the national struggle: "Palestinian women are the most advanced women in the Arab world. We are more educated, and girls are active politically. If we were in our own land maybe we would have developed in a different way, but I still think we would be more advanced."

Um Khalid frequently expresses her opinion on women's changing position in society. When she says with approval, "Boys and girls are equal now," she means girls have equal opportunities for education,[12] the right to choose a husband, and the right to participate in the national movement. While she tries to instill in her daughters the value of an education and encourages them to do well in school, she also places on them a heavy load of housework. Aware of its negative consequences, she laments, "I know that I demand too much help in the house from Muna and her studies suffer because she has little time to study after school."

Um Khalid still believes it is better for girls to marry young so that "they gain some freedom to go out, to be active." Marriage to her is a somewhat liberating move away from parental control, probably because in her case her husband does not prevent her mobility outside the home. She was quite adamant that her daughters were free to marry whomever they wish. When her husband was helping a young cadre by mediating with his girlfriend's parents, who opposed her marriage, Um Khalid got into a heated argument with her neighbor, who advocated the "old way of getting married." They didn't speak for some days after this row, and Um Khalid chalked it up to her neighbor's "backwardness."

The future marriage of her daughters is still a primary concern. One of the reasons she sought a job was to be able to buy Muna "nice clothes and gold jewelry, since she is at an age when she has to take care of her appearance."

Fatmeh: Triple Burden   Born in Lebanon, Fatmeh is a thirty-year-old mother of four children. Originally from a small village near Safad, her family set up home in a camp in South Lebanon. She is politically active on a number of levels—teacher, community activist, and member of a political organization—while her husband is a prominent Resistance leader in the camp where they reside. She describes him as a "liberated man"—he helps with the housework and child care and encourages her to be active politically.

Married at sixteen to her high school teacher, hers was a "love marriage" that her parents did not oppose. Until five or six years ago, Fatmeh stayed at home to raise her four children. Once her youngest daughter entered nursery school, she began to feel "empty." Contrary to the usual pattern of dilution of activism with marriage, Fatmeh took up politics after marriage and children. She enrolled in a teacher's training course, enabling her eventually to become full-time headmistress of a Resistance-affiliated kindergarten. Subsequently she also became an official member of a political organization. Fatmeh has a triple load—housework, a full-time salaried job, and political activities.

She negotiates between these three sets of demands with minimal tension and conflict. Fatmeh lives in the midst of a helpful extended family, although she and her husband and children live in their own apartment. Alleviating domestic pressures are in-laws residing next door, a "liberated" husband, and children old enough to do household chores. Her mother-in-law arrives daily about 6:00 a.m. to prepare the children for school—she dresses them, fixes their breakfast, and walks them to school. Fatmeh and her husband share in preparing their own morning meal an hour or so later, which is often shared by visiting comrades, and then they go off to work. Abu Tariq, her husband, is a teacher in the local UNRWA school and a full-time militant. The midday meal is a family affair with all pitching in to help. Although the bulk of the housework is done by Fatmeh, the children have daily chores and when Abu Tariq is in town he helps. Because he travels for the Resistance he is occasionally away from home for several weeks at a time. Fatmeh's eldest daughter often does the housework, although Fatmeh insists that she doesn't oblige her to.

Fatmeh would return home from eight hours of work to greet four children and face an evening of meetings or national events and, on occasion, a room full of visitors. Yet she was relaxed and hardly seemed fazed. Contrary to the stereotypical image of the harried Western working mother, she was a model of relaxation.

Layla: A Cadre Layla, a thirty-two-year-old cadre and mother of one, grew up in a lower middle class neighborhood of Beirut bordering on Sabra-Shatila camps. In 1948, her family came to Beirut as refugees from 'Akka, in northern Palestine. With a bit of capital and some Lebanese relatives to ease the transition, they were able to start a small business in Beirut and avoided having to reside in the camps.

Layla joined the Resistance in the late 1960s, and in the course of her work she met her husband, who was in another organization. While theirs was not an arranged marriage—their families didn't know each other—Layla will not characterize it as a "love marriage." She says she chose to marry him because he is "democratic" with women, "has no sense of possessing them," and "understood my character, whereas others didn't." She claims they weren't in love but that they were good for each other given their political commitments and interests. She also felt confident that marriage would not interfere with her political work.

Layla has one child and hopes to have another. She doesn't really want two but feels it is not fair to her daughter to be an only child. Her reasoning about having a second child was based on a sociological analysis of Arab society: "This is a family-oriented culture. The state is weak —we need our families for material and emotional support."

When her child was born, Layla took forty days' paid maternity leave from the Resistance and her mother, who lives in the neighborhood, came every day to help her. When she returned to work the baby was sent to the nursery from eight to two. Her afternoon and evening activities diminished slightly, but her husband did take over care of the child when she went out at night. During the war, when both were fighting, their child was in day care and they took turns staying at home on alternating evenings with her. Layla griped that leaders whose wives went abroad or did nothing during the war complained when she asked for time to see her daughter. Small daily household tasks were shared, but her husband did the bulk of the housework. Layla detested housework and avoided it as much as possible. They employed a maid off and on depending on their own work schedules. After the war, as a cadre she held administrative posts that required a presence in the office from eight to two, in addition to frequent evening meetings and travel abroad. When military crises erupted, which were not infrequent, she had to stay in the office sometimes for several days on end. Their parents' middle class income, as well as her husband's job in a Resistance-affiliated publishing firm, facilitated her activism. Labor-saving household devices, such as a washing machine, food processor, and vacuum cleaner, were gifts from his parents and brothers working in the Gulf, whose assistance also made possible the hiring of a maid several days a week to clean and cook.

Layla's political activism fluctuated over the past decade, but not for the usual reasons. Usually women go in and out of the organizations in response to life events such as marriage and the birth of children. Layla dropped out twice, once in 1970 and again in the aftermath of the 1975–76 civil war, both times for political reasons. She disagreed with the leadership over what she considered mistakes commited during the 1969–1971 confrontation with Jordanian government forces and the civil war in Lebanon.

Discussion The case of Um Khalid illustrates several crucial aspects of how housewives respond to protracted and violent conflict. It is as an active housewife that Um Khalid most forcefully illustrates how women in camp settings stretch their domestic and social roles to include new activities. Sustaining such role expansion requires unusual strength, and for this reason Um Khalid exemplifies an ideal to which many women may aspire, rather than a large category. Yet other politicized housewives can be found in Shatila, combining management of a large household with political work and sometimes a salaried job as well. Although the national movement encouraged the active housewife in ways that included employment, job training programs, after school activities for children, and nurseries, two points must be made. Mobilization campaigns did focus on unmarried women rather than housewives. Second, the active housewife did not emerge as a direct consequence of the Resistance but has existed since the beginning of the Palestinian struggle and should be seen as an indigenous and specifically women's response to protracted conflict.

For active housewives like Um Khalid, domestic labor remains primordial and overwhelming because of a large family, low income, and the lack of change in the domestic division of labor. As a consequence of sharing domestic work among family members, the proximity of her mother-in-law, and an encouraging and helpful husband, Fatmeh, on the contrary, enjoys substantial time for political activities. She is aware that her situation differs from others and considers herself quite lucky. She manages her situation with few tensions or conflicts, unlike Um Khalid, who has eight children, an unhelpful husband, and no relatives to ease the burden of excessive housework. Yet even she manages to do some community work. Layla had relatives nearby, a helpful and ideologically committed husband, and only one child. But all three women felt they had something to contribute to the struggle and that they had a right to do so.

The case of Um Khalid illustrates how ordinary women are caught between domestic demands and political loyalties—on the one hand the desire to work, the need to earn a salary, and an urge to contribute to the struggle and on the other the need to carry on with domestic duties and child care. Although aware of the opportunities for women to be politically active, she found her domestic duties too arduous and time-consuming to allow more than a part-time teaching job and attendance at public events. Full-time work remained out of the question while the two young-est children were still at home. Resistance-sponsored kindergartens were available, but the monthly fee (approximately $30.00 in 1982) was too expensive for a family of ten.

Um Khalid's case shows how women's tasks as child minder, domestic manager, and wife have not weakened, but have been expanded to in-clude national activities. Mothering has assumed new dimensions. Moth-ers now are expected to help children with homework, follow their progress in school, be knowledgeable about child health, nutrition, and psychological development, and arrange for after-school activities in clubs and social and political organizations. Women may be giving birth to fewer children, but the actual amount of time spent in mothering might not be substantially less. The women over twenty-five years of age in the literacy courses were there to learn to read and write in order to help their children with homework and expressed feelings of shame if their children knew they were illiterate.

Sharing of housework between men and women is rare except among highly politicized and ideologically motivated middle class activists like Layla and her husband. In families like Um Khalid's, the sharing of domestic work is usually between kinswomen; in nuclear families it is between mothers and daughters. Um Khalid values her daughters' educa-tion and thus plays a delicate balancing act, often fraught with guilt, between putting her daughters to work in the house, which frees her to pursue her teaching job and attend events, and yet encouraging them to study. As daughters are increasingly able to extend their schooling, often leading to aspirations for higher education and jobs, there is a growing questioning of housewivery and motherhood as women's sole roles. These aspirations can be rather abruptly cut short by domestic demands. This is particularly the case with the eldest girl in a large family. In such families, the eldest daughter often has the least education. In a family of ten children, for example, the eldest daughter's education was ended by her mother's need for help in looking after the nine younger children. Yet this family placed a high value on education for both boys and girls. Eventu-ally the sons went on to university. One of the younger daughters is a medical student; the other studies business.

Although some women manage the load of domestic work, activism, and employment, tensions run high. There are complaints about domestic labor hindering educational and political pursuits. This is more so among women like Um Khalid, who are the older part of a generation of active women on a scale much more extensive than in the 1920s and 1930s. Activism among this now elderly generation posed little serious challenge to domesticity. Despite grumbling—"We women do all the work," or,

"A woman's work is never finished"—few women of Um Khalid's age openly criticize the cultural rules that place responsibilities for household management on their shoulders. Most women of her generation are proud of their many children. Younger, educated women increasingly aspire to work and be politically active and thus feel thwarted by domestic requirements even when they have the obvious advantages of smaller families and access to Resistance-sponsored social services in child care, health, and education.

Family organization plays a crucial part in how women manage activism. The most apparent structural transformation has been toward neolocality (establishment of a new residence with marriage), accompanied by continued extended family obligations and rights. Layla and Fatmeh live in nuclear families, but both have kin living in the same neighborhood upon whom they rely for assistance. Such shifts in household organization put more emphasis on the conjugal unit and thus on love and companionship as the basis for marriage.

The transition in residential forms has both negative and positive consequences for women's domestic labor and mobility. Um Khalid's extended family circumscribed her mobility while broadening and tightening the locus of social control. Yet cooperative labor patterns among women freed her from continuous, heavy household chores. Nuclear family life places on her (and her eldest daughter) the burden of domestic chores, but lessens the locus of social control, thus removing an obstacle to her mobility. The presence of her mother-in-law was essential in freeing Fatmeh to engage in extradomestic activism, yet she sometimes resented her monopolization of the children. Layla's family and her in-laws lived close by and were available for emergency baby-sitting and financial assistance.

These three cases illustrate the dynamics of marriage and political activism. For Fatmeh, marriage wasn't an obstacle to activism; indeed, she entered politics after marriage and childrearing. Layla continued as a cadre after marriage, whereas Um Khalid was unable to sustain her activism for a variety of reasons, mainly her husband's distance from household matters and a large number of children. In contrast, both Layla's and Fatmeh's husbands were active in the home and valued and encouraged their wives' political involvement. To a large extent, the successful management of competing loyalties and demands depends on the nature of the marriage—whether the husband encourages political activity, prohibits it, is indifferent as was Abu Khalid, and shares in domestic work. Thus marriage, in and of itself, is not always the crucial factor it appears to be. What is just as critical is whom a woman marries.

Another crucial factor in how women manage activism and domesticity is related to changing ideologies of marriage. Women like Layla, who remained active after marriage, have tended to treat their conjugal relation as a revolutionary relationship distinct from society's norms of marital relations. In an experimental move, there is an agreement that political commitment is as important as the marital bond. In such marriages, which are few, husbands usually share in housework and encourage their wives' activism. To maintain such a situation after the birth of a child is difficult. Extended family situations are crucial at such junctures in relieving women of the onus of child care. Commitment to gender equality must be buttressed by smaller families and more institutional supports.

Women's political commitment and participation are closely correlated with the female life cycle. The peak in women's political participation is between the ages of approximately eighteen and twenty-three or before marriage. Political activity rapidly diminishes with marriage. By opening nurseries and kindergartens, the Resistance intended to alleviate some of the burden of child care from women in anticipation of their increased activism. Child-care facilities were of little use to Um Khalid; the size of her family made it prohibitively expensive.

The role of class is somewhat paradoxical. Before marriage, middle-class women have relatively greater freedom to engage in political work. Yet after marriage, somewhat isolated in nuclear households, their child-care problems are more acute than those of women in the camps, who usually have easier access to extended kin networks. Moreover, it is these middle-class women who must often manage a triple burden as they undertake salaried work, in addition to political membership, to maintain a middle-class standard of living. If their husbands are full-time militants their salaries support the family. Those who continue political work after marriage are usually politically astute and highly committed and either have access to family child care or have few enough children that Resistance nurseries are affordable or have enough financial resources to enable them to hire other women to do their domestic tasks.[13] The latter is the recourse of upper- and middle-class women like Layla. Camp women active after marriage usually rely on the functionally extended family for child care.

Political activism can have minimal impact on the sexual division of labor, as in Um Khalid's case. For most, it restructures the patterns of domestic labor between women. In the case of poor women with few resources, domestic labor is shared between kinswomen, usually mothers and daughters, particularly the eldest. For middle-class women with access to financial resources, poor female foreign migrant labor become their "shock absorbers." The express purpose of hiring maids is so that women (not men) can be relieved of domestic work in order to engage in politics or salaried work. The availability of maids and kin mediates between extradomestic commitments and domesticity. Men's exemption from housework does not entail an adjustment or restructuring of the sexual division of labor; it simply shifts the burden elsewhere.

Coping with Family Opposition

In chapter 4 we saw the kinds of opposition women faced during the mobilization process. Opposition doesn't stop once women are in the organizations. In coping with family opposition women walk a fine line between cultural norms of female propriety, which families are invested with maintaining, and political aspirations, which can compel women to defy these norms. Nearly every woman who decides to join the Resistance faces opposition from her family. Families fear a damaged reputation in the community as a result of women's public exposure and proximity to men. Such opposition is an expression of fears a daughter won't find a husband because of a reputation for improper comportment.

The first question one political organization poses to a new recruit is whether she feels able to deal with her family's opposition; if not, they explain to her that she probably can't give much to the struggle. In fact, women's struggles with their families were seen as a vital stage in their development—if she cannot face her family she will not be of much use to the movement.

The majority of women deal patiently with their families, using an approach summed up by Selwa as "talking them into understanding the importance of women's participation in work and the national struggle." When Selwa wanted to work in a neighborhood kindergarten her father opposed it on the grounds that it is dishonorable for women to be employed outside the home. Eventually she succeeded in winning his approval by persuading him, "An honorable girl is honorable wherever she is." The assumption is that it is preferable not to break family ties abruptly and alienate older, traditional sectors of the population, but to try to "politicize them into acceptance" and gain approval gradually.

Though women leaders and mobilizers discourage confrontation in the family, preferring that girls move cautiously and adopt a tactic of politicizing their parents as part of a mass mobilization strategy, confrontation is clearly one alternative mode of interaction. In the early period of the Resistance presence in Lebanon, a small number of middle-class girls, determined to devote themselves full time to political work, broke completely with their families. Layla, for example, decided that national struggle should take precedence over family and notions of honor:

Initially, my parents agreed to my political work because I was writing articles and giving speeches, though they did have reservations. When I started going to meetings with men they started to react negatively. The more I was involved, the more they worried—mainly about gossip and my honor. They couldn't really say no to me because I had always done whatever I wanted. When they said, "Don't come back home!" I didn't. I didn't let them threaten me. I tried not to have an outright confrontation with them—no love affairs or outings to movies or parties, anything of which they disapproved. I wanted them to know that I was only doing political work when I was away from home and that I wouldn't do anything to affect the family honor. It was when I left to live in the camps that they told me never to come home. They threatened to burn my books, throw out my bed and my favorite jasmine plant. Later they sent me very emotional letters asking me to come home. I would write back that I was working for our people. Later we reconciled when I moved back to Beirut and started visiting them.

Layla's situation contrasts markedly with that of women in the camps, for whom such a break would be much harder. However painful it may have been, she felt able to sustain herself without her parents' support or even tolerance. Camp women can hardly contemplate such a break. The locus of social control for them is more closely knit, as the clan and extended family reside in fairly close proximity and thus are better located to exert authority. It is also a question of visibility. If a camp girl breaks with her family, news and shame travel quickly within the community, whereas middle class families can more easily hide absence. When a local teacher told eighteen-year-old Khadijeh's brother and father that he had seen her selling calendars for a political organization in the streets of the camp, they were livid. The brother announced to the household his intention to kill his sister for this public display of shame. Her mother sent her sister to warn her not to return home. Khadijeh sought the help of Fatmeh's husband, Abu Tariq. In the meantime, Khadijeh's brother took all her clothes, dumped them on the front steps, and burned them in order to prevent her from leaving the house once she returned. Abu Tariq accompanied her home and talked to her brother for several hours, trying to calm him down. Nothing was resolved, but he felt the threat of violence had subsided and Khadijeh was safe.

Middle-class girls like Layla are educated enough to support themselves should the need arise. The structural and social conditions of camp life, overcrowded and close, and intense community life render the actions of women much more visible and thus subject to control than those of urban women who live in the midst of more diffuse family structures, with weaker community integration and control and more liberal notions of women's proper comportment. In any case, few women break their family ties, preferring instead to negotiate a solution. Indeed, the temporary break between Layla and her family could be seen as a form of negotiation. She presented them with a fait accompli, which they eventually chose to accept. Khadijeh was constantly negotiating with her family, though with little actual tangible outcome. Weeping at work over a fight with her brother and father that morning, she cried, "It's like the Palestinian-Israeli conflict. It goes on and on with no solution in sight."

Domesticating the Workplace

With domestic labor as a constant, women find paid labor in the following sectors: seasonal work in Lebanese agricultural enterprises near rural camps (Rashidiyyah and Burj al-Shamali in the south and Wavell in the Biqaʿ), salaried work in Resistance institutions and offices (in the Information Department, the Red Crescent, Samed, etc.), as full-time salaried cadres, and employment in the private sector. A common source of income for camp women is piecework embroidery. In addition, it is not uncommon for women to work in their homes as seamstresses. Others practice the art of maquillage for weddings and engagement parties. No statistics are available on Palestinian women agricultural or piecemeal workers or paid militants. However, there are statistics on women workers in Shatila, which as an urban camp would be more likely to have larger numbers of women workers.[14] Damur probably has a high rate as a result of its demographic profile—primarily widows and their children. They work either in agriculture or in the Samed factory.

Entry into the world of work has been both eased and legitimized by a physical setting that doesn't sharply separate the realms of home and work. The type of work women do in the Resistance and in its institutions and workshops is, by and large, an extension of their traditional domestic labor (social work, sewing, embroidery, teaching, cooking, cleaning, etc.). Mass work and employment or training in Resistance workshops are noteworthy for their accommodation of family responsibilities. Mass work articulates well with domesticity. Centered around informal visiting, there are no fixed hours, and as it is carried out close to home, children can be brought along if need be. Indeed, the presence of children raises the respectability of mass workers and gives them an adult status while reducing the threat these women might pose. Children signify stability and, of course, marriage and the unambiguous status it confers.

Women fashioned an informal, familylike atmosphere in the workplace, imbuing it with domestic qualities. The small factories and work-shops in the camps are less formal and bureaucratic than offices and institutions in the urban areas. To the outside observer, the familylike atmosphere in the workplace is striking. Twenty women form the average workshop. Children occasionally pass by to see their mothers, and babies are brought in by kin to be breast-fed. The absence of time clocks and stringent production schedules allows women to respond to family crises, such as a sick child or parent, without entailing conflict between work and family obligations. For women unable to be physically present at the workshop, arrangements to work at home on a piecemeal basis can be made. Numerous women work this way, as is obvious from the frequent sight of women embroidering dresses and cushions at home. Working at home lessens the likelihood of conflict with fathers and husbands over leaving the house and accommodates salaried labor with delivery and care of newborns. Randa, the supervisor at the workshop in Damur, used to visit ten or twelve women daily, delivering the brightly colored cotton thread for embroidering the Palestinian cross-stitch design. She would collect the finished pieces and pay the women for each one.

While motherhood is extolled as an honored natural event and a national duty, its meaning for women's everyday performance of work and activism varies widely. The PLO offers liberal maternity leave (from forty days to two months) with full pay and no loss of position or seniority and fairly flexible work schedules in the workshops and facto-ries.

While mass work and workshop employment may be compatible with child-care duties, for cadres located in offices it is less so. Usually more distant from home, it is not as easy to take children to the office, where a more formal air prevails. Work hours are often longer and sometimes require travel, unscheduled meetings, and long night hours. The work-place is neither predominantly female nor in the immediate neighbor-hood. The conflict between domesticity and work is more acute, espe-cially during military alerts. During the 1981 Israeli bombings of Beirut, activist couples tried to arrange for one parent to stay with the children while the other worked, fearing that if both were killed the children would become orphans. Despite the availability of emergency child-care facilities, some women hesitate to leave their children for any length of time in the event they are targets of attack or the teacher panics and leaves the children; in addition, parents fear separation in the event of an invasion or large-scale bombing.

Women's salaried employment is a double-edged sword in terms of its influence on relations within the family. There is little doubt that it informed a shifting balance of authority in the family. On one hand, by working or joining the Revolution women were posing a challenge to authority structures in the family based on age and gender. On the other hand, their monetary contributions strengthened the family economically. Camp families strive to send their sons for higher education, and women's salaries aid this endeavor, as well as being a factor in raising the household standard of living. Increased household income allows families to meet their financial obligations to other, more distant kin. Women's income helps to keep intact families, social units with powers of control over their members.

Whereas a young unmarried man's salary often assists in supporting his family, working women are able to fulfill this role, freeing young men for Resistance work and higher education. Women's economic contribution doesn't automatically translate into independence, but it does strengthen her voice and authority in the family. When women bring in money to the household their role in decision making, which has never been marginal, is enhanced. Equally relevant in bolstering their power and status in the family are new educational levels that often far outstrip those of their fathers; this, together with the political language they acquire in the workshops and offices, equips them to argue more persuasively with their families and to defend their positions vigorously. One of the more common arguments used by women in confronting family opposition to activism is to label opposing kin as "unpatriotic" or "traitors." In a society where nationalist sentiment is pervasive, such appellations carry substantial emotional weight. Activist and working women can be politicizers of their families. Arriving home from work, they initiate lively discussions, bringing news and analyses of the latest political and military events, as well as information about new services and projects in the camps, thus linking the family with the larger world outside the home and neighborhood.

Many women give a major part of their earnings to their husbands or fathers. Often women will use some portion of their salaries to invest in boosting their chances of marriage. Fashionable clothing and gold jewelry are thought to make women more attractive as potential brides. Women may have acquired a greater voice in the decision-making process within the family, but the structure of subordination and the division of domestic labor remain fairly constant. Although fathers and husbands sometimes oppose women's activities outside the home, the need for an additional income is slowly eroding such attitudes, as is the increasing prevalence of politically inspired ideologies that deem such opposition "backward" and "reactionary" and thus a hindrance to the national struggle.

In sum, the impact of the Resistance on gendered forms of power and the division of labor has been more uneven than uniform. Women's actions in defense of the community and participation in community level national affairs, however novel, do not necessarily indicate a transformation in power over women or a restructuring of the division of labor. In short, structures of domination are reproduced and transformed simultaneously. This process of seemingly contradictory historical momentum is mediated by the endowment of the domestic domain with political qualities and the superimposition of domestic qualities on the political realm. More mediating movement is apparent on the intra-gender rather than inter-gender level. The politicization of the domestic sector is probably inevitable in situations where mass mobilization is a political strategy and the community itself, clearly bounded from its surrounding environment, is the target of attack.

7

The Loss of Autonomy and the
Transforming of Gender

■

Academics usually attempt to locate a scholarly product by labeling it according to a specific paradigm or theory. Studies of gender have assumed their dynamic and innovative position in social sciences, in part, because they don't always fall into neatly delineated theoretical categories. Indeed, they are constantly testing and rejecting one paradigm after another. I hope that this work will not be labeled as falling into a specific category. A scholarly product is the distillation of the author's own personal experience of a situation and the nature of her relations with those she is studying. Equally, how, in this instance, an ethnographic encounter is formulated and translated into an ethnographic product is also a consequence of the author's academic training, which is itself situated in the larger intellectual context of time and place. Marcus and Fisher have described the contemporary era in anthropology as one in which "every individual project of ethnographic research and writing is potentially an experiment" (1986:ix). This study is "experimental" in that, as Marcus and Fischer write about it, it is characterized by theoretical "eclecticism, the play of ideas free of authoritative paradigms . . ." and "openness to diverse influences embracing whatever seems to work in practice . . ." (ibid:x).

One basic question or theme does, however, weave its way through this study. How did women's experience of exile and the emergence of a militant national movement that guided a society in assuming control of its destiny in a conscious, militant fashion inform transformation, and yet constancy, in gender relations and meaning? Ortner counsels: "To say that society and history are products of human action is true, but only in a certain ironic sense. They are rarely the products the actors themselves set out to make" (1984:155). In a discussion of the practice-centered approach in contemporary anthropology she points out that fundamental change is more often a "by-product" of action rather than an *"intended* consequence" (ibid.). This certainly holds true for Palestinian gender relations at the official level of discourse, particularly that of the largely male leadership. But women in participating in the national struggle shook off cultural constraints to confront a coercive reality that they aimed, with varying degrees of consciousness and intent, to transform. Thus human agency—society and history as processes with a central human subject—to rework E. P. Thompson's critique of a perception of history "as a process without a subject" (1978:79) is central to this analysis of gender. Women did not simply yield to the overwhelming force of circumstances. Indeed, they actively mediated and shaped the cultural specificities of history's impact on their lives.

The intent of the Resistance leadership, largely male, and that of individual women who joined the Resistance movement and women leaders in the union and the women's sections of the political organizations differed in a number of respects. For the Resistance leadership, and male members in general, the issue of gender relations did not constitute an intellectual or organizational zone of prestige. With only a minimally articulated vision of a future Palestinian society and state, gender questions did not generate much official interest. For women, naturally, the question was of paramount concern and very personal interest. In joining the Resistance they faced unavoidably, immediately, and continuously the question of gender and power, for to participate was to challenge extant gender constructs with new, experimental forms of behavior and definitions. When they joined the national movement some of them also envisioned new forms of relations between men and women. In any case, female activism held up for inquiry and critique, public and personal, the conventional norms of gender in Palestinian society.

In contesting the rules of gender, an internalized sense of domination was confronted. This was not necessarily the intention of the national movement, which encouraged the expansion of women's national consciousness and commitment. But not only an internalized sense of domination was exposed. Women who subscribed in general terms to the sexual division of labor and the basic parameters of the gender order demanded the rights due their sex precisely for adherence to the normative gender order under extremely stressful conditions. In both cases it was women's action, itself contextualized in a matrix of the external forces that enforced exile and militancy and a cultural system that established limits and meaning to behavior, that gave rise to new forms of consciousness and ideologies.

Critics may charge that this was just another situation like Algeria, where women participated in a national liberation movement in the 1950s to free their country of French colonialism that resulted in patently little fundamental change in gender relations. The reality that resulted from this matrix of intentions, disguised intentions, new forms of consciousness, and consequences defies easy categorization or labeling. Comparison must be tempered by contrast. Algeria and Palestine experienced extreme, and are experiencing in the case of the latter, prolonged forms of settler-colonialism, and in both societies militant national liberation movements emerged. But for women the situation is vastly different. Palestinian women have a history of a woman's movement spanning the century. Their movement, in its early years, was self-initiated and self-sustained. They have actively organized to define and defend their role in the revolution.

In spite of differences in the history and structure of the women's movement and in the outcome of the struggle—in 1962 Algeria achieved independence from France—Palestinian women often ominously refer to the Algerian situation as a possible future outcome of their own situation. Protracted national crisis and a high level of violence against civilians compelled Algerian women to act, as did a national movement that had an interest in mobilizing women for clandestine forms of struggle. Involvement in the Algerian national struggle by a small group of intrepid women, however, did not significantly empower women as a group within the state structure or economy or in their private lives and relations. M'rabet, writing about postrevolutionary (1960s and 1970s) Algeria, argues that the petit-bourgeoisie leadership, with its references to nationalism and tradition as the embodiment of cultural authenticity, manipulated traditional ideologies, a salient mobilizing sentiment against colonial domination, in order to consolidate their class position (1977). Presenting the coincidence of class and gender subordination, M'rabet suggests that the state was unwilling to make the cost investments—education and subsidies for domestic labor and child care—necessary for women's integration into the public sector on an equal basis with men. Nor can the unemployment factor be ignored. To avoid social unrest as a consequence of high levels of unemployment, women were discouraged from seeking employment and priority in jobs was accorded to men. Cultivating the support of the Islamic clergy also played a significant part in the Algerian state's neglect of the issue of women (Lazreg 1985).

South Yemen provided a quite different set of historical and political circumstances. The apparent success of South Yemini women in avoiding demobilization in the wake of national liberation and state re-formation attests to the necessity of scrutinizing state commitment to gender equality. One of the basic strategies of the Yemini state in pursuit of social development was to integrate women into the labor force to enlarge the human resource base, to integrate them into the political process to expand the support base of the regime, and to transform family structure and relations. Unlike Algeria, Yemen suffered a labor shortage and women were a largely untapped resource. Furthermore, the Yemini state expressed its commitment to gender equality by curbing the power of the religious judiciary and introducing a Family Code that substantially revised a number of Islamic legal codes governing women's status in the family. A law was pressed into service to alter the family toward a nuclear structure and more egalitarian relations. New laws were intended to be instrumental in forming new personalities and identities grounded less in family and more in women's role in production and politics (Molyneux 1985).

Both Algeria and South Yemen, for different reasons, point to the need to examine both ideological promotions of gender equality as a moral and developmental issue, expressed in a reformed legal system, and women's access to economic opportunities, channels of power, and legal equality. The history of the Palestinian women's movement itself and the nature of its relationship to the national political structure point to the thorny and divisive, yet central, question of autonomy to define one's issues and priorities. The Palestinian experience underscores the extent to which women's consciousness, in its various forms, and its relations to action are fundamental elements in trying to determine the direction in which such movements are headed.

Granting a mutually influential relationship between political economy and ideology and culture, are there historical instances when a specific constellation of forces emanating from the political economy in the global scene in which a society is located assumes enhanced influence in shaping social forms? The identification of determining factors, or materialities, in this case national dispossession, exile, and militancy, need not preclude a prominent role for human agency. Indeed, it is human agency and culture that impart specificity to social forms in the face of an increasingly homogenizing global economy and culture. It was women who made a conscious, though at times hazily defined, decision to prod and poke at the gender map. Eventually their gender-busting behavior began the process of refashioning. Yet their intentions were not always crystallized in an articulate, definitive platform of actual demands or analysis. For Palestinian exile society in Lebanon as a whole it was a moment of experimentation with new forms of social relations and the organization and wielding of power. It was to come to a climactic, disastrous end in the summer of 1982.

The relationship between practice and ideology is one of mutual influence and reinforcement, but at specific historical instances, in this case extreme national crises, the role of action assumes prominence in shaping ideology. The actions and experiences of Palestinian women informed changes in cultural ideologies. On the one hand, ideologies of gender were stretched by reinterpretation to include female activism. On the other hand, however, there were boundaries to ideology beyond which challenges to meaning became more problematic. Extremes in activism, such as military heroism, went beyond the bounds of concepts of femininity, and thus women in these positions were perceived and categorized as gender neutral. In short, the extant gender system could not handle such radical departures and a kind of ambiguity set in. This period and state of ambiguity presented a situation where practice chipped away at conventional definitions and boundaries. This was the opportunity for new ideas to take shape.

Anomalies and an unevenness characterized the process of change. In trying to capture the process and direction of change, it makes sense to highlight seemingly significant aspects as it oscillates between transformation, reproduction, and reformulation. In examining change it is important to focus on the changes in meaning of extant relations and structures. One might argue that a uniform pattern of radical change in the Palestinian gender order was precluded by the lack of a well-developed, articulated alternative conception of gender around which to model practice that would dilute the hegemony of extant forms. Instead, widely disparate social forms appeared as a consequence of women and men experiencing and organizing to confront enemies and exile. Anomalies and unevenness are located at this juncture in social life. Social forms emerged that reinforced and reaffirmed the cultural meaning of certain aspects of gender relations. Other forms certainly gave indication of novelty. For example, on the one hand, the phenomenon of politicizing domesticity was a permutation on and a reformulation of the meaning and function of domesticity in a highly charged and insecure political atmosphere. It was an expression of the extent to which the community was under assault and the sentiment of sharing the burden together accompanied by a belief in the right and duty of women to participate. Activism extended the substance and meaning of the private domain, but it did not necessarily alter the gender associated with its maintenance. On the other hand, married activist couples sharing equally in housework and child care was a novel phenomenon, indicating a transformation in the gender map. By and large, the kinds of tasks women performed in the struggle and the nature of forms of social control exerted over their behavior were reformulations of male hegemony. Thus social change appears to be intimately related to a continuous process of confronting the forces that nuance the details of daily life.

While I have argued that women were prominent actors in fashioning their position in a new Palestinian social formation, their actions took place within the institutional and ideological parameters established and promoted by the national movement. While involvement in the Resistance may have awakened women to forms of domination and the potential for equality and while it did provide the institutional framework and ideological legitimacy for gender changes, the national movement also declined to be an arena for a radical restructuring of the gender order. It imposed limits on women's actions and access to power. Women's perceptions of themselves were in dissonance with those of a leadership that continued to propagate the idea of women's participation in national politics, but in a secondary manner, vacilating between conception of female persona as sex and citizen. Supporting institutions were not extensive enough to handle the increasing disarticulation between domesticity and activism of the full-time cadres.

Activist women were caught between the demands of loyalty to the national movement and knowledge of the inextricability of their struggle from the Palestinian struggle and an awareness of the need for an autonomous struggle. In accepting the *nature* of their linkage to the national movement they also accepted the concept of secondary struggles. I stress the nature of the linkage, not the idea of linkage itself. A movement can be linked yet autonomous. *Autonomous* is not to be confounded with *separatism*. By *autonomous* I simply mean a movement by and for women that could act independently in the development of its theory, organizational structure, and the policy positions adopted, as well as in the allocation of its resources, but at the same time remain vitally cognizant of and analyze women's condition in the context of the broader Palestinian condition and remain committed to and active in the larger struggle for national self-determination.

While Palestinian women recognized the benefits that accrued to men through their domination of women, they were vitally aware that equality with men in the then-current objective circumstances of the Palestinian people would only be equality in subordination and dispossession. Their profound and unshakable belief in the inextricability of their struggle for gender equality and rights with that of the national movement derived from such an awareness. In sum, internalized domination was being confronted and transformed by a set of practices arranged by women themselves in response to movements in the larger, more encompassing structures that shaped daily life. Such practice gave rise to a process of redefining and reinterpreting gender ideologies.

The Summer of 1982: The End of an Era

Given the extreme and abrupt difference in the conditions of the Palestinian community in Lebanon from the time I completed my fieldwork in May 1982 and those that prevailed just a few months later, a brief update on the research community is warranted. The events that transpired during the summer of 1982 ended what is now nostalgically referred to by Palestinians who departed Beirut as *"ayyam Beirut"* (the era or days of Beirut). By the last week of May 1982, I considered my fieldwork completed. I had planned to spend the summer filling in any gaps in my data. On Friday, June 4, I left Shatila camp in the midafternoon. As soon as I reached home I heard the familiar sound of Israeli warplanes. But this day the drone and sounds of bombing lasted longer than usual. Curious as well as concerned, I joined my neighbors gathered in the street in front of our building to watch this horrific drama in the sky. We wondered what areas were being hit. In those few hours little did we foresee that the situation of the Palestinian community in Lebanon and the political map of the country would change in a way that few of us could even imagine possible. Once again the clear-cut, overwhelmingly raw power of external forces and political events was propelling the immediacies of daily life.

That night, a friend and her daughter from the al-Fakhani area came to stay at my home, feeling that it was in a relatively safe area. We ended up staying together throughout much of that summer of siege and invasion. On several occasions we fled from my house with only a few minutes' notice upon the hurried warnings of the local militia that Israeli gunboats were going to shell our seaside neighborhood. At such times we walked with hundreds of other West Beirutis in the darkened, littered streets of the city searching for a safe spot to sleep.

By Monday, June 7, when it was abundantly clear that a full-scale Israeli invasion of Lebanon was under way, several other friends had joined us to stay at my house. I was one of the fortunate ones whose apartment building had a well. During the Battle of Beirut, in an attempt to make life unbearable for those in West Beirut, the Israelis cut off the water and electricity supply and prevented any food or medicines from entering that part of the city. In my neighborhood, under the control of a local Lebanese militia, every household contributed about $3.00 toward the purchase of a pump. Once a week each building had use of the pump to draw water.

Although I stayed in West Beirut throughout most of the summer of 1982, I was no longer an ethnographer. This was not a terribly difficult transition to make, since I had lived in Beirut for a number of years as a non-fieldworker. How could I do research in such a situation? I had neither the energy nor the inclination to define myself as an observer at such a time. A strong, overwhelming sense of solidarity in face of invasion and siege bound together the residents of West Beirut—Muslim and Christian, Arab and foreigner. Facing the siege together forged the sense of empathy that Kirschner (1987) described as an essential component of the interaction between self and other. But to distance oneself, the other component of ethnographic interaction, was emotionally, as well as physically, impossible. Remaining in West Beirut meant sharing in the daily struggle to survive the siege and the deadly, indiscriminate bombardment to which the city was exposed.

During those months, as best I could, I kept up with the women who had so generously contributed to making this book a possibility. Um Khalid left Shatila in the first few days of the war. Along with many other families from the camp, they found refuge in a nearly completed but unoccupied high-rise residential building in Ras Beirut. Her husband was one of the few cadres to remain in Shatila. I heard through women working in relief efforts that people from Shatila had occupied a building in the Minara section of Ras Beirut. By asking women in the streets who looked by their dress to be camp Palestinians where Shatila famlies had taken refuge I was able to locate Um Khalid. I visited as often as possible during the siege.

Once the Resistance had withdrawn from Beirut in early September and it seemed the war was over, Um Khalid and her family returned to Shatila. The Habib Accords, agreed to by the United States, the PLO, and the government of Lebanon, contained provisions assuring the protection of the Palestinian civilian population remaining in Lebanon (see Cobban 1984 and Khalidi 1986). During that first week I visited several times. The atmosphere was eerily quiet but tense. The camp, always a bit shabby-looking, had taken a severe battering during the war. The Lebanese army was posted around the camps, armed with weapons acquired from the departing Resistance forces. Few offices were open, and a sense of ambiguity prevailed, accompanied by uncertainty as to their future treatment and status in Lebanon. Financial insecurity compounded matters. How were people to cope without the employment provided by the Resistance and the now vastly reduced PLO social service sector? A community that had felt itself proud, increasingly self-sufficient, and protected was now vulnerable, humiliated, and anxious as to its fate.

The assassination of Lebanon's newly elected president, Bashir Gemayel, on September 14 precipitated Israel's invasion of West Beirut and a massacre of Palestinian civilians in the Israeli-surrounded Sabra-Shatila camp area.[1] Um Khalid and her family survived the massacre, although their house was very badly damaged. I ran into her and her children in the streets of Ras Beirut several days after the massacre, when the situation had calmed enough for people to venture forth from their homes. Her husband, like many Palestinian men, had gone into hiding to avoid capture by the Israelis and the Lebanese forces. She looked bewildered and haggard from those three or four nerve-shattering days of massacre. Her refuge was a school that had been turned into a relief center for people displaced by this latest Israeli invasion. A day or two later, she returned to Shatila. I went also, though I feared being stopped by any of the various armed groups now roaming West Beirut and openly hostile to Palestinians or anybody associated with them. I drove into the camp with a physican friend who was as scared as I was, particularly given that several doctors and nurses had been murdered during the massacre. I was nervous about my own reaction to the horror and destruction that had just been unleashed on Shatila, a place that I had known as friendly and secure. Collapsed buildings were indistinguishable from one another and blocked roads such that I could not figure out how to go from one area to another. Offices were trashed and blockaded with barbed wire. Piles of books and papers were burning in scattered piles. Public facilities were equally destroyed or damaged. A kindergarten near Um Khalid's house whose usually brightly furnished, sunny rooms had been host to camp children was an empty shell. A beautiful piece of architectural design—an octagon built around a central courtyard with a fountain—it was now occupied by homeless families. One room was a makeshift clinic hastily put together to replace one bulldozed during the attack.

Um Khalid was nervous and exhausted but tried to maintain her composure. She was now alone with the responsibility of caring for and feeding eight children. I felt daunted by her situation. I knew she had no money coming in and was worried about how she was going to feed her children. She no longer had running water—it now had to be carried about half a mile daily in large plastic containers. Her home had a huge gap in the wall, and anything of value had been stolen during the massacre. She was deathly afraid for her children—that her teenage son would be killed or taken away by the Lebanese Forces or other unknown armed elements and that her daughters would be raped or humiliated. I tried to give her some money, which she adamantly and proudly refused. Only when I told her the money was for new school clothes and notebooks for the children did she relent and accept it. Knowing that I would soon leave Beirut, I gathered as many warm items of clothing as I could and gave them to her daughters. I felt helpless to do much beyond these small measures. Soon afterward, Um Khalid and her children moved to ʿAyn al-Hilweh camp, which she felt was safer than Beirut. The next year she delivered her ninth child, a son, Muhammad. A mutual acquaintance visited me in the United States and told me that Um Khalid cries when my name comes up in conversation. I remind her of the "good days" when Palestinians enjoyed autonomy and security.

Layla was seven months pregnant with her second child when the war started. She also left her home and sought safer shelter in another part of West Beirut. As soon as the war was over she and her husband and children left for the Gulf. Family members living there were able to offer a refuge. Eventually she immigrated to the United States.

Fatmeh and her husband did not fare as well during the invasion. A well-known activist, her husband fled to the hills when the Israelis took ʿAyn al-Hilweh camp after a particularly fierce battle with local forces. He was able to make his way behind Syrian lines and then to Damascus. He hid in the mountains for several weeks, exhausted and filthy. The generosity and kindness of Lebanese villagers who provided food and sanctuary prevented his capture.

Fatmeh and the children remained in the camp. She was forcibly taken from her home several times in the summer of 1982 for interrogation by the Israelis. Her courage and refusal to reveal names and give them any information earned her tremendous respect and a reputation for bravery and steadfastness that quickly spread through the Palestinian information network to Beirut and beyond. She remains in ʿAyn al-Hilweh and has resumed her work as a headmistress. Her husband returned several years later.

Dalal fought in the al-Fakhani area during the invasion. I saw her frequently that summer, as she would pass by my house in her free time or while making hurried trips to the al-Fakhani area with friends to try to retrieve a few belongings from their then deserted homes we would pass by her house to drink tea and talk to the fighters. She left Beirut with the Resistance evacuation in late August and now lives in the United States, where she is active in Palestinian community affairs. She married and has three small children. I lost track of most of the other women who gave so generously of themselves to make this study possible. I do know that quite a few stayed in Lebanon after the war and several were arrested.

The Aftermath

Sitting in her office in 1981, Rima, an activist, mused, "Have changes in women's position advanced enough and are they stable enough to withstand a crisis situation such as our expulsion from Lebanon or a drastic decline in the power of the Resistance?" At the time, her question seemed to have little more than hypothetical relevance. In retrospect, she had posed a question that would soon be sadly relevant. Information gleaned from friends who have continued to live in West Beirut, press reports, and article provides a general overview of the post-1982 period.

In beginning to answer Rima's question we must look at the manner in which the Resistance presence ended to ascertain how it affected women. Just as important is the set of daily objective circumstances that faced women in the aftermath of the demise of the Resistance in Lebanon. The parameters of consciousness and action continued to be nuanced by crisis. But this was a crisis of extreme proportions in the context of near powerlessness on the part of the community to define its situation, let alone change it. How one fared and responded also must be located in a class context. Class affiliation and the access to resources it allows, the options it implies, were significant in nuancing how one experienced new crises and reacted to them.

The departure of the Resistance left an institutional vacuum in the camps. Camp residents were suddenly deprived of medical care, childcare and educational facilities, employment opportunities, welfare services, and the protective services formerly provided by the Resistance. The period of kidnappings and arbitrary arrests by Lebanese army security forces and Phalangist militiamen, which often resulted in death, ended in February 1984 when Lebanese Shite and Druze militias forced their withdrawal from West Beirut. The gradual reassertion of a Palestinian military presence in the camps and the south was accompanied by vicious battles with the Shite Amal militia, highlighted by the three-year

Battle of the Camps and their siege from May 1985 to January 1988 (Cutting 1988). Amal continued the practice of kidnappings, murder, and rape.

Women's priorities were focused on survival—theirs and their families —and how to feed the children and protect the men who remained. Women were not demobilized, because the war was not over. There was no safety and enveloping isolation of home to return to. Men were certainly not in any position to protect women. Their tactics to avoid arrest meant lying low, rarely leaving the quarter, if not the house. Women were compelled to seek work to feed their children. In those families with men detained or missing it was women who braved kidnapping and insults and went looking for them, on occasion crossing into East Beirut, seeking husbands and brothers in prisons and detention centers located there. They had to find and exchange information about charity and donor agencies to cope with the destruction of homes and loss of breadwinners and simply to feed their children. All of this required mobility under extreme forms of danger of rape, humiliation, kidnapping, and arrest by the varied assortment of militias and armed men who freely roamed West Beirut after the Resistance's withdrawal. Not only did they no longer enjoy the protection of the Resistance; they no longer had the benefits of its social service sector.

Poverty, widowhood, and fear colored the daily lives of camp women. Older women faced poverty better than did the young; they had experienced the exodus of 1948 and the initial chaos of transformation into refugees. They knew how to stretch resources and seek out new ones. The younger generation of women, who had known only the "good days" of the Resistance, had little experience dealing with the dizzying number of donor offices that sprang up to assist the victims of the war and massacre. The responsibility of looking after children seems to have prevented complete breakdowns. "Who would look after my children?" was the response to talk of women losing control of themselves and being unable to deal with the situation facing them (Sayigh and Peteet 1986:131). Sentiments of domesticity guided women's response to these new forms of crises.

Some Palestinian women remained politically active throughout the 1980s, but for the vast majority their goal was to survive and keep intact their families and community. The vast majority of female cadres left with the departing Resistance forces in August and September of 1982. Those few cadres who remained were initially hesitant to take up political activities given the grim prospects of arrest. They were known and feared that if they were too openly even circulating in the camps they might be arrested. In addition, there was minimal overt political activity in the

215

immediate wake of the massacre. But over the course of the next few months some women were compelled to public political action by events that impinged directly on their daily lives and those of their families. The disappearance of so many men and the kidnapping and arrest of others prompted camp women, many of whom had not previously been active, to undertake incredibly dangerous acts. They publicly protested the arrest of their male kin, organizing demonstrations and leading groups of women to demand of politicians the release of their men.[2] They received little direction from above, many being the spontaneous actions of groups of women or individual women (Sayigh and Peteet 1986). These were done in the tradition of female consciousness—to ensure the continuity of domesticity and to carry out its tasks. Thus women assumed new tasks as demanded by the force of circumstances. They did so in culturally pre-scribed gender-specific ways. But their own actions were also obviously derived from the effects on women of thirteen years of Resistance cam-paigns and mobilization programs and the ideological changes in gender that accompanied these. In short, women displayed, although in greatly diminished form, a sense of empowerment that was not crushed by the defeat of the Resistance forces. The fact that such protests could be met with cruel, dangerous, even life-threatening responses points to the tenac-ity of women to continue acting to preserve their communities and fami-lies.

Some urban middle-class women demobilized or diluted their political activities. The relatively greater anonymity of urban life afforded them the opportunity to mask former identities and affiliations. This was easier for them to do than for camp women cadres. The intense and close nature of social life in the camps made it difficult for those few remaining cadres in the camps to completely halt their activism. Kin, neighbors, and Resis-tance members and friends turned to them for help in reestablishing their lives. It was assumed they would have access to Resistance emergency funds. Middle-class cadres could more easily assume nonpolitical activi-ties, employment, and social life. Yet other middle-class cadres worked clandestinely for the Resistance, delivering messages and funds to the camps and the cadres from the exiled leadership. In spite of their being better positioned to escape rape,[3] murder, arrest, and kidnapping, middle-class Palestinian women, activists or not, faced actions designed to rid Lebanon of a Palestinian presence. Militiamen from the Phalangists and Major Haddad's South Lebanon army conducted a campaign of harass-ment, property confiscation, and murder against Palestinians, especially in the southern coastal cities of Saida and Sur. Armed gunmen confiscated homes without warning, ordering residents to go to the refugee camps.[4] In December 1986, Nabila Brayr, a well-known Palestinian activist and employee of an international agency (UNICEF), was shot dead at a roadblock by unidentified gunmen widely thought to belong to the Shi'ite Amal militia. Nabila had courageously continued her relief and development work during the "camp wars" with Amal, angering those forces arrayed against the remaining Palestinian community in Lebanon.[5] Nabila's tragic death was widely reported in the regional and international press (though not the Lebanese press). The women victims of rape, murder, and detention received little if any mention.

How did the ideologies of gender nourished during the "good days" of the Resistance change? Certainly, national consciousness did not diminish. If anything, Palestinians became more "Palestinian," in distinction from Arab, given their political abandonment by nearly all Arab countries and the massacres perpetuated by other Arabs. Strategies for survival assumed primacy vis-à-vis ideology and liberal aspirations. For example, in the wake of 1982 Um Khalid and her husband arranged a marriage for their eldest daughter, sixteen-year-old Muna. Previously Um Khalid had high hopes that Muna would finish high school, then complete a technical training course and marry at a later age. A young suitor with employment in the Arab Gulf offered the prospect of giving Muna more security and stability than she would find in Lebanon. She would be spared potential rape or death, and it would be one less child to feed, clothe, and be responsible for. Can this course of decision making and action really be deemed regression, an abandonment of principals? Or does it make more sense to cast it as a move to better one's chances of actual immediate survival and long-term security in the midst of chaos and uncertainty?

Palestinian women did not demobilize in the same fashion as Algerian women after national liberation. Unlike Algeria, where the national struggle ended with independence and the assumption of state control by the national liberation forces, this was a defeat, a tremendous setback to the Resistance. It is futile to discuss whether or not women's issues and struggle were assigned a secondary status. For the Palestinians remaining in Lebanon the focus during this immediate post-war period was more on survival and less on organizational and ideological questions and tensions.

In the eight years since the invasion and the end of *ayyam Beirut,* regional and international events have continued to transform Palestinian society in the diaspora. The PLO suffered a serious split that fractured its constituent organizations, including the Women's Union. Without renouncing their historic claim to Palestine, the PLO has recognized an Israeli entity and entered into dialogue with the United States. But of most significance for the whole Palestinian community in the diaspora and inside historic Palestine is the *intifada,* the uprising against Israeli occupation. This is the most sustained rebellion waged by the Palestinians. While costing Israel economically and morally, it has gained the attention and respect of large segments of Western public opinion. Women are visible participants in the *intifada,* carrying on a now well-established tradition of political activism. This is another experimental moment for the gender order as women's resistance to twenty years of occupation shatters the seeming naturalness and acceptability of foreign domination (for a young generation that has known no other form of political life) and holds up for questioning the gender order.

Notes

■
Introduction

The quotation at the beginning is a statement uttered by a Palestinian woman to the foreign press in Rashidiyyah camp in the aftermath of the 1982 Israeli invasion of Lebanon.

1. *Resistance* refers to both the PLO in its many forms—its institutions, constituent political organizations, and leadership—and to the generalized ethos of struggle by the Palestinians in Lebanon under the leadership of the Palestinian national movement. For a general overview of the PLO see Cobban (1984). For an in-depth study of its social institutions see Brand (1988). See Brynen (1990) for a historical review and analysis of the Resistance in Lebanon.

Fida'iyyin (sing. *fida'i*) are those who sacrifice themselves. In popular Palestinian lexicon, it means guerrillas, those who engage in armed struggle in the name of the Palestinian Resistance movement.

2. The best study of the Palestinian exile experience in Lebanon remains that by Sayigh (1979).

3. Israeli historian Benny Morris lists the refugee figures presented by the various parties involved. The United Nations Economic Survey Mission and the United Nations Relief and Works Agency for Palestine Refugees in the Near East (UNRWA) proposed a number of 726,000, while the various Arab governments estimated 900,000 to 1,000,000. The British gave a figure of 810,000. The official Israeli number was 520,000, although they acknowledged the accuracy of the UN figure of 726,000. They preferred the lower number, fearing that if they were ever compelled to allow the return of the refugees, official recognition of the higher UN or Arab figures would present them with an overwhelming number of claims (1987:297).

4. Figures taken from Abu-Lughod (1980:29). For estimates of the Palestinians in Lebanon at the time of research see Kossaifi (1980:20,28). All statistical figures regarding the Palestinian refugee population in Lebanon are, at best, rough estimates. The Lebanese government hasn't undertaken a census of its own population since 1932 for fear of its political-sectarian implications.

5. *Palestinian Statistical Abstract 1984–1985*, no. 6 (Damascus, Syria: Palestine Liberation Organization, Economic Bureau, Central Bureau of Statistics, 1986), p. 42.

6. I use the term *ordinary* to distinguish between formally active women and those who are inactive in political organizations, though they may be mobilized during crises to assist in defense of the camp or they may be supporters of an organization.

7. The anthropological literature on public/private domains in the Middle East is not negligible. See Aswad (1978), Nelson (1974), and Altorki (1986), among others.

8. In English, *cadre* means the nucleus around which an organization, political or military, can be built. The Arabic use of the term implies a person who is being trained, politically and militarily, in an organization's theory and practice in order to be an effective member able to rise to positions of leadership and recruit and train others.

9. See Elshtain (1987) for a historical perspective on women and political conflict and Ridd and Calloway (1986) for an anthropological or sociological perspective on women and conflict in Europe and the Middle East.

10. See Harstock for a theoretical discussion of gender and power (1983:145–185).

11. Hobsbawm and Ranger (1983) discuss the recent "invented" nature of many seemingly long-standing, immutable "traditions" both in the West and the third world.

12. Samed, an industrial and social institution producing goods for local consumption and for export and providing jobs, initially to martyrs' widows and daughters and now to camp women and men, is the prototype institution for economic self-sufficiency.

13. Zionism is considered by a number of scholars as a unique form of settler colonialism predicated on colonization of the land rather than the people. Aside from dispossessing the Palestinians, it expelled a number of

them and has not allowed them to return. Unlike most colonial movements, which were intent on exploiting indigenous peoples, Zionism rid Palestine of the bulk of its native inhabitants and refuses to accord them national recognition. See Flapan (1979), Weinstock (1973); Rodinson (1973), and Zureik (1979).

14. Powdermaker (1966) details her own research methods and techniques in a number of quite varied cultural settings to illustrate the contingent and flexible nature of research strategies and methods of recording.

15. Kirschner (1987:218) explores the relationship between the construction of knowledge and gender, positing a closer association between women ethnographers and empathy with the "other."

16. *Ukht* (sister) is the title of address for women members of Fateh. In the leftist Democratic Front for the Liberation of Palestine and the Popular Front for the Liberation of Palestine, women members are called *rafiqah* (comrade), as are male members *(rafiq).*

1. Gender and Culture in Exile

1. There is much contentious debate about Lebanon's treatment of the Palestinians. This topic has not been examined definitively and arouses much passion in all sectors of the political spectrum. The most that can be said with certainty is that significant sectors of the Lebanese progressive movement initially supported the Palestinian national movement. But countless Palestinians have stories of mistreatment, humiliation, and abuse at the hands of the Lebanese, both civilian and military, that span the whole of the exile period.

2. For an extensive study of the Palestinian community in Lebanon see "The Demographic Characteristics of the Palestinians in Lebanon," in *The Economic and Social Situation and Potential of the Palestinian Arab People in the Region of Western Asia,* by TEAM International for the Economic Commission for Western Asia (ECWA) (January 1983), p. 20.

3. See ibid. for a brief discussion of each camp.

4. The influx of Palestinians from other camps in Lebanon during strife also caused village boundaries to blur, as did the influx of Lebanese Shi'a fleeing war-torn South Lebanon.

5. Most of Shatila's residents were originally from the Galilee villages of Majd al-Krum, al-Barwah, Dayr al-Qasi, Saffuriyyeh, 'Amqa, al-Safsaf, Sha'b, al-Yajur, Kwaykat, al-Farradeh, Sahil Manshiyyat 'Akka, and Jaffa (not in the Galilee). At first most of these families had sought refuge in South Lebanon, and then they later moved to Shatila, where an International Red Cross center was located.

6. See "Demographic Characteristics," p. 68, for background information on Shatila camp.

7. Ibid.

8. After the 1982 Israeli-sponsored Phalangist massacre of Palestinians in Sabra-Shatila camp, women downplayed their individual suffering, saying,

"We are all suffering together. There is no one who has not lost someone" (Rosemary Sayigh, personal communication). The reference to the commonality of suffering may be a means of avoiding the atomization of a community under attack and threats of dispersal.

9. For accounts of this period and some of the groups involved see Cobban (1984), Kazziha (1975), and Sharabi (1970).

10. For an account of their history, organization, and divergences from Fateh see Cobban (1984) and Kazziha (1975).

11. Caulfield points out that the concept of cultures of resistance has been neglected in the analyses of national liberation movements and cautions an awareness of their duplicity. The search for authenticity as the cultural expression and source of legitimacy of a resistance leadership and strategy can be a backward movement if oppressive traditions are upheld as epitomizing authenticity (1974b:69–70).

12. See Hobsbawm and Ranger (1983) for an interesting discussion of the invented nature of what usually passes for tradition. See Caulfield (1974b) for an examination of women's roles in cultures of resistance.

13. See the *Palestinian Statistical Abstract 1981,* no. 3 (Damascus: Palestine Liberation Organization, Economic Dept., Central Bureau of Statistics), for data on male and female employment.

14. Before 1948, the female illiteracy rate was over 90 percent. In contrast, in 1971 77.8 percent of camp girls between the ages of six and nine were enrolled in primary schools; 66.7 percent of girls aged ten to fourteen were pupils (ibid.).

15. See the report on "Sex Discrimination against Girls in Nutrition and Health," by Selwa Masri, in *Girls' Adolescence: The Lost Opportunity,* summaries of presentations and recommendations of UNICEF's MENA Regional Workshop on Girls' Adolescence (Amman: March 23–26, 1985), pp. 26–27. The report states that girls are immunized at lesser rates than male children, female mortality rates from diarrhea and dehydration are higher than for males, boys are breast-fed for a longer period of time than girls, and malnutrition was more common among girls than boys and boys receive better quality food and health care than female children.

2. The Palestinian Women's Movement: Organization and Representation

1. See Khalidi for a commentary on the study of the Palestinian peasantry (1988:207–213).

2. Huda Sha'rawi's memoirs, recently translated into English, render an intimate glimpse into the Egyptian feminist's private life, intellectual and political development, and attempts to shape her own life (Shaarawi 1987).

3. PLO literature here refers to the numerous pamphlets, booklets, and statements published by the PLO Information Office and the General Union

of Palestinian Women and the *PLO Bulletin*. Such sources contain few references.

4. *Aliyah*, in Hebrew, means "a going up" and is used to refer to waves of Zionist immigration to Palestine. It can also be used to describe an individual move to Israel as well.

5. Khalidi (1988) details several revolts or violent incidents over alienation of the land to settlers: Tiberias region, 1901–2; 'Afula, 1910–11; Petah Tiqva, 1886; and Rehovot, 1892.

6. Some PLO literature refers to this demonstration as taking place in January and some in February, and most mark it as the beginning of the women's movement.

7. In an interview I had with Mogannam in 1985 (conducted jointly with Rosemary Sayigh) she said, "When I wrote my book I put down everything and my husband would correct it." As for her reasons for writing the book, "In every book of history you never heard anything of the women. They denied her a place. I just wanted the English-speaking people to know that the Arab woman is just like any other woman in the world."

8. The Arab Executive Committee, the main Palestinian political body, acted as the liaison between the Palestinian community and the Mandate Government.

9. In Sayigh's interviews with Um Samir and Zlikhah al-Shahabi both noted the unity among the women. Um Samir said, "Even women whose husbands collaborated with the Zionists worked with us," and al-Shahabi commented that splits in the national movement did not affect the women (Sayigh 1987:29–30).

10. The members of the Executive Committee were: Madames Khalidi, Jamal Husayni, Musa ʿAlami, ʿAwni ʿAbd al-Hadi, Shukri Deeb, Bulos Shahadeh, Subhi al-Khadra, and Matiel Mogannam and Misses Shahinda Duzdar, Zahia Nashashibi, Fatmeh Husayni, Khadijeh Husayni, and Zlikhah al-Shahabi. The fourteenth is not listed (Mogannam 1937:76).

11. For a study of the political significance of women's networks in Turkey see Aswad (1974).

12. Another reason women organized separately was the practice of elite benevolence to the less well off. One facet of the complex patron-client ties may have been elite women's charitable work with their family bloc's clients. Was women's social work an extension of social relations designed to support or underline patron-client ties? It remains to be seen to what extent women's organizations were based on family political blocs and whether they aimed at mobilizing clients, since under the AWE's aegis they were ostensibly operating as an organization, not as family blocs.

13. There is a discrepancy concerning the date of this event. Mogannam states that the visit was in 1932 and the women's speeches in 1933 (1937: 93–94).

14. *al-jahiliyya* refers to the period before Islam and means the "era of ignorance," before God's revelations to the Prophet Muhammad.

15. For a description of the collective punishment of a village see Newton

(1971). The subsequent Israeli use of collective punishment was based on the continued application of the British Emergency Regulation invoked during the Mandate period in Palestine. The Israelis still use collective punishment as a form of political control and intimidation to quell resistance in the occupied territories and Lebanon.

16. *Al-nakbah* means "disaster" or "calamity" in Arabic and is used by Arabs to refer to the 1948 Arab-Israeli war and the exodus of the Palestinians from their homeland.

17. Some of the women killed in action and now considered martyrs were Hayat Balbissi of Nablus, Jamileh Ahmad Sulh, Ziba 'Atiyyeh, and Helwa Zaydan, who died fighting in Dayr Yasin.

18. In the Bedouin code governing the conduct of warfare, ideally women and children are granted immunity from intentional slaughter, rape, kidnapping, and theft of their private property. Dickson, describing women and warfare, writes: "The laws of the desert hold her inviolable. Her men may be killed, her sons may have to scatter and flee for safety, but the women of the tent are safe . . . they know that the victors will not touch a hair on their heads" (1949:124). Whereas Dickson contends that the ideal Arab conduct of warfare normally limits attacks on women, al-Hibri suggests that kidnappings of women occurred during *al-jahiliyyah* and the early Islamic battles but notes that Islam prohibits Muslims from taking Muslim women captive during warfare (1982:209).

19. Dodd and Barakat's (1969) research among refugees of the 1967 war ascertained that many people fled the West Bank out of fear for their kinswomen's honor. Refugees from 1948 often cite the same factor, along with forcible expulsion, as the reason they fled.

20. The Irgun Tz'vai L'umi was a small Jewish military organization formed in Palestine in 1930. Ideologically based on the thinking of Vladimir Jabotinsky, it asserted that "only active retaliation would deter the Arabs," and it included Transjordan in Greater Israel. Lohamei Herut Israel (also known as Lehi or the Stern gang after its leader Abraham Stern) split from the Irgun in 1940 (Raphael Patai, ed., *Encyclopedia of Zionism and Israel*, [New York: Herzl Press and McGraw-Hill, 1971], 1:552–553 and 733).

21. See Morris for a detailed account of the fall of Haifa and 'Akka and the events leading up to the exodus of their Arab inhabitants (1987:107–110).

22. Brand (1988) explores in detail the reconstitution or formation of a variety of Palestinian institutions in the period between 1948 and the emergence of the Resistance movement.

23. See ibid.:84–98. Palestinian women in Egypt did not establish a women's organization until 1963. Brand gives an account of its history and activities.

24. For lists of women's organizations see Giacaman (n.d.) and Haddad (1980).

25. People who experienced the events of 1948 often speak of the first years of exile in terms of mourning over a lost loved one.

3. Ideas and Action: Political Consciousness

1. Tal al-Za'ter, a refugee camp on the eastern fringes of Beirut, was home to around 13,000 people in 1972. During the 1975–76 Lebanese civil war, it was subjected to an eight-month siege (January–August 12, 1976). Upon the camp's falling to right-wing besiegers, thousands of inhabitants were massacred. The rest fled to West Beirut, and many eventually resettled in Damur (see note 8) or in other refugee camps.

2. In this book frequent reference is made to "girls." It is used in a very precise manner in Arabic. In Arabic, unmarried females, assumed to be virgins, are referred to as "girls" *(banat)* regardless of age. Only married females are referred to as "women." To render the image of Palestinian girls and women as they are conceptualized and referred to in their own society, on occasion I used the English equivalent of the Arabic.

3. For a detailed discussion of the concepts female and feminist consciousness see Kaplan (1981).

4. Piven (1985) derived this term from E. P. Thompson's "moral economy" of the English crowd.

5. See Kaplan (1981) where she argues this point and Piven's (1985:271) examination of literature on peasant rebellions where in a similar fashion "tradition itself armed people to enter history."

6. The Phalangists are a right-wing military and political group founded in the 1930s by Pierre Gemeyal. Predominantly Maronite in composition, they fought in the 1970s and 1980s to maintain Maronite hegemony and diminish the Palestinian presence in Lebanon.

7. Dikwaneh is a predominantly Christian suburb on the eastern outskirts of Beirut, once adjoining Tal al-Za'ter camp.

8. Damur was attacked by the Joint Forces (an alliance of Lebanese progressive parties and Palestinian organizations) during the civil war in January 1976. Its inhabitants fled and the town was settled in the fall of 1976 by Palestinian refugees from Tal al-Za'ter.

9. In a study of Palestinian identity, Mansour noted that "a large number of the girls are acutely aware of the injustice done to women but feel uneasy about moving away from the traditional cultural model" (1977:79).

10. In the wake of the 1982 Israeli invasion of Lebanon and the subsequent PLO withdrawal from Beirut, conflict has continued to dominate the everyday lives of Palestinians in the camps. The years from May 1985 to January 1988 were marked by a series of battles with the Shi'ite Amal militia, known popularly as the "camp wars."

11. For an account of women and children as specific targets of torture and murder during the 1982 Sabra-Shatila massacre see Kapeliouk (1984).

12. See Dubois, Buhle, Kaplan, Lerner, and Smith-Rosenberg (1980) for a discussion of this topic.

13. Boesen (1983) contends that women's cultures among the Pakhtun of Afghanistan pose no challenge to male dominance but do express a different consciousness of society and women's role in it.

225

14. The term *responsible (mas'ul)* refers to one's superior in rank and responsibilities in a political organization and implies a relationship of hierarchy; the responsible is in a position to give orders and command obediance. In striving for equality among members of organizations, the Resistance opted for such terms to avoid the even more pronounced hierarchy implied by formal military terms.

15. See note 3.

16. Excerpted from an interview with Jihan Helou, General Secretariat of the General Union of Palestinian Women, in the *PFLP Bulletin* (April 1982), no. 61, p. 33.

17. Personal communication, Rosemary Sayigh.

18. Kaplan (1981) examines women's participation in strikes in Spain in light of female consciousness and its revolutionary potential.

19. See Eisenstein (1978) for a Marxist-feminist perspective on women's liberation more relevant, by and large, to women in the industrial Western world. In Marxist-feminist theory, women develop a revolutionary feminist consciousness in response to the contradictions engendered by wage labor in the public sector and domestic work; exploitation in each is informed by and legitimized by their position in the other. The number of full-time wage earning Palestinian women was not substantial; the employed were more likely to be unmarried girls. Exploitation in the workplace is seen as a result of national rather than gender domination. With the advent of the revolution, increasing numbers of women entered the work force, although in Palestinian institutions where overt exploitation of women was not so obvious. Higher level managerial positions were occupied by men in most instances. Women received equal pay and benefits and liberal maternity leave. The high drop-out rate upon marriage tended to deflect attention away from an awareness of women's concentration in low-skilled, low-paying jobs.

4. Mobilizing Women

1. For a discussion of the prospects for civil society in this stage of incipient Palestinian state formation see the paper by Elia Zureik presented at the seminar on "State and Society: Authority and Legitimacy in the Modern Arab World," Georgetown University, 1989.

2. Mohanty (1988:65–66) critiques Western feminist discourse on third world women for its premise that women are "socially constituted as a homogenous group identifiable prior to the process of analysis." In this mode of analysis, women are defined "primarily in terms of their *object status* (the way in which they are affected or not affected by certain institutions and systems)."

3. For an account of one woman's determination to enlist in the ranks of the revolution in spite of family opposition and ambivalence on the part of the National Movement see Khaled 1973.

4. In March 1968, about 300 Palestinian guerrillas inflicted heavy casualities on approximately 15,000 invading Israeli Defence Forces at Karameh,

Jordan. In the aftermath of this display of guerrilla fighting spirit and abilities, recruits flooded PLO offices all over the Arab world. Cobban reports that ". . . 5,000 new recruits applied to join Fatah within the next 48 hours" (1984:42).

5. See Barakat (1977) for a comprehensive examination of the student movement in Lebanon prior to the civil war.

6. Day of the Land is celebrated every 30 March by Palestinians in the diaspora, in Israel, and in the Occupied Territories. On this day in 1976, Palestinians in the Galilee organized large demonstrations to protest Israeli land expropriations.

5. *Action, Ideology, and Gender in the National Movement*

1. Khalil Al-wazir, better known by his nom de guerre, Abu Jihad, was the PLO's Deputy Commander in Chief of the Military until his death at the hands of an Israeli hit team in 1988.

2. For an interesting discussion of women's military training and its antic-ipated effects on the restructuring of gender relations and family organization in Qadhdhafi's Libya, see Attir (1985).

3. Khalidi notes that it was becoming apparent to the PLO leadership that in the event of an Israeli invasion Syrian and Soviet support would be limited. Preparations included a general PLO military buildup (1986:34–36, 59).

4. The *ashbal* were acclaimed as heroes for their defense of ʿAyn al-Hilweh and Rashidiyyah camps in South Lebanon during the 1982 Israeli invasion. Their determination not to surrender and to recapture sectors lost to the Israeli Defence Forces, using RPGs (Rocket Propelled Grenades used as antitank weapons) tied down the Israelis. When Rashidiyyah finally surren-dered, the Israelis were reportedly stunned to see the camps' defenders were a group of young boys.

5. In an angry article criticizing the limited role of women in the PLO and denouncing male attitudes toward women, Selwa al-ʿAmed (1981) points to intellectuals' and fighters' widely disparate attitudes toward women, noting the progressiveness of the latter.

6. Dalal Mughrabi, a young woman from Shatila camp, died leading a commando raid into Israel in mid-March 1978. The incident sparked off the subsequent Israeli invasion of South Lebanon.

7. al-ʿAmed (1981).

8. The speech was published in the *PFLP Bulletin* (April 1982), no. 61:35–36.

9. See Brand (1988) for a discussion of the emergence of the GUPW in the diaspora communities.

10. For the text of the communiqué issued by the GUPW see *International Documents on Palestine 1974* (1979), pp. 479–480.

11. For the text of the political program of the Twelfth Palestine National Council, commonly known as the Ten-Point Plan, see ibid.:449–450.

12. For the text of the PFLP communiqué announcing its decision to withdraw from the PLO Executive Committee see ibid.:500–503.

13. This act was not maliciously directed against women. Other unions and members and officials have been censored for diverging from the PLO consensus.

14. In discussing the historical evolution of the discourse on feminism and noting the wide divergences in how the term is used Offen writes: "As things stand now, scholars have to invent their own definitions of feminism" (1988:131).

15. MacKinnon argues that the issue of sex is central to feminist theory, method, and practice. She equates the central position of the concept of sex in feminism to that of work in Marxism (1982:1–3).

6. Activism and Domesticity

1. The family often assumes new forms as it responds to colonial intrusion and to economic marginality. Brown explores how Dominican women's serial relationships with men are a specifically female strategy to maximize resources and adapt to extreme poverty (1974). Stack demonstrates how an extended cluster of female kin coalesce to ensure domestic survival and continuity among poor blacks in the United States. This strategy of providing mutual assistance ". . . represents the collective adaptations to poverty . . ." (1974:128).

2. See Myntti (1984) and Taylor (1984) for discussions of the impact of male migration on women in Egypt and North Yemen.

3. Altorki (1986) explores changing family patterns and relations in the wake of abrupt large-scale transformations in Saudi Arabian society as a consequence of the dramatic rise in oil revenues since the 1960s.

4. Islamic law usually grants custody to paternal kin. See Esposito (1982).

5. The national movement's assumption of control of the means of violence and foray into the realm of family matters is discussed in Peteet (1987).

6. Father's brother's daughter marriage has been the subject of much anthropological attention. See Abu-Lughod (1986), Barth (1970), Bourdieu (1977), Khuri (1970), and Murphy and Kasdan (1959).

7. In criticizing anthropological approaches to the question of power and political behavior, Collier seeks to demonstrate that women do "seek power: the capacity to determine her own and others' actions" (1974:90).

8. In a study of a squatter settlement in Jordan, Shami and Taminian (1985) show how women gain power and status within the household as the number of children (sons, in particular) they bear increases.

9. See Abu-Lughod (1986) on honor and shame among an Egyptian Bedouin community, which marks a departure from previous interpretations.

10. A study of Palestinian refugees of the 1967 Arab-Israeli war found that significant numbers fled their homes in fear for their kinswomen's honor (Dodd and Barakat 1969).

11. See Altorki (1986) on the greater incidence of neolocal residence and

its relation to the question of love as the basis of marriage in contemporary Saudi Arabian society.

12. The UNRWA provides free education to refugees only through intermediate school. Families will usually sacrifice to save money to send sons to private secondary schools. There is a significant female drop-out rate around twelve to thirteen years of age because of the cost of private secondary education and the onset of sexual maturity.

13. In the 1970s and early 1980s, foreign female migrant workers, mainly from Sri Lanka, the Philippines, and Thailand, entered the Lebanese labor market, primarily as household workers. They replaced poorer Arab women who, in the days before petrodollars raised the standard of living, used to do such work. As immigrant workers they had no labor rights and thus were poorly paid and sometimes subject to abusive behavior by their employers.

14. A 1979 PLO survey of Shatila's 1,410 Palestinian households (total population: 8,278) found only 167 employed women, primarily in production, service, technical, and clerical fields.The total number of camp Palestinian women employed in Lebanon reached 1,610 out of a total of 14,894 employed camp Palestinians (male and female) in 1980. Yet neither of these figures includes piecework embroidery, agriculture, or the variety of home industries such as sewing and maquillage. See *Socio-Economic and Demographic Characteristics of the Palestinian Arabs in Lebanon, Shatila Camp, Nov. 1979, Statistical Surveys no. 4* (Damascus: Palestine National Fund, Central Bureau of Statistics, PLO, 1979), table 17, and *Palestinian Statistical Abstract 1981* (Damascus: Economic Department, Central Bureau of Statistics, PLO, 1981), p. 234.

7. *The Loss of Autonomy and the Transforming of Gender*

1. For details of the invasion and the massacre see Khalidi (1986) and Kapeliouk (1984).

2. For a description of one such event see Robert Fisk, "Lebanon Women Seek Lost Men," *London Times,* December 7, 1983, reprinted in *Journal of Palestine Studies* (Winter 1983), 12(2):197–198.

3. For an account by an Israeli soldier of the gang rape of a Palestinian woman see Israel Segal, "Torturing Together in South Lebanon," *Koteret Rashit* (Hebrew), March 16, 1983, reprinted in English in *Journal of Palestine Studies* (Summer 1983), 12(4):175–177.

4. See David Hirst, "No Palestinians in the Land of Lebanon," *Guardian* (London), February 7, 1983, reprinted in *Journal of Palestine Studies* (Spring 1983), 12(3):219–221.

5. For an account of Nabila Brayr, her work, and her death see Zahra al-Bahr, "Nabila Silbaq Breir: A True Martyr," *Middle East International,* February 6, 1987, pp. 21–22. In 1976, her parents and sister were murdered in their East Beirut home by gunmen believed to be from the National Liberal Party of Camille Chamoun.

References

Abu Ali, Khadija, 1975. *Introduction to Women's Reality and Her Experience in the Palestinian Revolution.* (Arabic.) Beirut: GUPW.

Abu-Lughod, Janet. 1980. "Demographic Characteristics of the Palestinian Population." In *Palestine Open University Feasibility Study,* part 2, annex 1, table 6, p. 29. Paris: UNESCO.

Abu-Lughod, Lila. 1986. *Veiled Sentiments: Honor and Poetry in a Bedouin Society.* Berkeley: University of California Press.

Abu-Lughod, Lila. 1987. "Locating Anthropological Discourse: Theory and Method in the Anthropology of the Arab World." Paper presented at the symposium on "Theory and Method in Modern Middle East and Islamic Studies," Georgetown University, November 1987.

Al-'Amed, Selwa. 1981. "Some Notes on the Situation of Women in the Palestinian Resistance." *Shu'un Filastiniyya* (April), no. 113, pp. 9–20. (Arabic.)

References

Al-Hamdani, Leila. 1987. "A Palestinian Woman in Prison." *Khamsin* issue on *Women in the Middle East.* London: Zed Books. pp. 40–59.

Altorki, Soraya. 1986. *Women in Saudi Arabia: Ideology and Behavior Among the Elite.* New York: Columbia University Press.

Amos, John. 1980. *Palestinian Resistance: Organization of a Nationalist Movement.* New York: Pergamon Press.

Antonious, George. 1965. *The Arab Awakening.* New York: Capricorn Books.

Antonius, Soroya. 1979. "Fighting on Two Fronts: Conversations with Palestinian Women." *Journal of Palestine Studies* (Spring), 8(3): 26–45.

Aswad, Barbara. 1974. "Visiting Patterns among Women of the Elite in a Small Turkish Village." *Anthropological Quarterly* 47(1):9–27.

Aswad, Barbara. 1978. "Women, Class and Power: Examples from the Hatay, Turkey." In Lois Beck and Nikkie Keddie, eds., *Women in the Muslim World,* pp. 473–483. Cambridge: Harvard University Press.

Attir, Mustafa. 1985. "Ideology, Value Changes, and Women's Social Position in Libyan Society." In E. Fernea, ed., *Women and the Family in the Middle East: New Voices of Change,* pp. 121–133. Austin: University of Texas Press.

Badran, Margot. 1988. "Dual Liberation: Feminism and Nationalism in Egypt, 1870s–1925." *Feminist Issues* (Spring), 8(1):15–34.

Barakat, Halim. 1977. *Lebanon in Strife: Student Preludes to the Civil War.* Austin and London: University of Texas Press.

Barth, Fredrik. 1970. "Father's Brother's Daughters Marriage in Kurdistan." In L. Sweet, ed., *Peoples and Cultures of the Middle East,* 1:127–136. New York: Natural History Press.

Bayat-Philipp, Mangol. 1978. "Women and Revolution in Iran, 1905–1911." In Lois Beck and Nikkie Keddie, eds., *Women in the Muslim World,* pp. 295–308. Cambridge: Harvard University Press.

Boesen, Inge. 1983. "Conflicts of Solidarity in Pakhtun Women's Lives." In B. Utas, ed., *Women in Islamic Societies,* pp. 104–127. London and Malmo: Curzon Press.

Boserup, Esther. 1970. *Women's Role in Economic Development.* New York: St. Martin's Press.

Boulatta, Kamal, ed. 1978. *Women of the Fertile Crescent: Modern Poetry by Arab Women.* Washington, D.C.: Three Continents Press.

Bourdieu, Pierre. 1977. *Outline of a Theory of Practice.* Cambridge: Cambridge University Press.

Brand, Laurie. 1988. *Palestinians in the Arab World: Institution Building and the Search for State.* New York: Columbia University Press.

Brown, Susan. 1975. "Love Unites Them and Hunger Separates Them: Poor Women in the Dominican Republic." In R. Reiter, ed., *Toward an Anthropology of Women,* pp. 322–332. New York: Monthly Review Press.

Brynen, Rex. 1990. *Sanctuary and Survival: The PLO in Lebanon.* Boulder, Colo.: Westview Press and Francis Pinter.

Caulfield, Mina Davis. 1974a. "Culture and Imperialism: Proposing a New

Dialectic." In D. Hymes, ed., *Reinventing Anthropology,* pp. 182–212. New York: Vintage House.

Caulfield, Mina Davis. 1974b. "Imperialism, the Family, and Cultures of Resistance." *Socialist Revolution* 4(2):67–85.

Cobban, Helena. 1984. *The Palestinian Liberation Organization: People, Power and Politics.* London: Cambridge University Press.

Collier, Jane Fishburne. 1974. "Women in Politics." In Michelle Rosaldo and Louise Lamphere, eds., *Woman, Culture & Society.* Stanford, Calif.: Stanford University Press. pp. 89–96.

Crapanzano, Vincent. 1980. *Tuhami: Portrait of a Moroccan.* Chicago: University of Chicago Press.

Cutting, Pauline. 1988. *Children of the Siege.* London: Pan Books.

de Reynier, Jacques. 1971. "Deir Yasin, April 10, 1948." In Walid Khalidi, ed., *From Haven to Conquest,* pp. 761–766. Beirut: Institute for Palestine Studies.

Dickson, R. P. 1949. *The Arab of the Desert.* London: George Allen & Unwin.

Dodd, Peter, and Halim Barakat. 1969. *River Without Bridges: A Study of the Exodus of the 1967 Palestinian Arab Refugees.* Beirut: Institute for Palestine Studies.

Dubois, E., M. Buhle, T. Kaplan, G. Lerner, and C. Smith-Rosenberg. 1980. "Politics and Culture in Women's History: A Symposium." *Feminist Studies* 6(1):26–4.

Dwyer, Kevin. 1982. *Moroccan Dialogues: Anthropology in Question.* Baltimore: Johns Hopkins Press.

Eisenstein, Zillah. 1978. *Capitalist Patriarchy and the Case for Socialist Feminism.* New York: Monthly Review Press.

Elshtain, Jean Bethke. 1987. *Women and War.* New York: Basic Books.

Esposito, John L. 1982. *Women in Muslim Family Law.* Syracuse, N.Y.: Syracuse University Press..

Farsoun, Samih. 1970. "Family Structures and Society in Modern Lebanon." In L. Sweet, ed., *Peoples and Cultures of the Middle East,* 2:257–307. New York: Natural History Press..

Fernea, Elizabeth, ed. 1985. *Women and the Family in the Middle East: New Voices of Change.* Austin: University of Texas Press.

Fernea, R. A., and J. Malarkey. 1975. "Anthropology of the Middle East and North Africa: A Critical Assessment." In *Annual Review of Anthropology,* vol. 4.

Flapan, Simha. 1979. *Zionism and the Palestinians.* London: Croom Helm.

Fluehr-Lobban, C. 1980. "The Political Mobilization of Women in the Arab World." In J. Smith, ed., *Women in Contemporary Muslim Societies,* pp. 235–252. London: Associated University Press, Bucknell University.

Foucault, Michel. 1977. *Power/Knowledge: Selected Interviews and Other Writings 1972–1977.* Edited by Colin Gordon. New York: Pantheon Books.

References

Giacaman, Rita. n.d. "Palestinian Women and Development in the Occupied West Bank." Unpublished paper.

Granqvist, Hilma. 1931. *Marriage Conditions in a Palestinian Village*, vols. 1 and 2. Helsinki: Sodorstrom.

Haddad, Yvonne. 1980. "Palestinian Women: Patterns of Legitimation and Domination." In E. Zureik and K. Nakhleh, eds., *The Sociology of the Palestinians*, pp. 147–175. London: Croom Helm.

Harstock, Nancy. 1983. *Money, Sex and Power: Towards a Feminist Historical Materialism*. Boston: Northeastern University Press.

Hegland, Mary. 1982. " 'Traditional' Iranian Women: How They Cope." *Middle East Journal* 36(4):483–501.

al-Hibri, Aziza. 1982. "A Study of Islamic Herstory: Or How Did We Ever Get into This Mess?" In A. al-Hibri, ed., *Women and Islam*, pp. 207–219. London: Pergamon Press.

Hirst, David. 1977. *The Gun and the Olive Branch*. London: Faber and Faber.

Hobsbawm, Eric and Terence Ranger. 1983. *The Invention of Tradition*. Cambridge: Cambridge University Press.

al-Hout, Bayan. 1979. "The Palestinian Political Elite During the Mandate Period." *Journal of Palestine Studies* (Autumn) 9(1):85–111.

International Documents on Palestine 1974. 1977. Beirut: Institute for Palestine Studies.

Jamal, Leila. 1981. "Contributions by Palestinian Women to the Struggle for Liberation during the British Mandate." *Palestine Bulletin* 7(13): 30–34.

Kandiyoti, Deniz. 1987. "Emancipated but Unliberated: Reflections on the Turkish Case." *Feminist Studies* (Summer), 13(2):317–338.

Kapeliouk, Amnon. 1984. *Sabra and Chatila: Inquiry into a Massacre*. Translated and edited by Khalil Jahshan. Belmont, Mass.: AAUG.

Kaplan, Temma. 1981. "Female Consciousness and Collective Action: The Case of Barcelona, 1910–1918." In N. Keohane, M. Rosaldo, and B. Gelpi, eds., *Feminist Theory. A Critique of Ideology*, pp. 55–76. Chicago: University of Chicago Press.

Kazziha, Walid. 1975. *Revolutionary Transformation in the Arab World*. London and Tonbridge: Charles Knight.

Keesing, Roger. 1985. "Kwaio Women Speak: The Micropolitics of Autobiography in a Solomon Island Society." *American Anthropologist* 87(1): 27–39.

Khaled, Leila. 1973. *My People Shall Live: The Autobiography of a Revolutionary*. London: Hodder and Stoughton.

Khalidi, Rashid. 1986. *Under Siege: PLO Decisionmaking During the 1982 War*. New York: Columbia University Press.

Khalidi, Rashid. 1988. "Palestinian Peasant Resistance to Zionism Before World War I." In Edward Said and Christopher Hitchens, eds., *Blaming the Victim: Spurious Scholarship and the Palestinian Question*, pp. 207–233. London and New York: Verso.

Khalifeh, Sahar. 1985. *Wild Thorns.* Translated by Travor LeGassick and Elizabeth Fernea. London: Al Saqi Books.

Khuri, Fuad. 1970. "Parallel Cousin Marriage Reconsidered: A Middle Eastern Practice That Nullifies the Effects of Marriage on the Intensity of Family Relationships." *MAN* 5:597–618.

Kimche, Jon. 1971. "Deir Yasin and Jaffa, April, 1948." In Walid Khalidi, ed., *From Haven to Conquest,* pp. 775–778. Beirut: Institute for Palestine Studies.

Kirschner, Suzanne, R. 1987. " 'Then What Have I to Do with Thee?': On Identity, Fieldwork, and Ethnographic Knowledge." *Cultural Anthropology* (May), 2(2):204–211.

Kossaifi, George. 1980. "Demographic Characteristics of the Arab Palestinian People." In E. Zureik and K. Nakhleh, eds., *The Sociology of the Palestinians,* pp. 13–46. London: Croom Helm.

Lazreg, Marnia. 1985. " 'You Don't Have to Work, Sisters! This is Socialism.' " Paper presented at the annual meeting of the Middle East Studies Association of America, New Orleans.

MacKinnon, Catharine A. 1982. "Feminism, Marxism, Method, and the State: An Agenda for Theory." In Nannerl O. Keohane, Michelle Z. Rosaldo, and Barbara Gelpi, eds., *Feminist Theory: A Critique of Ideology,* pp. 1–30. Chicago: University of Chicago Press.

MacKinnon, Catharine A. 1983. "Feminism, Marxism, Method, and the State: Toward Feminist Jurisprudence." *Signs: Journal of Women and Culture* 8(4):635–658.

Mansour, Sylvie. 1977. "Identity Among Palestinian Youth: Male and Female Differentials." *Journal of Palestine Studies* 6(4):71–89.

Marcus, George E. and Michael M. J. Fischer. 1986. *Anthropology as Cultural Critique: An Experimental Moment in the Human Sciences.* Chicago: University of Chicago Press.

Marsot, Afaf. 1978. "The Revolutionary Gentlewoman in Egypt." In Lois Beck and Nikkie Keddie, eds., *Women in the Muslim World,* pp. 261–276. Cambridge: Harvard University Press.

Miller, Ylana. 1985. *Government and Society in Rural Palestine 1920–1948.* Austin: University of Texas Press.

Mogannam, Matiel. 1937. *The Arab Woman and the Palestine Problem.* London: Herbert Joseph.

Mohanty, Chandra. 1988. "Under Western Eyes: Feminist Scholarship and Colonial Discourses." *Feminist Review* 30:61–88.

Molyneux, Maxine. 1985. "Legal Reform and Socialist Revolution in Democratic Yemen: Women and the Family." *International Journal of the Sociology of Law,* 13:147–172.

Morris, Benny. 1987. *The Birth of the Palestinian Refugee Problem, 1947–1949.* Cambridge: Cambridge University Press.

M'rabet, Fadela. 1977. "Excerpts from Les Algeriennes." In E. Fernea and B. Bezirgan, eds., *Middle Eastern Muslim Women Speak,* pp. 320–358. Austin: University of Texas Press.

References

Murphy, Robert and Leonard Kasdan. 1959. "The Structure of Parallel Cousin Marriage." *American Anthropologist* 61(1).

Myntti, Cynthia. 1984. "Yemeni Workers Abroad: The Impact on Women." *MERIP Reports* (June), no. 124, pp. 11–16.

Nader, Laura. 1974. "Up the Anthropologist—Perspectives Gained from Studying Up." In D. Hymes, ed., *Reinventing Anthropology*, pp. 284–311. New York: Random House.

Nashif, Taysir. 1977. "The Bases of Arab and Jewish Leadership during the Mandate Period." *Journal of Palestine Studies* 6(4):113–121.

Nelson, Cynthia. 1974. "Public and Private Politics: Women in the Middle Eastern World." *American Ethnologist* 1(3):551–563.

Newton, Frances. 1971. "Searchlight on Palestine 1936–38." In W. Khalidi, ed., *From Haven to Conquest*, pp. 357–366. Beirut: Institute for Palestine Studies.

Offen, Karen. 1988. "Defining Feminism: A Comparative Historical Approach." *Signs: Journal of Women and Culture* 14(1):119–157.

Ortner, Sherry. 1984. "Theory in Anthropology since the Sixties." *Comparative Studies in Society and History* 126:26–166.

Peteet, Julie. 1986. "Authenticity and Gender: The Presentation of Culture." Paper presented at the symposium "Arab Women: Old Boundaries, New Frontiers," Center for Contemporary Arab Studies, Georgetown University, April 1986.

Peteet, Julie. 1987. "Socio-Political Integration and Conflict Resolution in a Palestinian Refugee Camp." *Journal of Palestine Studies* (Winter), 16(2): 29–44.

PFLP Bulletin (November 1978), no. 32.

Philipp, Thomas. 1978. "Feminism and Nationalist Politics in Egypt." In Lois Beck and Nikkie Keddie, eds., *Women in the Muslim World*, pp. 277–294. Cambridge: Harvard University Press.

Piven, Frances Fox. 1985. "Women and the State: Ideology, Power and the Welfare State." In Alice Rossi, ed., *Gender and the Life Course*, pp. 265–287. New York: Aldine.

Powdermaker, Hortense. 1966. *Stranger and Friend: The Way of an Anthropologist.* New York: Norton.

Rabinow, Paul. 1977. *Reflections on Fieldwork in Morocco.* Berkeley: University of California Press.

Rapp, Rayna. 1979. "Review Essay: Anthropology." *Signs: Journal of Women and Culture* 4(3):497–513.

Rapp, Rayna, Ellen Ross, and Renate Bridenthal. 1979. "Examining Family History." *Feminist Studies* (Spring), no. 1, pp. 174–200.

Reiter, Rayna. 1975. "Men and Women in the South of France: Public and Private Domains." In R. Reiter, ed., *Toward an Anthropology of Women*, pp. 252–282. New York: Monthly Review Press.

Ridd, Rosemary. 1986. "Powers of the Powerless." In R. Ridd and H. Callaway, eds., *Caught Up in Conflict: Women's Responses to Political Strife*, pp. 1–24. London: Macmillan Education.

Ridd, Rosemary and Helen Callaway, eds., 1986. *Caught Up in Conflict: Women's Responses to Political Strife.* London: Macmillan Education.

Rodinson, Maxime. 1973. *Israel: A Settler-Colonial State?* New York: Monad Press.

Rosaldo, Michelle. 1974. "Woman, Culture, and Society: A Theoretical Overview." in M. Rosaldo and L. Lamphere, eds., *Woman, Culture, and Society,* pp. 17–42. Stanford, Calif.: Stanford University Press.

Said, Edward. 1979. *Orientalism.* New York: Random House.

Said, Edward. 1988. "Orientalism Revisited: An Interview with Edward Said." *MERIP Reports* (January–February), no. 150, pp. 32–36.

Said, E. et al. 1983. *A Profile of the Palestinian People.* Chicago: Palestine Human Rights Campaign.

Sayigh, May. n.d. *The Arab Palestinian Woman: Reality and Impediments.* Beirut: General Union of Palestinian Women.

Sayigh, Rosemary. 1979. *Palestinians: From Peasants to Revolutionaries.* London: Zed Press.

Sayigh, Rosemary. 1981. "Roles and Functions of Arab Women: A Reappraisal." *Arab Studies Quarterly* 3(3):258–274.

Sayigh, Rosemary. 1987. "Femmes Palestiniennes: Une histoire en quete d'historiens." *Revue d'etudes Palestiniennes* (Spring), no. 23, pp. 13–33.

Sayigh, Rosemary and Julie Peteet. 1986. "Between Two Fires: Palestinian Women in Lebanon." In Rosemary Ridd and Helen Callaway, eds., *Caught Up in Conflict: Women's Responses to Political Strife,* pp. 106–137. London: Macmillan Education.

Shaarawi, Huda. 1987. *Harem Years: The Memoirs of an Egyptian Feminist.* Translated and with an introduction by Margot Badran. New York: Feminist Press.

Shafiq, Munir. 1977. "Propositions on the Struggle of Women." *Shu'un Filastiniyya* (January), no. 62, pp. 200–227 (Arabic).

Shami, Seteney, and Lucine Taminian. 1985. *Reproductive Behavior and Child Care in a Squatter Area of Amman.* Cairo: Population Council.

Sharabi, Hisham. 1970. *Palestinian Guerrillas: Their Credibility and Effectiveness.* Beirut: Institute for Palestine Studies.

Smith, Pamela. 1984. *Palestine and the Palestinians 1876–1983.* New York: St. Martin's Press.

Stack, Carol. 1974. "Sex Roles and Survival Strategies in an Urban Black Community." In M. Rosaldo and L. Lamphere, eds., *Woman, Culture and Society,* pp. 113–128. Stanford, Calif.: Stanford University Press.

Tamari, Salim. 1982. "Factionalism and Class Formation in Recent Palestinian History." In R. Owens, ed., *Studies in the Economic and Social History of Palestine in the Nineteenth and Twentieth Centuries,* pp. 177–202. London: Macmillan Press.

Tawil, Raymonda. 1980. *My Home, My Prison.* New York: Rinehart & Winston.

Taylor, Elizabeth. 1984. "Egyptian Migration and Peasant Wives." *MERIP Reports* (June), no. 124, pp. 3–10.

References

Thompson, E. P. 1978. *The Poverty of Theory and Other Essays.* New York: Monthly Review Press.

Warriner, Doreen. 1948. *Land and Poverty in the Middle East.* London: Royal Institute of International Affairs.

Weinstock, Nathan. 1973. "The Impact of Zionist Colonization on Palestinian Arab Society Before 1948." *Journal of Palestine Studies* 2(2):49–63.

Zureik, Elia. 1979. *The Palestinians in Israel: A Study in Internal Colonialism.* London: Routledge and Kegan Paul.

Zureik, Elia. 1989. "The Socio-Cultural Basis of Authoritarianism in the Modern Arab State: The Palestinian Experience." Paper presented at the seminar on "State and Society: Authority and Legitimacy in the Modern Arab World," Georgetown University.

Index

'Abd al-Hadi, Madame 'Awni, 50
'Abduh, Muhammad, 42, 159
Abu Ghazalah, Samirah, 64
Abu-Lughod, Lila, 4, 11, 228n9
Activism, 10, 152-53, 192, 196-98,
    209, 215-16; an active house-
    wife, 188-191, 194; a cadre,
    192-94; and class, 197-98; and
    culture, 47, 173; and the division
    of labor, 197-98; and domestic-
    ity, 153, 175, 187-88, 192, 193-
    94, 195; and domination, 165-
    66, 206; an employed activist,
    191-92; and family opposition
    to, 198-200; and family organi-
    zation, 196; and life cycle, 197;
    and marriage, 196-97; in pre-

1948 Palestine, 39; and sex, 173;
    in war of 1947–48, 58, 60
'Akka, 48, 50, 51, 59, 192
'Alami, Musa, 49
Algeria, 206, 207, 217
Allenby, Lord Edmund, 50
Altorki, Soraya, 228nn3, 11
Amal, 214, 216-17, 225n10
American University of Beirut, 85,
    86
Amin, Qasim, 42, 159
'Arafat, Yasir, 27, 91, 167
Anthropology: and ethnography, 8-
    15, 204, 211, 221nn14, 15; of
    Middle East, 4; and theory, 4,
    205, 208; of women, 4
Arab Children's Home, 61

239